Estes and Lauriat
a History
1872–1898

ESTES AND LAURIAT

A HISTORY

1872–1898

❁

With a Brief Account of
Dana Estes and Company
1898–1914

❁

BY RAYMOND L. KILGOUR

❁

The University of Michigan Press
ANN ARBOR

TO RUDOLPH H. GJELSNESS

WHOSE DEEP INTEREST IN THE

HISTORY OF PUBLISHING

STIMULATED MINE

FOREWORD

Near the turn of the century, Boston lost two important publishing houses, Roberts Brothers and Estes and Lauriat, whose stories are well worth the telling. The records of the first were examined and described in one of the best of our all-too-few accounts of American publishing, *Messrs. Roberts Brothers, Publishers*, by Raymond Kilgour, author of the present history. The chronicle of the second of these publishers is related in this book. Thomas Niles of Roberts Brothers and Dana Estes of Estes and Lauriat, the builders of these businesses, both were men of force, self-confidence, and imagination who could devise and direct publishing enterprises.

Estes (Charles E. Lauriat directed the retail side of the business, which still continues), who died in 1909, stressed diversity and experimentation in types and methods of publishing, and this influence can be traced in many publishing practices of today. This gives Professor Kilgour's second venture into publishing history its special value.

As my own start in the business of books began with this old Boston firm, I am particularly happy that its record has now been so carefully examined, so admirably evaluated, and the spirit of its successes and failures so accurately caught.

The annals of book publishing are, happily, receiving increased attention from business and social historians. Book publishing is seen not only as a primary influence on thought and action, but as a business story from a difficult field, and provides a record of public taste as it changes from decade to decade.

Publishers of today, especially men and women newly entering the field, are fortunate that there is an increasing opportunity to read the history of publishing, a significant business which will deserve the label of "profession" as it increasingly recognizes the importance of preserving its records, thus making it possible for each new generation to build on the experience and practice of the past. Book publishing is not just enjoyable author relations or life in a pleasant atmosphere of cultured people, it is also a field of exacting and sensitive operations which must be studied, analyzed, and developed to fit changing times and new opportunities.

FREDERIC G. MELCHER

PREFACE

This history has had to be written without the aid of business records or correspondence of the firms involved. To the best of my knowledge no records are discoverable or accessible. The L. C. Page Company, which bought out Dana Estes and Company, first denied the existence of any records and then refused completely to co-operate, not even bothering to answer letters. While it may be doubted that they possess any extensive records, their refusal to make them accessible has forced me to work entirely from outside sources. Such an attitude is not at all characteristic of American publishers: other, and more important, firms with which I have had dealings have been most friendly. Nor were the descendants of Dana Estes any more helpful; even though they may have possessed little of value for the history of the publishing houses, they were quite indifferent as regards that small amount.

The heart of publishing, of course, is the making of decisions on what books are to be undertaken, where the markets are, and how they can be reached. The history of publishing must also record what reception the books had, and their influence on readers and on publishing trends. It is invaluable to have the business background of each publishing venture, if it is available, but the truly vital thing is what books were published and what effect their success or failure had upon the policies of the firm. Most interesting, naturally, is the study of the success of the lesser works along with those of great literary merit, because it frequently indicates best the real tastes of the reading public. For this study the *Publishers' Weekly* is the *sine qua non,* along with a wide range of reviewing periodicals. Thus, while it is regrettable that no records were available for this history, it is not likely that the really important features of the two houses have been overlooked, unless by my own shortcomings.

I am particularly grateful to Frederic G. Melcher, who took time from his many activities to send me a long letter giving his reminiscences of Estes and Lauriat. He worked in the bookstore from 1895 to 1898, then, under Charles E. Lauriat, from 1898 to 1913, a total of eighteen years. He knew the partners and the firm's many associates and provided intimate details that would have been unobtainable elsewhere. Since I have incorporated his notes in this history I feel somewhat less concerned about the lack of records and correspondence.

My daughter Katharine, who has read many of the children's books mentioned in these pages, provided me with the viewpoint of a younger generation. She has read widely enough in nineteenth-century children's literature to be quite sympathetic in her judgments.

Many librarians have been helpful in making available to me the resources of their institutions. I should like to express my gratitude to the Peterborough Public Library, of Peterborough, New Hampshire, to the Boston Public Library, and especially to the University of Michigan Library, where most of my research was carried on. Specific and grateful acknowledgment is due the New York Public Library for permission to quote in full a letter by Dana Estes found in its collections.

Funds for the printing of this book were generously provided by the Horace H. Rackham School of Graduate Studies of the University of Michigan.

Peterborough, New Hampshire
August, 1956

Contents

Illustrations

(Illustrations follow page 96)

Estes and Lauriat
a History
1872–1898

Chapter One

ANTECEDENTS

IN 1872 Boston proudly displayed seventy-three booksellers and publishers as evidence of its intellectual vitality. From its beginnings it had been a bookish town, ever since Hezekiah Usher, about 1647, had set up the first bookstore in the colonies; by 1685, John Usher, Hezekiah's son, was importing large quantities of English books as well as publishing American authors. With the nineteenth century the book trade grew in prestige and in numbers. Not only were there many publishers and booksellers handling religious books, textbooks and the like, but a succession of fine literary firms, such as Carter, Hilliard and Company, Little, Brown and Company, The Old Corner Bookstore, John P. Jewett and Company, Samuel G. Drake, T.O.H.P. Burnham, Augustus Flagg, William H. Piper, and Lee and Shepard, provided fare for every taste. Samuel G. Drake's was the first exclusively antiquarian bookstore in the country, directed by a distinguished author and editor. Little, Brown's bookstore carried their own publications along with the finest British importations. John P. Jewett, on Cornhill, commonly called "Booksellers' Row," was a typical bookseller, supplying the clergy, school committees, and the country trade with books and stationery.[1] Jewett, a close friend of Wendell Phillips and John A. Andrew, was also an ardent anti-slavery man, who won fame by publishing *Uncle Tom's Cabin* in 1852. Another well-known bookseller on Cornhill was William Veazie, who dealt in all classes of literature, with no theological or antiquarian specialties.

By the fifties the book trade, which up to then had centered closely on Cornhill and the adjacent part of Washington Street, formerly called Old Cornhill, began to broaden out, and booksellers and publishers appeared farther along Washington Street and nearby on Court, School, Bromfield, and Franklin streets. In 1855, twenty-nine bookstores and publishers were on Washington Street as against twenty-five on Cornhill.[2] By 1872 the majority were doing business on Washington Street from Dock Square, near Faneuil Hall, to the Old South Meeting House, though a few firms had gone up to Tremont Street. Boston counted seventy-three booksellers and publishers in this year, thirty-three of them on Washington Street, which was now, unequivocally, "Booksellers' Row." Many of the thirty-three were small firms with specialties, but ten, at least, were important, including the American Tract Society agency, Crocker and Brewster, Gould and Lincoln, H. O. Houghton, Little, Brown and Co., A. K. Loring, Noyes, Holmes and Co., W. H. Piper, Roberts Brothers, and A. Williams in the Old Corner Bookstore. And this list, of course, does not mention some of the largest and most famous, such as T.O.H.P. Burnham, Lee and Shepard, D. Lothrop, and J. R. Osgood, successor to Ticknor & Fields, all of them located a short distance away. Concentrated as it was in a small area, the book trade had to be vigorous to survive the competition, while the constant pressure of new publications, new imports, and the demands of an amazingly varied clientele roused the Yankee mind, rarely lacking in resources, to new heights of ingenuity.

In Boston the closely knit book trade had always assumed that bookselling was an art that demanded long and expert training. No bookseller could hope to achieve any reputation in the trade unless he had served an apprenticeship in some of the older establishments. The Old Corner Bookstore was famous as a school for bookmen, and every new publisher counted his clerking years, either there or elsewhere, as the equivalent of professional study, with his "A.B." in bookselling coming after six or ten years of work. Some even continued for an "A.M." for twenty years or more. There were great advantages in this method of growth: not only was the training thorough and on a high level of taste as well as of practicality, but also a network of friendships was established that helped to keep the trade sane and honorable through good times and bad. A new firm was almost never set up by an upstart from the outside but rather by someone who had risen through the ranks, and the trade wished him well in his venture, for had they not done the same? An excellent example is Thomas Niles, who, after years of training under William D. Ticknor, in the company of James T. Fields, set up as a publisher with the bookbinding firm of Roberts Brothers and, in ten years, made it one of the outstanding publishers in the country. Lee and Shepard had been founded by two men who learned their trade with other publishers, one of them the famous old firm of Phillips, Sampson and Co. The really important firms were headed by men who had had unusual opportunities for training and had been content to spend long years as subordinates before attempting their first flight.

In August, 1872, a new firm, modestly and with some trepidation, made its announcement to the trade. In a circular addressed to book collectors and bearing the unpretentious heading "Interesting to Book Buyers," one read:

DANA ESTES AND CHARLES E. LAURIAT HAVE THIS DAY FORMED A COPARTNERSHIP UNDER THE NAME AND STYLE OF ESTES & LAURIAT FOR THE TRANSACTION OF A GENERAL BOOKSELLING, PUBLISHING AND IMPORTING BUSINESS
and have purchased the stock, goodwill and lease of store formerly occupied by W. H. Halliday & Co., 143 Washington St., opp. 'Old South Church,' Boston.

Mr. Dana Estes having been connected with the Boston Book Trade for the past thirteen years, during the last five of which he has been principal salesman in charge of Lee & Shepard's Wholesale Department, and having an acquaintance with the trade throughout the whole country, feels that he can confidently invite his friends of the trade and the public generally to call and examine the stock selected by the new firm, believing it will compare favorably both in quality and price with any in the country.

Mr. Charles E. Lauriat having had seventeen years' experience in the old and new Book Business, the first six with William Veazie, and the last eleven with the popular house of W. H. Piper & Co., would inform his friends and the book-buying public, that in his new and attractive location, he will be pleased to have his customers look in upon him, when it will be his desire to cater to their wants in a manner that cannot fail to please.

The stock will be composed of the choicest selections of books from the English and American markets, the prices such as cannot fail to suit; and the many years' experience which he has had, may be of service to those in pursuit of Old and Rare Volumes.

The supplying of Public and Private Libraries has been for the past eleven years one of his specialties, and in this department his knowledge will be of use to those purchasing.

All orders sent by mail will be carefully and promptly executed, and the prices the lowest in the market. By strict application to business, he hopes to merit and receive a share of your patronage.

Having made arrangements for the New England Agency of Messrs. D. Appleton & Co., we shall have on hand at all times a full line of their publications, which we will supply to the trade and the public generally at the lowest current prices.

Boston, August 19, 1872.

A somewhat briefer notice appeared in the *Publishers' and Stationers' Weekly Trade Circular* on September 19, 1872.[3] In the same periodical's "Boston Letter" dated September 27, 1872,[4] a much longer notice told the trade of the establishment of the new business and described the first titles to be published. The writer of this article commented on the phrase "opp. 'Old South Church' ": "Everything for one-half mile on either side is described as opposite the Old South Church, making it the 'Broad church' par excellence." Of Charles E. Lauriat he remarked: "Whoever falls into his hands in searching for books may as well surrender at once, for with Mr. Lauriat 'success is a duty' and he never fails to sell." Their new store he thought "large and pleasant" and their opening prospects favorable.

It was certainly an excellent location for a bookstore, in the very heart of the book district. It was, indeed, directly opposite the Old South Church, while across the street was the office of the *Boston Evening Transcript,* the city's finest newspaper. Down the street, in the direction of Faneuil Hall, was the Old Corner Bookstore, on the corner of School Street, with W. H. Piper's next door. Little, Brown and Co. was still farther down, on the other side of Washington Street. Upstairs, in the same building with the new firm, was Roberts Brothers, who had just achieved a major publishing triumph with the works of Louisa Alcott. Estes and Lauriat were to have to do something brilliant to keep up with the modest establishment above them. But, to twist the saying slightly, they were in on the ground floor, where a bookstore should be, and their business, if it were to be a success, would have to be an expert combination of bookselling and publishing.

Although the circular sent out by Estes and Lauriat hinted at the professional experience of the founders, a few more details on their early careers are needed.

Dana Estes was born in Gorham, Maine, on March 4, 1840, the son of Joseph and Maria (Edwards) Estes. On the paternal side he was a descendant of Richard Estes of Dover, England, who came to America in 1684 as one of the early settlers of Maine. Among the books he prized was his ancestor's Bible bearing the note: "Richard Estes, his book, bought at sea of Thomas Edwards, 9th month, 1684—the 4th of ye seventh month come from ye Downes—the 27th of ye ninth month arrived in Boston." On his mother's side he was fourth in descent from Hugh McLellan of Gorham, who came from Londonderry, Ireland, in 1733, and who was a descendant of Sir Hugh McLellan of Argyle, Scotland.

Estes went to school in Gorham, and at the age of fifteen, when his family moved to Augusta, had his first business experience as a clerk in a wholesale and retail general store. In 1859 he came to Boston and took his first post in the book business with Henry D. Degen and Son. Since early childhood books had fascinated him, and he apparently made the book business his ambition.

Two years later, on the day Fort Sumter was fired upon, Estes enlisted in the Fourth Battalion Rifles, afterward the nucleus of the Thirteenth Massachusetts Regiment. He served as a private until he was disabled by triple wounds at the second battle of Bull Run, in August, 1862, at which time his only brother, Albert S. Estes, was killed. Incapacitated for further service, he returned to Boston and, after convalescence, took a temporary position with the bookselling house of William H. Hill, Jr., where he remained until his former employer, Henry Degen, returned from the war.

With Degen he formed a copartnership under the name Degen, Estes and Co. and carried on a small publishing and bookselling business on Cornhill. The firm made a specialty of children's toy books. After some years' experience, Estes decided that his interests did not lie in toy books and sold out to his partner, thereby freeing himself to accept a position as salesman with the thriving firm of Lee and Shepard, where he remained until 1872.

Dana Estes at thirty-two was a vigorous and ambitious man, full of confidence from his successful career with Lee and Shepard. His experience with this firm had led him to believe that the combination of a general bookselling business with publishing offered the surest prospects of success for the publishing business, and perhaps for both. He therefore sought a man intimately in touch with the retail book trade to become his partner in the new venture, and was able to induce Charles E. Lauriat to join him, on the understanding that Lauriat was to have sole charge of the miscellaneous bookselling department while Estes managed the publishing end, including the wholesaling and manufacturing divisions.[5]

Charles Emelius Lauriat was born in Boston on January 12, 1842. His grandfather, Louis Anselm Lauriat, a native of Marseilles, France, came to America in 1800, and carried on his trade of gold beating in Boston from 1822 to 1836. An adventurous soul, he was especially interested in science and, particularly, in balloons, and was the second person in this country to make a balloon ascension. This vigorous forebear of the bookseller made forty-five ascensions in the United States, some of them extremely hazardous. The grandson, whose parents were Emelius Anselm and Martha (Foster) Lauriat, did not inherit the adventurous traits of his ancestor, and, except for the ordinary vicissitudes of business, led a quiet life. Graduating from the Phillips Grammar School in Boston at the age of thirteen, the boy went to work in William Veazie's bookstore in 1855. This general bookstore was an excellent place for a lad eager to learn the book business, but, because of the change of locale of most of the book trade from Cornhill to Washington Street, Veazie went out of business six years later. Young Lauriat, who had learned much in these years and "taken his A.B. degree in bookselling," as George H. Sargent puts it,[6] went to work with William H. Piper and Co., at 131–133 Washington Street. Piper's was among the oldest bookstores in Boston—they called themselves the oldest in the sign which covered the entire front of the store—and also one of the largest establishments in the 1860's.[7] It was a place full of bustle, a firm inclined to flamboyant advertising, and they did a large business in new books as well as "rare and curious" items. The big sign on the store announced "For Sale at Very Low Prices" and "The Best Place in Boston to Purchase Books," with various enticements, such as "Illustrated Books, Old Books, Curious Books, Scarce Books, Books in Plain and Costly Bindings." All in all, it was an ideal place for wide experience, and Charles Lauriat, who remained there ten years, became well acquainted with the Boston trade and with that of other cities, since he became their "road man" and eventually was made manager. James M. Piper, brother of the head of the firm, later was associated with Lauriat's own bookstore. His early experience in traveling stood him in good stead when E & L's need for new stock sent him on trip after trip to Europe. Altogether, including the years when he was in business for himself after 1898, he went abroad thirty-five times, an amazing record, and a strenuous one.[8]

Beginning with his years at Piper's Charles Lauriat became acquainted with many of the literary and political celebrities of the age, and most of them visited E & L at frequent intervals to discuss old and new books. Among them were Oliver Wendell Holmes, Ralph Waldo Emerson, Frank B. Sanborn, Edward Everett Hale, Phillips Brooks, James G. Blaine, and Thomas B. Reed. Thus E & L, as combined bookstore and publishing house, served as an index of current tastes in bookselling and book collecting, since the partners were better able to gauge the public's capacity for certain types of literature than many publishers without such experience, and this combination undoubtedly imparted a practical slant to their publishing—their finger was always on the commercial pulse.

As we see it now, the years immediately following the Civil War show the decline of New England leadership, but the Boston of that day did not perceive it, nor did the rest of the country. New England had taken a leading part in precipitating the war, and New Englanders had had a rich share in the winning of it. It was an irony of fate that Boston should have begun to lose her supremacy from this moment of triumph, but her authority was still paramount for several years after emigration to the West had drained New England cruelly, leaving whole districts of farming land deserted: New Hampshire in 1860 had a population of 326,073; in 1870, war and emigration had shrunk it to 318,300.[9] Immigration from Europe was changing New England, not quite so rapidly but just as permanently. It was soon to be more fitting to call Boston the "American Dublin" than the "American Athens."

At this time, however, Boston had great prestige in politics and in literature. It set the tone of American speech, its magazines, the *North American Review* and the *Atlantic Monthly*, had unquestioned intellectual supremacy, it set the standard for culture. It has been said that the North before the war was as aristocratic in its intellectual life as the South had been aristocratic in its social regime.[10] The intellectual elite of Boston were still grouped in the Saturday Club, twenty-six men "all typical Boston gentlemen of the Renaissance,"[11] mostly authors and acknowledged leaders of national thought in this period. It was to change with the times, as lawyers, professors of science, and economists gradually replaced the men of letters. Boston was still intensely bookish and would remain so for many decades. Longfellow wrote in his journal: "Dined with Agassiz to meet Emerson and others. I was amused and annoyed to see how soon the conversation drifted off into politics. It was not until after dinner in the library that we got upon anything really interesting."[12] What Longfellow said in 1856 would remain true of many New Englanders and would gain even wider acceptance as Boston changed in later years.

The old New England love of learning was as strong as ever. The thirst for culture promoted the study of languages, not only French, German, and Italian, but Gaelic or Sanskrit if desired. There was, as a model, Elihu Burritt, the "learned blacksmith," who had retired to his farm to prepare grammars of Arabic, Persian, Hindustani, and Turkish, a formidable symbol indeed of the Yankee passion for self-improvement.[13] Many rustic Yankees had amazing erudition, such as the young Charles Dudley Warner, who memorized hundreds of poems while milking, or Bliss Perry's father, who studied his Latin grammar while plowing, turning the page after each furrow.[14] New England, especially in the Boston region, was rich in bibliophiles and bibliomaniacs. The passion for all types of books, the old and rare along with the abundant outpourings of Europe, guaranteed the existence of the many fine bookstores already functioning. Perhaps the houses of the Brahmins had only eastern windows,[15] but what they were looking for could not come from the west. These bookish people lived in admiration of European culture, which represented to them literary sophistication, poetry, intellectual freedom, and moral idealism.[16] There was also the fascination of the past, in some a type of nostalgia for the mother country, an Anglomania of which the patrician class of New England was frequently accused.[17] Before the growth of industrialism and the triumph of the business spirit, which caused the expatriation of a few, such as Henry James, New Englanders had gone to Europe to "collect the spoils of culture," to bring back whole libraries of books to aid in the development of their own culture, and they continued, after their return, to read avidly everything that Europe had to offer.

Perhaps, as time went on, the admiration of Europe turned into adulation. Howells, in *A Woman's Reason*, poked fun at those Americans, especially at Newport, who read only European writings and talked only of European affairs, much to the surprise of Lord Rainford, who had supposed that they would be interested in their own country.[18] Of course, New Englanders were not the only guilty ones, if there is any guilt concerned, and it is only because intellectual New England was perhaps more constant and more homogeneous in its admiration that it is emphasized here. This atmosphere would inevitably be reflected in whatever was published by Boston publishers or sold by Boston bookstores, and none of them could hope for success without a liberal supply of things European. That there existed no international copyright law to protect the writings of European authors was only coincidental, for Bostonians would have sought European writings, however they were obtained. Yet no one can deny that the piracy of foreign authors greatly aided most American publishers and, be it not forgotten, American readers. Therefore, any new firm, such as Estes and Lauriat, would expect to prosper very largely on its European importations, since the older American authors were almost entirely preëmpted by the established houses up and down the eastern coast. If it could find new American authors, well and good, but they would likely be New Englanders anyway, and it was more natural to hunt for novelties in Europe than in the provinces to the West.

Chapter Two

SCIENCE AND RELIGION

WHILE he was still a salesman with Lee and Shepard, Dana Estes had begun to plan his career as a publisher and was even inspired to do some writing himself. His marriage in 1867, to Louisa S. Reid, an English girl with marked literary interests, must have had something to do with it, for in 1868 appeared *Chimes for Childhood, a Collection of Songs for Little Ones,* graced by illustrations by Birket Foster, Millais, and other favorite artists of the day. This book of slightly over two hundred pages had a preface signed by Dana Estes and was, appropriately, published by Lee and Shepard.

It was editorial work of quite another sort that occupied him the months immediately before the founding of Estes and Lauriat. Estes was obviously caught up in the furor over science, particularly over Darwinism and evolution, that marked the late sixties and early seventies. The attack on the old classical system of education began in the years following the war, notably with the manifesto *The Culture Demanded by Modern Life* (1867), with its essays by Huxley, Tyndall, and Liebig, and its belligerent introduction by the ardent American, E. L. Youmans.[1] Charles W. Eliot, the prophet of the new technical system, turned Harvard over "like a flapjack," as Dr. Holmes put it.[2] Among the new "university lecturers" appointed by President Eliot in 1869 was John Fiske, who lectured on Positivism and Darwinism. This phenomenal scholar, whose grasp of history, philology, philosophy, and science had astounded his teachers in his undergraduate years, had already won the admiration of the great scientists and thinkers of England, notably Darwin, Spencer, Huxley, Tyndall, and Lewes. E. L. Youmans, perhaps the greatest single force for the propagation of scientific knowledge in the United States in that period, saw in Fiske the perfect expositor of the theory of evolution, and Fiske's Harvard lectures opened the great debate over evolution that convulsed much of American thinking for two decades. Dignified popularization reached its height in Fiske's lectures and writings; as Van Wyck Brooks remarks: "His methodical, orderly mind moved like a stone-crusher, reducing the boulders of thought to a flow of gravel that anyone could build a mental road with."[3] Darwin later said that he had never been able to understand Spencer until Fiske elucidated Spencer's theories.

Although Fiske undoubtedly gave impetus to popular interest in evolution, there was a large audience already won over to science. As was natural in America, the practical applications of science ranked foremost, but there were many readers for the occasional popular articles on astronomy, geology, botany, and zoology in the general magazines, and more books were needed to propound the latest theories and give relatively nontechnical summaries of current science. More and more articles on natural history appeared in the magazines and newspapers. The *Atlantic Monthly* had added the word "science" to its subtitle in 1868, making it read "A Magazine of Literature, Science, Art and Politics." John Burroughs was writing for the *Atlantic* in the sixties and seventies, as well as Nathaniel Shaler, the geologist, and Harvard's pride, Louis Agassiz. In 1872 the *Atlantic* added a separate department of scientific notes and book reviews, another indication of the increasing popular concern. Magazines elsewhere, such as *Harper's* and the *Galaxy* in New York, devoted considerable space to scientific articles and reviews, and the new *Scribner's Monthly* noted in 1873: "Ten or fifteen years ago, the staple subject here for reading and talk, outside study hours, was English poetry and fiction. Now it is English science. Herbert Spencer, John Stuart Mill, Huxley, Darwin, Tyndall have usurped the places of Tennyson and Browning, and Matthew Arnold and Dickens."[4]

The Astor Library in New York announced that scientific works had advanced to a popularity equal to that of works of general literature among the library's clientele.[5] Early in 1872 appeared the *Popular Science Monthly*, edited by Youmans and published by Appleton, the firm which also began the celebrated "International Science Series," with volumes by the great European masters such as Helmholtz, Darwin, Bagehot, Huxley, Lecky, and Tyndall.[6] The magazine included articles by such prolific popularizers as Richard A. Proctor, whose *Light Science for Leisure Hours,* immensely popular in 1871, served as a model for many American imitators. Jacob Abbott was turning out a series, "Science for the Young," for the Harpers; the famous "Science Primers," published by Appleton, edited by such brilliant expositors as Huxley, Roscoe, and Balfour Stewart, had begun to appear. With the sale of scientific books reaching large totals, since Mill, Darwin, Huxley, and Spencer sold better in the United States than in England—Spencer's works sold twenty thousand copies in America while scarcely the first small edition was being distributed in England—it is no wonder that a young man thinking about entering the publishing field should turn hopefully to scientific writings. While some of this resolution was undoubtedly prompted by the vogue of the moment, Estes had a continuing interest in science that is reflected in the works he published, although it tapered off somewhat after 1890. In 1872, however, the vogue was immense, and the budding publisher thought it might be profitable.

In the same "Boston Letter" which announced the founding of Estes and Lauriat[7] appeared the first list of new publications scheduled for the coming months. Among them were Professor Edward B. Tylor's *Early History of Mankind* and *Primitive Culture,* Guizot's *Popular History of France,* Miss E. B. Emery's *Queens,* a novel, and three additional numbers of "Half Hour Recreations in Popular Science": number 5, *On Nebulae, Meteoric Showers and Comets, and the Revelations of Spectrum Analysis Regarding Them . . . from the Works of Schellen, Roscoe, Huggins and Others;* number 6, *Unconscious Action of the Brain and Epidemic Delusions,* by Dr. W. B. Carpenter; and number 7, *The Geology of the Stars,* by Professor Alexander Winchell of the University of Michigan, author of *Sketches of Creation.*

The first numbers of "Half Hour Recreations" had been published by Lee and Shepard, and included: (1) *Strange Discoveries Respecting the Aurora and Recent Solar Researches,* by Richard A. Proctor; (2) *The Cranial Affinities of Man and the Ape,* by Professor Rudolph Virchow, of Berlin; (3) *Spectrum Analysis Explained and Its Use to Science Illustrated,* by Professors Schellen, Roscoe, Huggins, Lockyer, Young, and others; and (4) *Spectrum Analysis Discoveries,* by the same authors. All of these were adapted and compiled by Dana Estes, who carried them with him to the new firm when he left Lee and Shepard. Tylor's books had also been

announced by Lee and Shepard in August, but these, too, were assigned to Estes and Lauriat. Another series, "Half Hour Recreations in Natural History," was announced, to consist of several
volumes, each volume composed of twelve parts issued separately
at twenty-five cents each, the volumes to be $2.50.

The "Half Hour Recreations in Popular Science," small pamphlets that sold at twenty-five cents each, were Estes' contribution
to the popularization of science. Although he may have had advice
from scientific friends about certain selections, the idea of the
series was clearly his, and the series was a valuable attempt to
bring to the public, in compact form, the findings of current research on some of the engrossing topics of the period. Many of
these articles had to be adapted somewhat for the lay reader,
though others were by good popularizers whose articles could be
reproduced with no alteration. The first essay on the aurora, by
Richard A. Proctor, is an example of this latter class, while the
second, by Rudolph Virchow, was translated and adapted from his
article in the great *Sammlung gemeinverstaendlicher wissen-
schaftlicher Vortraege,* edited by Virchow and von Holtzendorff
from 1866 on.

The first book actually published by Estes and Lauriat ap-
peared in October, 1872, and was a combination of numbers four
and five of the "Half Hour Recreations" under the title *Spectrum
Analysis Explained, Including an Explanation of the Received
Theory of Sound, Heat, Light and Color. Compiled by the Editor of
"Half Hour Recreations in Popular Science" from the Works and
Observations of Profs. Schellen, Roscoe, Huggins, Lockyer, Young
and Others.* The original translation from the German of Dr. H.
Schellen of Cologne had been published by Appleton early in 1872,
so that Estes had the task of abridging and arranging the material
for popular taste, a task he accomplished quite well. A book of
about two hundred pages, it was called "an intelligible and pleasant
presentation of spectrum analysis," embodying things of deep and
curious interest, with numerous woodcuts and a few colored plates.[8]

The first series of "Half Hour Recreations in Popular Science"
took two years to complete, the collected papers appearing in the
fall of 1874. Several of the twenty-six numbers were granted reviews as they were published. The *Atlantic Monthly* rated Winchell's
Geology of the Stars "excellent," praising especially his summary
of modern research.[9] Winchell was a friend of Asa Gray and an
ardent defender, along with Gray and John Fiske, of Darwinism
and all the modern movements in science. The Boston *Literary
World* thought that Carpenter's *Unconscious Action of the Brain*

provided a useful key to anomalies of mental behavior which everyone has experienced, and was good reading as well.[10] Other essays, such as T. H. Huxley's *On Yeast*, T. Sterry Hunt's *Origin of Metalliferous Deposits*, Proctor's *Strange Discoveries Respecting the Aurora*, and Robert Hunt's *Coal as a Reservoir of Power*, had appeared first in scientific magazines such as the *Popular Science Monthly*, or *Van Nostrand's Engineering Magazine*. E. B. Tylor's *The Stone Age* received favorable mention in the *Popular Science Monthly*, as did several others. It was a praiseworthy achievement by an amateur, since all twenty-six numbers were interesting, and the judgment of the *Literary World* that the series constituted one of the freshest and most valuable compendiums of scientific information yet made,[11] which the *Churchman* supported by saying that the work "ranked among the best of the many works of this kind now being offered to the public,"[12] must have delighted the editor. The series soon had the flattery of imitation when another firm published "Half Hours with Modern Scientists."[13]

Several American publishers tried to get E. B. Tylor's *Primitive Culture*, one of the finest scientific works of the decade. Holt and Williams and Estes and Lauriat, the two firms that finally won out, published the work, by joint agreement, each paying the author generously. Tylor was probably the most famous anthropologist in the second half of the nineteenth century, the real founder of the science of comparative ethnology. His *Primitive Culture* soon became an anthropological classic, deemed one of the best presentations of primitive religion. This work, along with his *Researches into the Early History of Mankind*, originally published in 1865, was replete with erudition, yet lightened by an agreeable style and quiet humor. As the reviewer in the *Literary World* remarked: "The author's style, like Livy's, improves upon acquaintance"; he hinted that many readers would be frightened off by the size of the book, despite its great value.[14] The work was an admirable choice and did credit to Estes' initiative, all the more since he had to compete with several of the largest American houses.

The Boston magazines and newspapers noted that Messrs. Estes and Lauriat were prosecuting the publishing business with great energy, making a specialty of scientific books, some of them of exceptional value.[15] Besides the "Half Hour Recreations in Natural History" already announced, there was *The Unity of Natural Phenomena or the New Physics*, translated by Professor T. F. Moses of Illinois from the French of Emile Saigey. This was an excellent example of the French knack for presenting difficult subjects with attractive lucidity. More important was Elliott Coues's *A Key to*

North American Birds, which aimed to give a concise account of
every species of living and fossil bird on the continent north of
Mexico. Coues, who, at this time, was a captain and assistant sur-
geon in the United States Army, had already made a name for himself, though only thirty years of age, as a mammalogist and ornithologist, but this was his first important book. Divided into three
parts, it consisted of an introductory treatise on ornithology, suitable for layman or specialist; the key, which was an analysis of the
genera and subgenera in one continuous table; and the synopsis, in
which the species were arranged in classified form. Coues had won
his fame as a sparkling essayist on birds in the *American Naturalist* and in the London *Ibis,* but this work was a compact handbook,
giving plain and concise descriptions without any fine writing. It
was made as simple as possible, for use even by children, and was
well illustrated by woodcuts made from drawings by the author.[16]
Here was the admirable field book for the naturalist or sportsman
and a unique reference work for the library. The acclaim was practically unanimous on its publication, and, in successive editions, it
became what is known as a standard work, and was used well into
the twentieth century.[17] It also had to compete with the massive
History of North American Birds, published in this same period by
Little, Brown and Co., edited by Spencer F. Baird, T. M. Brewer,
and Robert Ridgway, all famous ornithologists.

Coues's book was the first published in conjunction with the American Naturalists' Agency in Salem, Massachusetts. The works were
prepared editorially in Salem, under the direction of S. E. Cassino,
but E & L published the books, took orders for them, and did most
of the general advertising, except that done in scientific journals.
Many excellent works bore the E & L imprint through this arrangement, and so pleasant and profitable was the relationship that
several authors continued with E & L after the agreement was
terminated in the eighties. Although many scientists may have
thought first of the editorial offices in Salem, the general public
associated E & L with the many books on birds and other natural
history topics, especially since the firm published numerous scientific books on its own. E & L were therefore aiding American
scientists in an area in which they could compete best with the great
Europeans, and from this first contact between Elliott Coues and
Dana Estes sprang a lasting friendship.

During the fall of 1872, while Tyndall was drawing unprecedented crowds to the Lowell Lectures in Boston, E & L announced
additional works: W. B. Helmsley's *A Hand-book of Hardy Trees,
Shrubs and Herbaceous Plants,* based on the French work by

Decaisne and Naudin and prepared by the assistant curator of Kew Gardens, a two-volume work with five hundred illustrations, priced at ten dollars; *Half Hours with Insects,* first of the "Half Hour Recreations in Natural History," written by Professor A. S. Packard, Jr., of the Peabody Academy of Natural Science, to be published in parts at twenty-five cents each; and C. J. Maynard's *The Birds of Florida,* also in parts, with elaborate illustrations. Estes' own compilations on popular science, necessarily spaced out over a period of years, and the works done in conjunction with the Naturalists' Agency, would also keep the firm active in the scientific field. It was the major interest of the moment and Estes determined to get all the business he could out of it.

Yet, even though E & L had opened their publishing with books on science, Estes wished to exploit other fields and shrewdly announced some religious books, perhaps as an offset to science for those conservative souls who looked on Darwin as the devil himself. An arrangement somewhat similar to that with the Naturalists' Agency was made with the bookseller-publisher Warren F. Draper of Andover, Massachusetts, and here again E & L set out to advertise and distribute the rather specialized works from this source. The professors of the noted Andover Theological Seminary, a stronghold of Congregationalism with unusually rigid Calvinistic tenets, supplied many of Draper's works, and great divines of the church were largely responsible for the rest. Under this aegis of orthodoxy E & L could rest secure against any imputations of irreligion, which would have been quite ungrounded in their case, and could count on a small but regular trade from the clergy of several denominations, who admired the scholarly productions of Andover, famous throughout the United States.

The first religious books appeared early in 1873. One was an "important book for Sunday-school teachers and students," *Jerusalem Ancient and Modern,* by the Reverend I. P. Warren, D.D., a compact work giving the history, topography, present conditions, excavations, and explorations of the Holy City, with appropriate maps and pictures. The Reverend J. S. Murphy's *Critical and Exegetical Commentary on the Book of Genesis* was the work of an accomplished Hebrew scholar, praised by reviewers for its orthodox soundness coupled with vigorous English style.[18] It was followed by volumes on Exodus, Leviticus, and a few other Old Testament books. The commentary on Genesis reached a fifth edition in a few weeks, and the whole group remained on the firm's list for many years. For really general success E & L counted on the Reverend Morley Punshon's *Lectures and Sermons.* This popular Methodist preacher was already known to American readers, and over four thousand copies were ordered in advance of publication. E & L gave it strong advertising, a front page in the *Publishers' Weekly* for April 12, 1873, where it was described as "An important book by a well-known man." One reviewer thought the style was sometimes gushing but found many passages truly eloquent and particularly enjoyed the essay on Macaulay.[19] It sold well: by April 23, five thousand copies had been printed and more were needed; and it helped to designate the new firm as a publisher of sound and solid authors.

Although Dana Estes had a real interest in science, he did not intend to become a publisher specializing in science, as Appleton was doing at the time. In fact, Appleton was doing it so well that it was difficult for other firms to obtain first-rate scientific writings to publish. Estes wished to be a general publisher who brought out some scientific works, no more than the Boston market would absorb, since New York had a sort of monopoly in science at the moment. Thus he continued to present the more popular scientific material, mostly natural history, as other general publishers were doing, maintaining a special interest in ornithology because of his friendship for Elliott Coues.

Except for the works by Coues, few of the books on science were of major value. Some were excellent works of popularization, such as A. S. Packard's on insects, and a few were notable for their elaborate and expensive illustrations. A brief survey of some of the more attractive and valuable books will suffice, since E & L did not win their fame through scientific publishing.

So successful was Coues's *Key to North American Birds*, which was published at the end of December, 1872, that a new edition was projected by April, 1873, which would comprise a *Check-list of North American Birds*, printed on one side only so that it could be cut up for labeling collections (the *Check-list* was also published as a separate pamphlet). In 1874, Coues's *Field Ornithology*, which gave directions for the collecting, preparing, and preserving of birds, came from the press and was enthusiastically received. As most reviewers pointed out, it was not a mere manual of taxidermy but a guide to the haunts of birds, warning against thoughtless destruction and serving as a stimulus to careful study.[20] It breathed the love of the woods and fields in passages where the author spoke poetically of the joys of bird hunting, joys which derived as much from the absorption of all the beauties of nature as from the finding of specific birds. The *Check-list* was appended to this work also, very appropriately.

Alpheus S. Packard, Jr., was another distinguished zoologist

on the E & L list in this first decade. Curator and then director of
the Peabody Academy of Science until 1878, he became professor of
zoology at Brown University. His *Guide to the Study of Insects* had
appeared in 1869, and E & L republished it after the success of his
later works. *Our Common Insects,* published in 1873, was splendid
popularization. Not only did it treat the more "polite" insects, if
such a term may be used of bees, flies, mosquitoes, and butterflies,
but also those unfortunate insects certainly not in good repute,
such as lice, fleas, ticks, roaches, and the like.[21] "Half Hours with
Insects," which appeared in parts from 1873 to 1877, was equally
trustworthy and attractive. The titles of the various parts were
well chosen and intriguing: *Insects of the Pond and Stream, Population of the Apple Tree, Insects as Mimics,* and *Insects as Archi-
tects* are only a few. They covered injurious insects as well as those
having no concern with man, and were advertised as valuable
for farmers, gardeners, collectors, and all intelligent readers.[22]
Packard's last book for E & L was *Injurious Insects of the West,* a
work of more practical application, and after this he transferred
to New York publishers. Many of the articles which appeared as
parts in "Half Hours with Insects" had first been printed in the
American Naturalist, of which he was editor in chief for twenty
years. All of these books by Packard were successful and remained
on the firm's list until 1898, being reduced in price after a few years
of steady sales.

There was even a book of sex education, by Professor Burt G.
Wilder, of Cornell, *What Young People Should Know.* Its aim was
to supplant quack literature on the subject and to be technically
accurate without salaciousness. As might be expected, the book
provoked mixed reactions: some praised its straightforward approach, its avoidance of prudery, noting that "Well-stated information never yet contributed to human inflammation" and, for its
only fault, finding it somewhat cumbered by technical discussions;[23]
others did not like the very idea of such a work and felt that this
book, though discreetly written in technical language, was not suitable for young readers.[24]

A ponderous but distinguished work, published by E & L for
the American Academy of Art and Sciences, was the five-volume
Works of Count Rumford, including a *Life of Count Rumford,* by
the Reverend George E. Ellis, the entire set selling for twenty-five
dollars. It was the first complete collection of the writings of this
brilliant American inventor and scientist, one of the real losses the
United States sustained in the Loyalist emigration. He was not only
a pioneer in popular science but also in economic reform, a man of

great versatility and initiative, this Massachusetts Yankee who became a count of the Holy Roman Empire. The *Nation* gave it a long and laudatory review, criticizing only Ellis' biography for not giving more details on the strictly scientific achievements of Count Rumford.[25] The work was handsomely printed and was sumptuous enough to use in the E & L display at the Centennial Exhibition, where one viewer remarked that Count Rumford was "a Tory who must feel out of place here."[26]

There were several excellent works in 1877, notably Elliott Coues's *Birds of the Northwest* and *Fur-bearing Animals of North America.* Coues remained in the Army until 1881 and his service took him to many parts of the West. In 1873 he was in the Dakotas, then served as the naturalist and secretary of the United States Northern Boundary Commission from 1873 to 1876. Always collecting and observing, he discovered many hitherto unknown bird species, and realized that this constant exploration of the West rendered all previous ornithological works out of date. His *Birds of the Northwest* was one of the most important works compiled on the Missouri valley area, and was filled with copious details from his personal observations.[27] The *Publishers' Weekly* remarked that the volume needed no recommendation beyond its full title and the author's name,[28] and the *Atlantic Monthly,* in a long and enthusiastic notice, called it "the work of a master, and one that will add to the reputation of the already distinguished author."[29] E & L unfortunately did not republish his classic *Birds of the Colorado Valley,* of 1878, which appeared as part of the Hayden Geological Survey series, and which contained some of the finest bird biographies that have ever been written, as well as delightful examples of English prose.[30] The *Fur-bearing Animals of North America* was a notable work, which profited from his extensive travels with the Army.

Another bird book, H. D. Minot's *The Land and Game Birds of New England,* was written by a young man still an undergraduate in Harvard College. This compact little book, crammed with fresh and original observations, was obviously by a field ornithologist, and was praised as being the best book on the subject then available.[31] The reviewers evidently did not realize that it was the work of such a youthful amateur, and welcomed with like acclaim a four-page leaflet entitled *The Summer Birds of the Adirondacks in Franklin County, N. Y.,* coauthored by Theodore Roosevelt, Jr., and H. D. Minot. This was Teddy's first published work, at the age of eighteen, and was undoubtedly inspired by his classmate's book on New England birds. It was prepared at the Naturalists' Agency and handled by E & L. Despite the authors' youth it gained immediate recognition in the scientific world and was incorporated in E. H. Howard's *Birds of New York* in 1910, there called the "first definite study of our Adirondack avifauna."[32]

Also of 1877 was *Ferns of North America,* the text by Professor Daniel C. Eaton of Yale, an accredited authority on fern lore, with illustrations by James H. Emerton, of Salem. It was published in parts, at intervals of two months, each part containing three large plates done by chromolithography and selling at one dollar. Since there were thirty parts, the book became a luxury item, one of the subscription works being handled in quantity by E & L in these years. The text was praised for its simplicity and accuracy, but the illustrations received the most acclaim for their faithfulness and their artistry. It was the favorable reception of this book that led to a series of lavishly illustrated books of popular science in the years to follow.[33]

Cuvier's *The Animal Kingdom* was one type of popular illustrated work: here the text was edited by Dr. W. B. Carpenter and other British scientists, but the appeal was in the illustrations, five hundred wood engravings and thirty-six colored steel plates by Landseer, all for six dollars. Another type was John Robinson's *Ferns in Their Homes and Ours,* a small book of eight chromolithographs of rare ferns, and J. H. Emerton's *The Structure and Habits of Spiders,* with text and illustrations by this successful artist, both inexpensive books. Dana Estes brought out his second series of "Half Hour Recreations in Popular Science," perhaps less attractive than the first series, but containing good essays by Tyndall, Archibald Geikie, Balfour Stewart, and Alexander Braun. Some of the topics were clearly of American interest, such as two essays on the telephone and the phonograph, with another on the illumination of beacons and buoys, which must have been close to the heart of Estes himself, who was already greatly interested in boats and yachting.

After 1880 the publishing of scientific works tapered off, with very few works of pure science and the rest largely books more important for their illustrations than their text. There were also practical books for the home, some of which were to be immensely successful. First came Miss Maria Parloa's *New Cook Book and Marketing Guide,* in 1880. Miss Parloa, who was principal of the School of Cookery in Boston and who had written other successful books, beginning with her *Appledore Cook Book* (1872), which celebrated the fare in summer-resort hotels, aimed her book at the beginner, especially with her introductory chapters on marketing, groceries, care of food, and kitchen equipment. She expounded clearly the various types of plain cooking and rich cooking, with abundant illustrations, and left an appendix of blank pages, "for those housewives who think they have got ahead of Miss Parloa," as one reviewer put it.[34] The book was hardly literature, but it could not fail to promote good digestion.[35]

Early in January, 1881, the publishers announced that it had sold over three thousand copies before publication, with five thousand more sold in the month following. In five months it sold ten thousand copies and the sales were doubled in a year. Said E & L: "It is pronounced by good judges the best cook-book ever made in America."[36] They devoted full-page advertisements to it in several magazines, one reading, in very large type: "Millions of dollars saved! to the wasteful people in this country by the use of this safe guide. It is the success of the season,"[37] followed by quotations from seventeen magazines and newspapers.

Setting out to exploit this vein, E & L next published Ellen H. Richards' *The Chemistry of Cooking and Cleaning,* a small manual by an instructor in chemistry in the Woman's Laboratory of the Massachusetts Institute of Technology. In 1882 Miss Parloa reappeared with *Camp Cookery,* "a dainty little volume," which gave directions for dressing and cooking game, handling utensils over the campfire, and such details. A few years later she brought out a *Kitchen Companion* and finally, in 1893, *Miss Parloa's Young Housekeeper,* a vade mecum for the complete novice. These, with revisions of her cookbook, were impressive sellers for E & L, who never tired of listing the thousands of copies sold.

From this time on, most of E & L's scientific books, with the exception of those by Elliott Coues and his disciples, became mixed up with gift books and subscription books, sold in parts. In 1881 we find *Beautiful Wild Flowers of America,* a quarto with colored plates from original drawings by Isaac Sprague,[38] text by the Reverend A. B. Hervey, being selections from Longfellow, Bryant, Whittier, Holmes, and others, and also *Beautiful Ferns of America,* another gift quarto, adapted from Eaton's book on ferns, of 1877, both books priced at six dollars. Mr. Hervey turned out a little book on *Sea Mosses,* also with colored plates, that had a scientific, not literary text, and won approval.[39] In 1882 came *Flowers of the Field and Forest,* colored plates by Isaac Sprague, which was also published in New York by Crowell. *Forest, Rock and Stream,* three years later, was a gift book without science, being composed of twenty steel engravings with descriptive text by N. P. Willis and a selection of flower verse. *Wayside Flowers and Ferns,* in 1886, had more sentimental text by Mr. Hervey and suffered a final degrada-

tion, in our eyes, at least, by being offered in three styles of soft
ornamental bindings called Burmese Plush, Wild Rose, and Peach
Blow. Yet, this same year, E & L published a sumptuous work, *The
Wild Flowers of America,* containing fifty chromolithographs from
paintings by Isaac Sprague and a fine text by George Goodale, a
Harvard botany professor, which sold for forty dollars. H. O.
Houghton started the publication of this work as early as 1877 and
it was later taken over by E & L, sold in twenty-five parts and
finally in two bound volumes. It was highly praised, both for illustrations and text, and was one of the better works of this sort the
firm published before the days of truly accurate color representation
of flowers.[40]

The books by Elliott Coues, having the double advantage of
great scientific reputation and abundant sales, remained on E & L's
list throughout the existence of the firm. That Estes and Coues were
great friends had something to do with it too, especially in the
eighties and nineties, when E & L had many irons in the fire. Coues's
Check-list of North American Birds was given a second edition in
1882. The first edition had covered 635 species; the next added 120
and provided a bibliography of Coues's scientific writings from 1861
to 1881, comprising about three hundred titles.[41] The following year
saw his *Ornithology of the World,* a popular work, containing about
seven hundred illustrations. In 1884 came the second edition of the
Key to North American Birds, much enlarged, with about five hundred illustrations, and containing his *Field Ornithology* as well. It
became the standard manual for the eighties as its predecessor had
been for the seventies.[42] Other books by disciples, usually with a
foreword by Coues, were published, such as Charles Dixon's *Rural
Bird Life* and Charles B. Cory's *Birds of Haiti and San Domingo,*
in a limited edition, in parts, with hand-painted plates in water
colors. Another work, suggested by Coues, was the translation of
Friedrich von Hellwald's *Naturgeschichte des Menschen* as the
History of Man, done by Professor J. S. Kingsley of the University
of Nebraska, assisted by a corps of specialists, W. H. Dall of the
Smithsonian Institution, F. W. Putnam of the Peabody Museum, and
Stephen Salisbury, of the American Antiquarian Society. It was a
semipopular work, copiously illustrated, with additional material
on American topics, particularly the American Indian.

Quite a new departure was the "Biogen Series" by Coues, the
first of which, *Biogen, A Speculation on the Origin and Nature of
Life,* came out in 1884 and was considered unique in print, binding, and contents. The argumentation was thoroughly scientific,
as befitted a naturalist, and a most novel contribution to the sub-

ject. In the second volume, *The Daemon of Darwin*, the author applied the theory of evolution to the development and probable destiny of the soul. The third volume, Henry S. Olcott's *A Buddhist Catechism*, with an introduction and notes by Elliott Coues, showed which way the wind was blowing. Coues, on a trip to Europe in 1884, in company with Dana Estes, met Henry S. Olcott and Mme Blavatsky, with the result that his curiosity about theosophy was fanned into ardent devotion. Soon afterward he founded the Gnostic Branch of the Theosophical Society in Washington and was one of the founders of the American Society for Psychical Research. Two new volumes, *Can Matter Think?* and *Kuthumi, or The True and Complete Economy of Human Life*, written by Robert Dodsley and edited by Coues, were brought out in 1886. Coues apparently yearned to be head of the entire theosophical movement in America, and his maneuvers to this end, along with his skepticism of the Mahatmic messages from the East, brought him in conflict with the whole society. In 1888 he still praised Mme Blavatsky as "the greatest woman of this age, who is born to redeem her times," but in May of 1889, when he failed to be elected president of the American section of the Theosophical Society, he denounced the Society as "Mme Blavatsky's famous hoax," and was expelled soon after. He then subsided into editing works of travel in the early West and revising his already famous ornithological works.[43]

The later years of E & L saw relatively few scientific works. The third edition of Coues's *Key to North American Birds* appeared in 1886, the fourth in 1890. The book was now so popular that it had several formats, notably the Sportsman's Edition, printed on thin paper and bound in flexible Russia-leather covers. The nineties saw only such minor works as G. B. Goode's *American Fishes*, J. S. Kingsley's *Popular Natural History*, and Charles B. Cory's *Hunting and Fishing in Florida*. Practically all the scientific publishing of any value came within the period 1872–1886 when E & L published more scientific books than any other Boston firm.

By 1880 Dana Estes had lost his keen interest in science, especially since he had won publishing triumphs in other fields. His interest had always been that of the amateur, and although he retained it to the end of his publishing career, he saw that it was futile to compete against the professional productions of an Appleton or a Wiley. He was inclined to stick with a favored author through thick and thin, especially if that author showed personality in his nature writing.

When Estes began publishing by himself after 1898, there were a few more books on natural history, most of them for ornithologists. It was wholly fitting that Dana Estes and Co. should publish the final edition, its fifth, of Coues's *Key to North American Birds,* in 1903. This massive work, whose scientific value had long been acknowledged, was made more artistic by the addition of two hundred new illustrations by Louis Agassiz Fuertes, the most noted bird painter of his day. It is this edition that still may be found on the reference shelves of many large libraries, as it is inevitably in all specialized zoological collections. Fuertes also illustrated another book for the firm, Mason Walton's *The Hermit's Wild Friends* (1903), which recorded the whimsical nature notes of the hermit of Bond's Hill in Gloucester, Massachusetts.[44]

In 1907 Dana Estes discovered a nature writer after his own heart, a simple, straightforward observer who wrote without sentimentalizing. This was Charles W. Townsend, whose first book, *Along the Labrador Coast,* appeared in the fall. His trip to Labrador was made for scientific purposes, and his technical findings were published as *Birds of Labrador* by the Boston Society of Natural History. *Along the Labrador Coast* related his other observations, displayed his interest in the history and the people of that bleak coast. The *Nation* thought it made enjoyable reading, and most other reviewers agreed.[45] His second book, *A Labrador Spring,* was also praised for its sound information and human interest.[46]

Best of all was his *Sand Dunes and Salt Marshes* (1913), a book which embodied over forty years of hunting, watching, and walking through the Ipswich marshes along the Massachusetts coast north of Boston. Like his other books, it was a sober account, more in the style of Gilbert White than of Donald Culross Peattie, but a book that well reflected his loving concentration on all forms of life in that region, though his favorite birds got most attention. The reviewer in the *Nation* liked it for what Lowell found refreshing in Gibbon, his "honest incapacity of imagination."[47] Actually there is much contagious enthusiasm in the book, and it is almost surprising that such an apparently barren subject could be made so interesting. The illustrations, from the author's photographs, were beautifully appropriate, and the whole book was handsomely made.[48] It is still delightful reading and thoroughly to be recommended to anyone interested in such regions of sea, sand, and smell.

This was the last scientific book for Dana Estes and Co. and a worthy close to their nature publications. L. C. Page liked it well enough to advertise, soon after his purchase of Dana Estes and Co., "a really excellent book from the Estes list."[49] Since he advertised only two or three titles from their list, this was praise indeed. E & L and their successor, even though general publishers, had managed to turn out several important scientific works and a good number of useful but minor nature books. And in this field, somewhat contrary to the firm's policy in most others, the majority of the authors were Americans.

Throughout these years of science publishing, religious books kept pace, but dropped off almost entirely after 1885. In the first five years of E & L they ran neck and neck, eighteen scientific works, including three series titles, as compared with sixteen religious books. In their annual catalogues E & L also listed, sometimes separately, sometimes not, the large back list of Warren F. Draper, amounting in 1880 to over eighty titles, a sizable proportion of E & L's list. While many of the religious books published and advertised by E & L were sound, solid achievements, they did not have the prestige of the scientific publications. A few titles, taken at random, will show the type of books published: Alexander Buttman's *A Grammar of the New Testament Greek;* William Smith's *Dictionary of the Bible;* Ralph Emerson's *Augustinism and Pelagianism;* Frederick Gardiner's *A Harmony of the Four Gospels in Greek* and *The Principles of Textual Criticism;* John W. Haley's *The Discrepancies of the Bible;* Austin Phelps's *Ministerial Culture;* and a *History of the Books of the Bible* by Calvin E. Stowe, Harriet Beecher's husband. Many of them were grammars, dictionaries, commentaries, and text publications, such as the *Codex Vaticanus,* but the majority were doctrinal treatises written usually from the Andover viewpoint, though E & L published a few books by Baptists, Methodists, and Episcopalians, as, for example, the Reverend Alvah Hovey's *Religion and the State,* a work on church taxation and exemption by the president of Newton Theological Seminary (Baptist).

Some of the firm's subscription books, in the early years, were religious. *Kitto's Family Bible,* with colored engravings, steel plates, maps, and one thousand wood engravings, which sold in forty parts at fifty cents each, was a general favorite. One might select *Pictorial Sunday Reading,* which contained selections from the Bible, "80 elegant illustrations and 650 pages, printed on superior toned paper"; this was sold in twenty parts at fifty cents each. The *Pilgrim's Progress* was marketed in thirty parts at thirty cents each, while Fleetwood's *Life of Christ, Also the Lives of the Apostles and Evangelists,* "profusely illustrated," was available in thirty parts at fifty cents a part. These popular works, along with the very scholarly material from Andover, satisfied Estes' need for a certain percentage of religious works on his list. After 1885, however, when the firm was making big money from juveniles and several varieties of subscription books, the religious publications dropped out, and except for children's works, it is impossible to find ten religious titles in the later years of E & L. Thus, both science and religion sank into the background when there was an opportunity to make large profits from standard authors in sets, children's books, and illustrated works on travel.

Chapter Three

EARLY SUBSCRIPTION BOOKS
AND SOME OTHERS

EVER since Colonial days the selling of books by traveling agents
has flourished in America. The peddler, of whatever wares, had
become a vital part of the American scene, especially in the nineteenth century, and much of the literature of the time testifies
to his peculiar temperament and his ubiquity. In a predominantly
rural nation, in the days before rapid communications, he served as
the advertiser of novelties, he brought a glimpse of the up-to-date,
urban culture that most country people yearned for, and he frequently did it with gusto: "I call them missionaries," said Gail
Hamilton in her essay about peddlers in *Twelve Miles from a
Lemon*.[1] " 'There's odds in deacons,' the country folk say; how much
more in peddlers. My own especial prejudice is against the peddler
who carries a little black glazed carpet-bag and in favor of him who
comes in a large, long, high, red cart. *He* gives hostages to society."
She tells of the villager's delight when the bright cart of the tin
peddler hove into view: " 'Any tin ware to-day?' he asks you,
cheerily." While he shows his wares he tells about his family, gives
news of the next town, perhaps explains his philosophy of life. And
then there are the men with black carpetbags, or the clerical-looking
men who accost the villager with a jaunty air and ask her to accept
a box of soap as a present!

And finally the book agents! "When I see a poor man traveling
up hill and down across our country-side, expecting to earn his

bread and butter by the commission he is to receive on the sale of his books, and think of the sparse farm houses where he is to sell them, the farmers mowing the marshes knee-deep in salt water, and the women rising at midnight to cook their suppers, I am just not moved to tears. . . . Is there no corn in Egypt that you must come up to Canaan to gather these scanty gleanings? The minister may generally be counted on as secure prey, and sometimes a freak will take a farmer or two of us, to the peddler's advantage."[2] He may be selling Bibles, with a shrewd mingling of religion and trade, and can induce hardfisted farmers to buy more Bibles, even if they already have some, to leave as part of their property. Some more obnoxious agents, selling religious books and newspapers, bore into the house and hold an inquiry on your way of life and your personal history. "They have just intelligence enough to be curious, but not enough to be decent."[3] Yet, despite Gail Hamilton's opinion, many book agents, carrying the most dubious wares, must have been given a welcome, often a hearty one, by those living out on lonely country roads, for they had news and fresh subjects of conversation, and they frequently could sell the trash they carried because they were jovial and loquacious.

During the first half of the nineteenth century, book peddling of this type, usually known as the subscription-book trade, had thriven mightily. By the time of the Civil War whole organizations had been formed to market these books, such as Payne and Holden, General Subscription Agency for the West, whose corps of agents could canvass Ohio, Indiana, Illinois, and other states if the terms were sufficiently liberal.[4] The regular book trade suffered a marked depression in 1868, but subscription publishing felt none of it. "Demobilized soldiers found that they could make a living by canvassing for such works as Greeley's *American Conflict*, which sold 225,000 copies, . . . Richardson's *Field, Dungeon, and Escape* and his *Beyond the Mississippi*, which between them rolled up sales of nearly 200,000 copies."[5] This was the start of the great period of subscription selling. Many of the best-selling books were not in the hands of the trade at all and were not sent to magazines and newspapers for review.[6] "Canny publishers saw that a far vaster public than they had dreamed of was eager to buy books if the books could be taken to the buyer."[7] Frank Compton's statement that probably 90 per cent of the book buyers in the decades following the Civil War never entered a bookstore does not seem overly exaggerated, since these people were, as he put it, "far removed from bookstores, physically and spiritually."[8]

The *New York Times*, in 1872, thought that the subscription-book trade might eventually drive the regular book business out of existence. The high prices of books and the increasing resources of public libraries were two important reasons. The *Times* described the two distinct branches of publishing: the regular trade, in bookstores and book auction sales, serving mostly the inhabitants of cities and towns, and the more quiet but vastly extended business through book agents in country districts. The books of one branch of the trade were often never heard of among the customers of the other. The *Times* believed that the agency business was certain to become the profitable branch, both for author and publisher, and would continually improve. It would turn out books with better pictures, books of a more original and reputable character, and it would gradually fill up the farm houses of the country with literature "both solid and attractive." "It is with books, perhaps, as with articles in shops, the customer likes to be persuaded. Since most Americans live away from libraries, reading-rooms and book shops, the agent is the merchant of the thoughts of the world to them."[9]

The editor of the *Publishers' and Stationers' Weekly Trade Circular* disagreed with the *Times* and surveyed quite fairly the status of the subscription trade at this time. He granted the many services done by the colporteur in earlier days, when the Bible, Foxe's *Book of Martyrs,* and the *Pilgrim's Progress* were the staples. The success of the publishing business in America was built upon foundations laid by him, and there was still a broad field of endeavor in the West and South. But the book agency business, as now conducted, he remarked, was the abuse of a good thing, for "enterprising people" could, by going from house to house, sell almost any sort of book. It was a good thing that 227,000 copies of Kitto's *History of the Bible* had been sold, or that such books as Smith's *Bible Dictionary* and so fine an art work as *Picturesque America* should be brought into many homes. It was not a good thing, he thought, that five-dollar bills—the hard-earned savings, it might be, of weeks—should be extracted from lean purses for such worthless books as collections of feeble essayists whom the trade would not publish or "wicked and demoralizing volumes salaciously baited," such as *The Mysteries of Life in the City of Satan.* The great proportion of books from Hartford were actually bad or humbug. (Whether he included Mark Twain in this judgment is hard to say.) "A gorgeous binding, usually in bad taste, thick but cheap paper, outrageously poor woodcuts, the largest type with the thickest leads, make a big, gaudy book which a glib tongue or persistent boring cheats folks into buying, when the reading matter it contains is worth, if anything, a dollar and a half."[10]

George Ade doubted that the public really wanted many of these subscription books. Every well-furnished home had to keep something on the center table, where the Bible was usually flanked by subscription books, which were thick and heavily gilded to keep company with the bulky and expensive Bible.[11] The agents knew how to sell these books, and it could be a profitable business, since the agent's commission was often 30 per cent. On a $3.50 book an agent would make $1.00, and he might make $100 a month, the minimum figure cited by experts writing on the subscription-book trade. Many agents would not handle low-priced books, so that most subscription books averaged five to ten dollars a volume, or bulked up in numerous parts, each reasonably priced. But the advantage of the agent was not in price but in "push," and if the regular trade was apathetic, it stood to lose.[12]

It was no wonder, then, that many shrewd publishers, established in the regular trade, set up branches for subscription selling, thus going over to the enemy. They counted on a small number of titles, large printings, and an army of canvassers. In comparison with the printing of one thousand to twenty-five hundred copies for the ordinary trade-book edition, the subscription book, to be successful, demanded an initial printing of perhaps fifty thousand copies, with several new printings of similar scope in case of popularity. Mark Twain wanted his books sold by subscription; *The Innocents Abroad* came up to expectation, selling more than 125,000 copies in three years. Many of the larger publishers, therefore, set up separate departments for subscription selling, since there was no need to pay for newspaper and magazine advertising, only to engage experienced book canvassers. Of course, the regular book trade tried to intimate that subscription-book selling was beneath the noble profession of bookselling; even though there was a larger profit for the author, such methods of sale would not be employed by authors of established reputation, who would lower themselves by seeking a constituency of a lesser grade.[13] The sale of a book should be proportioned to its merits, the trade asserted, rightly enough, and not made "subordinate to the arts of importunity and trickery."[14]

It only remained, then, for the subscription trade to condescend, now and then, to supply the regular book store with subscription books. In 1873 a New York firm offered to supply the trade with subscription books in large or small quantities, thus exploding the fiction that subscription books were obtainable only from agents.[15] This was rather unusual, and most subscription-book publishers were very concerned over the diversion of their books to the trade. E & L later had a legal battle with Mark Twain over this very point, proving that agents frequently broke their contracts with the subscription house to make quick sales of certain popular items to retail booksellers. By and large the dike held, and the profits of book canvassing remained accordingly high. The trade magazines of 1872 and 1873 were particularly worried by subscription selling, judging from the frequent editorial laments; and it was in this atmosphere that E & L set out to make their first experiments in the two kinds of bookselling.

In their very first announcement of publications, in the fall of 1872, E & L had listed Guizot's *Popular History of France,* to be published in six volumes. Subsequent advertisements, early in 1873, indicated that the work was planned as a regular trade publication at three dollars a volume. On April 12, 1873, the *Publishers' Weekly* had a letter from "Dana" lamenting the apathy of the trade, since a *"very important"* book had been announced for months and dealers had been urged to send advance orders, yet not five copies had been ordered by the book trade of the whole country.[16] The editor attempted to soothe "Dana's" impatience, noting that the Boston firm was too recent to have made any reputation for its books.[17] More advertisements of the Guizot appeared, then, late in November, E & L informed the trade that the work would be published in parts and sold by subscription.

In a letter to the *Publishers' Weekly* Dana Estes offered the following defense:

> We send herewith a few sample sheets of Guizot's *France.* We fully intended to publish this book *for the trade.* We announced it for one year and found no encouragement to do so. We have had a single agent take more subscriptions in a single week than the entire book trade of the country called for on a year's advertising. If booksellers will not order a standard book like this, we cannot afford to manufacture it and wait for them to do so. We can find enterprising agents who can sell it even in panic times. . . . We are endeavoring to make this book as fine a book of its class as has ever been turned out, and *we must have it sell* in some way. If the booksellers won't sell it, agents must have it.
>
> Yours faithfully,
> Estes and Lauriat[18]

Advertisements were put in all the regular magazines and papers for agents, "experienced book canvassers," not only for Guizot's *France* but for other historical works projected by the firm. Perhaps the panic of 1873 had as much as anything to do with E & L's entrance into the subscription field, for they had clearly planned to publish only for the trade. However it came about, it was a momentous decision for E & L and opened the door to their future prosperity, although, at this time, it seemed more like a desperate bid for survival.

If it had not been a bad year, the book trade would surely have been more responsive to the announcement of Guizot's *France*. It was as good a book as Dana Estes thought it, and was destined for a long success. It was offered, to subscribers only, in fifty-five parts, paper covered, at fifty cents each, or a total of $27.50. Subscribers could also have it in six royal octavo volumes in a variety of bindings, ranging from cloth, at $33, full library sheep, at $39, half morocco, at $45, to full morocco or full tree calf, with gilt edges, at $60. This "great work" the publishers confidently believed a specimen of bookmaking "unexcelled by any book made in America." It was a work whose publication would require several years: the French edition began to appear in Paris in 1870, the London edition, in a translation by Robert Black, first came out in 1872, published by Sampson, Low, Marston, Low, and Searle. E & L made arrangements with Hachette in France and the British publishers to have the sole rights in America. They secured electrotypes of all the original woodcuts, most of them by Alphonse de Neuville, the great French illustrator, to the number of three hundred, and added forty steel engravings by "celebrated artists," a necessity for any "dignified" work. Heavy paper and "beautiful letter press" were also promised. "Persons wanting a good and reliable History of France need have no hesitation in subscribing for this as it is the only one of a popular nature, and by a standard historian, to be had in the English language. . . . The world-wide reputation of Guizot is a sufficient recommendation to the work, and a guarantee of its being thoroughly correct and an intensely interesting history."[19]

Guizot was, indeed, a historian of world-wide reputation. His early works on the civilization of Europe, the civilization of France, and the English revolution had proclaimed him a brilliant and original scholar who opened new paths for philosophical history. Eminent as a diplomat and a statesman, he was driven out of office by the revolution of 1848 in France, but, after a brief period of exile, he returned to France to live the rest of his days in comparative seclusion. He had entered politics through a sense of duty and did not find it a calamity when events retired him to a scholar-ly life. Only a month after he reached England, in March, 1848, although he had barely escaped with his life, this self-possessed man was writing to his friend, Barante, "I shall set to work again." To another friend he sketched out his scholarly aims, to finish his *History of the English Revolution,* his *History of Civilization in France,* and his *History of France as Told to My Grandchildren.*[20] This latter work, which was to become the *Popular History of France,* he had begun as early as 1839, at his country home at Val-Richer, in Normandy, where he had written three chapters. "I think I could write in six volumes a history which would be of real value in itself, both interesting and readable in its form, and likely to become generally popular." Although this history had actually been started for his grandchildren, it was made suitable for readers other than children as he continued it.[21]

He interrupted the *History of France,* however, to complete other works, notably his *Memoirs,* which served as a justification of his political career, and he did not start in again in earnest until 1869, at the age of eighty-two. Its publication in Paris was hindered by the Franco-Prussian War and the first volume did not appear until early 1872. Several laudatory articles were published about it in French magazines, notably the *Revue des deux mondes,* and Guizot wrote to a friend of his, Vitet: "It was, indeed, in the first place for the instruction of my grandchildren, but not for them alone, that I began, and, God willing, shall finish this important work. I fancied that I might help restore France in her present ruins by setting before her a faithful picture of the recoveries of former days in her long life. It is only our faith in a resurrection which enables us poor creatures to endure the idea of death. It ought to be the same thing for nations. They are not dead as long as they are and feel themselves to be alive, they do not fall into decrepitude as long as they do not yield to it, and can look back to former resurrections in their history."[22] Guizot gave all his time to the history in these years, completing the final volume of the French edition just before his last illness in 1874. This work of his old age was a favorite with him, and a day or so before his death he asked to hear some passages from his history, especially those about the Huguenots, and he gazed for a long time at the portrait of Coligny. He had brought French history up to 1789 when his strength failed, and his daughter, Mme Guizot de Witt, completed the portion on the French Revolution from his notes.

The six volumes of the history were published by E & L from 1872 to 1876. The red and black title page seems a bit garish to our taste but evidently aroused no objection then, and was even admired. Two more volumes were later written by Mme de Witt and added to the British edition, bringing the history down to the revolution of 1848, but E & L never published them, although they were willing to import them, in a uniform binding, for those who wished to supplement the original set. The early parts, when they appeared, were lavishly praised, although most of the reviews awaited the completion of the work in 1876. Charles Sumner said of it: "To a most interesting subject Guizot brings the experience of a statesman, the study of a professor, and the charm of an accomplished writer. I am glad you are to place this recent work within the reach of all American readers."[23] Wendell Phillips thought that everything from the pen of Guizot was remarkable for thoroughness of investigation and exact statement.[24] Reviews in the major periodicals agreed that it was well written, that it was popular in the best sense of the word, since it omitted tedious details of battles and sieges in order to emphasize the great historical milestones, which only a true historian could distinguish from the mass.[25] The style was clear, never lush or pulsating, like Michelet's, but firm and powerful when the scene itself was great or terrible, so that the controlled emotion was all the more effective. Guizot was not a brilliant writer, but he made the work interesting by his full delineation of character and his concentration upon great personages and great events. As he notes in his "Letter to the Publishers": "When we wish particularly to get an idea of the chief features of a country, we mount the heights. . . . And so we must proceed in history when we wish neither to reduce it to the skeleton of an abridgment nor extend it to the huge dimension of a learned work. Great events and great men are the fixed points and the peaks of history . . . and, with rare exceptions, it is always on the great deeds and the great personages of history that I have relied for making of them in my tales what they were in reality—the centre and the focus of the life of France."[26]

The various reviewers each had favorite passages: some praised and quoted pages on Charlemagne, some the sections on the literary figures of the age of Louis XIV, some the pages on Joan of Arc, while others found interesting opinions on Voltaire. Guizot was a strong partisan of constitutional monarchy and an equally strong Protestant, but his impartiality was noted by all critics.[27] A true philosophical historian, he was always moderate, just, tolerant, and logical, virtues frequently eschewed by modern historians of similar pretensions. It was a history especially adapted to the tastes of British and American readers, since one of his basic ideas was that government should belong to the middle classes, which possess both wealth and intelligence and which, by their self-interest and ability, will assure the prosperity of the social body.[28] And it was also a history of France by a deeply religious man and a Protestant to boot, points which a book canvasser could profitably stress. Charles Kendall Adams considered it the best popular history of France, adding that no other country could boast of a history so well adapted to the needs of intelligent young men and women.[29]

Most reviewers had good words for the superior typography and the numerous illustrations. The pictures were rated fully equal to those of the French edition, and many liked the skillful choice of subjects by Neuville. Professor Niemeyer of the Yale School of Fine Arts pleased the publishers by saying that nearly every illustration was an artistic conception vividly presenting the incident which formed its subject,[30] and C. K. Adams thought them well drawn and admirably suited to enhance popular interest. Neuville, who was a pupil of Delacroix, was, in the 1870's, at the height of his popularity as a depicter of battle scenes, in which he knew how to delight his French clientele by depicting the French soldiers of the debacle as always chivalrous and brave, the Prussians coarse and brutal. The illustrations for Guizot's history constituted one of his major efforts, and make one realize that ideal representations of this sort, when cleverly done, add much more to the vividness of history than any number of reproductions of architectural façades and historical artifacts, to which so many modern works are limited. The American edition also included genealogical tables and a detailed index, both superior to the corresponding sections in the English and French editions.

And last, but not least for E & L, the history sold beyond expectations and became the first great success of the firm. Frank Luther Mott ranks it next to the best sellers of this decade, which had to achieve a sale of 375,000 copies to fulfill his requirements.[31] It is impossible to estimate the total sales of this work, since it was being issued, under subsidiary imprints, up to the turn of the century, but Estes always spoke of it as the foundation stone of E & L's fortunes. A supplement and an abridgment brought additional profits several years later, and the prestige of this work helped market other works by Guizot and other large-scale histories, done in the same lavish style.

As soon as Guizot's *France* was commenced, several historical works were announced, some by subscription and others as regular trade publications. In January, 1874, Charles Knight's *Popular*

History of England was advertised, after being printed and bound in England for E & L. This history, originally published from 1856 to 1862, had been republished in 1871. It was akin to Guizot's *Popular History of France* only in its general purpose, for Charles Knight, whatever his merits as a popularizer and a noble champion of popular education, was not a great historian.[32] The work was generously illustrated with woodcuts and was eminently readable, with great detail on the later centuries, a book that would sell as a parallel work to Guizot's for those who read history for pleasure. The eight-volume set was priced from $25, in cloth, to $60, in full tree calf. At the same time both E & L and Putnam published the abridgment of Charles Knight's autobiography, which had appeared in three volumes, in 1865, as *Passages from the Life of Charles Knight*. This fascinating book described the many ventures in bringing culture to the masses that had made Knight a famous name in England and America.

Charles Knight, with his *Penny Cyclopaedia, Pictorial Bible, Popular History of England, Pictorial Shakspere,* and *Old England,* revolutionized the methods of adapting serious matter to popular taste, accomplishing it mainly by a simple yet clever mingling of readable text with attractive and interesting illustrations. He was one of the foremost in employing abundant woodcuts to enliven his books, along with the more sober and highly regarded steel engravings.[33] He was a truly philanthropical publisher, since some of his early publications, such as the *Penny Magazine* and the *Penny Cyclopaedia,* were great popular successes in number of copies distributed, but financial losses for the publisher, because of the low price and heavy excise tax. He had found it expedient to sell works in parts, by subscription, and it was highly appropriate that E & L should publish the life of so distinguished a subscription publisher. It might be added, however, that E & L were not imbued with the same philanthropic purposes as Knight, even though they republished many of his works. They simply found them admirable for subscription selling and made a good profit on them. Thus they published, in later years, his *Shakspere* and *Old England,* both sumptuously illustrated and suitable for sale in parts. A year later, E & L brought out a new, American reprint of the *Popular History,* still in eight volumes, but with a continuation to 1874 by William Nassau Molesworth, whose three-volume history of England from 1830 to 1874 was a highly regarded work at this period, especially lauded by the mighty Gladstone himself.

Early in 1874 E & L published Lord Campbell's *Lives of the Chief Justices of England,* a new edition in four volumes of this work, which had originally appeared in 1857. It was not ranked as highly as his *Lives of the Lord Chancellors,* published in 1849, and which E & L republished the following year in ten volumes. Neither of these works was new, and Little, Brown and Company, just a few doors away, were also publishing an edition of the *Chief Justices.* Even though these works were old, they were reviewed in several periodicals,[34] and all reviewers commented on their handsome appearance. E & L advertised the work, with typical bombast, as "the most brilliant contribution to British history made within our recollection," but the facts hardly bore out this claim. "Plain John Campbell," who made a pretense of humility while striving with every art of the politician to become Lord Chancellor—which he did—was scarcely a judicious historian. Both his *Lord Chancellors* and *Chief Justices* were works hastily written in spare moments, crammed with unacknowledged citations, and marred by numerous inaccuracies and by petty sneers and insinuations against both living and dead, though the dead fared considerably better than certain of the living. Some of the writing was lively, anecdotes and personal details abounded, so that the books were readable for lawyers and laymen alike; the very personalities and animosities of the author gave spirit to the pages, for Campbell was an energetic hater. Despite all the defects, the works were invaluable repertories of facts, and entertaining in the bargain.[35]

Probably the major reason for republishing Campbell's *Chief Justices* was the appearance of Sir Joseph Arnould's *Memoir of Thomas, First Lord of Denman,* which E & L published in June, 1874, in two volumes, uniform with Campbell's set, making six volumes in all. The *Nation* gave it a long review, centering chiefly on the career of Lord Denman, praising the work and the fine appearance of the books themselves.[36] All of these books were costly, the *Chief Justices* ranging from eight to fourteen dollars, and the memoir of Lord Denman at seven dollars for two volumes. This was surely a bid for the legal trade, just as their religious books were a bid for the clerical. Several other works, more specifically legal still, were published in 1874 and 1875, such as S. N. Phillips' *Famous Cases of Circumstantial Evidence* and Sir George Stephen's *Adventures of an Attorney in Search of a Practice,* both older works. More interesting, perhaps, was Edward Foss's *Memories of Westminster Hall,* a two-volume work dealing with famous judges and trials, among them the amazing Tichborne Case and older cases, such as the trials of Algernon Sidney, Dr. Henry Sacheverell, Queen Caroline, and Tom Paine. This, too, was handsomely printed and bound.[37]

The next important project was the "Epochs of Modern History Series," eighteen small volumes appropriately priced at one dollar each, which covered medieval and modern history to 1865. It was a British series, edited by Edward E. Morris, later professor of English at the University of Melbourne. It was a set distinctly aimed at the general reader, giving him an abundance of facts, clearly presented, with sober and generally objective interpretations. The books were too small to allow space for illustrations, but had good maps and genealogical tables. Some of the authors did an excellent job, and many of the little brown-cloth volumes are still useful for the reader who wishes to get a fairly detailed factual survey of a period such as the Thirty Years' War or the reign of Edward III. Samuel R. Gardiner did the volume on the Thirty Years' War, Mandell Creighton on the age of Elizabeth, William Stubbs on the early Plantagenets, and James Gairdner on the houses of Lancaster and York. Frederic Seebohm wrote the *Era of the Protestant Revolution,* which won praise from several sources as reasonably impartial, clear, dramatic, and readable, a book which only the most bigoted Catholic or Protestant would reject.[38] This was followed by George Cox's *The Crusades,* very useful as a survey, and S. R. Gardiner's *The First Two Stuarts and the Puritan Revolution,* all of which were favorably received.

W. F. Allen, who reviewed most of the series for the *Nation,* was quite enthusiastic about these works. Although correcting minor errors of detail and disputing certain opinions, he found many of them the best small treatises available on the topic, and this was probably the soundest judgment of the whole group. They are now considered out of date, though works by such masters as Stubbs, Seebohm, Creighton, or Gardiner would still have merit as brilliant surveys.[39]

Almost simultaneously appeared another series, the "Epochs of Ancient History," in ten volumes. These were quite successful, but have not lasted as well as the modern series. A few of the great authorities of the day were included, such as Charles Merivale, Wilhelm Ihne, A. M. Curteis, and M. W. Capes, but even their works brought mixed praise and blame, to a much greater extent than did the modern series. With the exception of the volume *Rome and Carthage,* which is still useful, this series has faded.[40]

Modeled on the "Epochs" were the "Epochs of English History," edited by Mandell Creighton, which included eight volumes. In general, these were not by distinguished authorities, although Frederick York Powell wrote on *Early England up to the Norman Conquest* and Mandell Creighton on *The Tudors and the Reforma-*

tion. The periods were too inclusive to be treated handily in such small volumes, and the authors, although good popularizers, had little to bring to the subject in the way of authoritative interpretations. Yet, like similar works of today, such as the "Pelican History of England," they had the virtue of quick and simple surveys, useful summaries of recent scholarship for the non-scholarly public.

In publishing the "Epochs of History" E & L had strong competition from Scribner, Armstrong and Co., who were publishing the series in New York. E & L, in their first advertisement, announced: "This is the only authorized edition of these valuable books,"[41] but the books were identical in appearance, imitated exactly from the British edition published by Longmans, Green and Co. They were advertised vigorously from both New York and Boston, and the *Publishers' Weekly* finally commented that the publication of the "Epochs" was not a "trade fight" between the two firms but a matter of amicable agreement.[42] Both the aggressive advertising and the inherent merits of the little books made them sell in prodigious quantities, and one constantly finds either the E & L or Scribner editions in many second-hand bookstores today. Scribner had given E & L quite a fright by threatening to publish Guizot's *France* in a uniform edition with Mommsen, Froude, and others published by the New York firm, but they were able to settle this problem, as well as that of the "Epochs of History," without open hostility. In 1874, E & L were glad to get off so easily; five years later, they would have taken on Scribner without a qualm, but no one tried to grab any of their titles when they were strong except the cheap-book publishers, who were the enemies of the entire book trade.

So remarkable was the success of Guizot's *Popular History of France* that E & L even imported the French text in 1876, noting that over a hundred thousand copies of the work had been sold. One wonders how many copies of this expensive edition, priced at $37.50 in paper covers and $42.50 in cloth, were sold to those who preferred the learned savor of the original French. Shortly thereafter, E & L announced the publication, in forty parts, of Guizot's *Popular History of England,* by special arrangement with Hachette in Paris and Sampson, Low in London. This shorter work, written before his French history, was found practically complete after his death. It was published in 1879, in four large volumes, and was given the same wealth of illustration which had made the *France* so notable. Here again were pictures by Alphonse de Neuville, Emile Bayard, André Marie, P. Leyendecker, and other French illustrators who had worked on the Hachette edition, and also by an

English group, headed by Sir John Gilbert, with steel engravings by lesser British artists. Another volume was added in 1881, covering the period from 1837 to 1874, but was almost entirely the work of Guizot's daughter, Mme Guizot de Witt.

Guizot was often accused of being an Anglophile, and his Protestant faith, his love of constitutional monarchy, his general familiarity with English history and politics, as well as English literature, all contributed to strengthen whatever natural bias may have existed. His several historical studies on England, in his earlier years, had displayed great ability: John Stuart Mill and Taine both praised his *History of the English Revolution.* He was probably the only French historian fitted to write on England with both knowledge and objectivity, and a good history by a foreigner always reveals certain interpretations that the native historian may overlook altogether. It was also a general history, with considerable detail, though falling short of Knight's *Popular History* in this regard. Charles K. Adams considered it a work that could always be consulted with profit as well as interest, for it was the work of a great historian,[43] but few thought it on the same level as the history of France.

The work was fully as handsome in appearance as the French history, and was also given a thoroughly detailed index. It was equally expensive, the cheapest edition, in cloth, selling at $20, and the morocco and full-tree-calf bindings at $40. With the extra volume, the cheapest edition cost $25.50. The English history was no such amazing success as its predecessor, but many copies were sold right up to the end of the century, a cheaper duodecimo edition having been issued in 1879 in an attempt to match the cheap reprint versions.

E & L were interested, naturally enough, in anything about Guizot, and prepared an attractive volume for his daughter's biography, *Monsieur Guizot in Private Life, 1787-1874,* which came out in 1880. It bore a handsome medallion of Guizot on the front cover, and was bound in a sturdy brown buckram that seemed an appropriate garb for a work about this tranquil figure. It was, of course, his home life rather than his public life that was described in the book, which was written to prove that this man, whom his enemies and much of the world called hard, cold, and formal, was a fond and devoted father and friend. It was filled with letters that revealed his kindness, his deep loyalty to his many friends, and his constant concern for his family, amid all the troubles of state. One reviewer called him "perhaps the greatest, certainly the purest and noblest Frenchman," a man of particular "interest to New England readers who trace the past and present greatness of the country to the intense moral earnestness of Puritanism."[44] Most reviewers thought the book valuable because it corrected the false impressions of the man, so generally held, and only lamented the rather extreme filial reverence that pervaded it.[45] The book was so popular with the readers of Guizot's other works that it was published in both trade and subscription editions, the latter being uniform in format and binding with the histories of France and England.

The Picturesque World; or Scenes in Many Lands, beginning publication in parts in 1875, was a subscription work in the ever-popular field of travel and description. Appleton had already published *Picturesque America*, a magnificent collection of the finest in wood and steel engravings, and *Picturesque Europe* was under way, both large works in forty-eight parts. *Picturesque America* had acquired forty-two thousand subscribers in New York City alone and won corresponding success all over the country.[46] E & L sought to capitalize on this popularity with their series, also in forty-eight parts, with one hundred steel engravings and five hundred wood engravings, "the finest specimens of wood engraving which have ever been produced in any country," as the prospectus modestly averred. Characteristically, the steel engravings were more emphasized, in line with the taste of the period, although the wood engravings were more likely to be enjoyed by later generations, of different tastes.

There were pictures from the Orient and Occident alike, with some of North America to compete with Appleton's. The views, to quote the prospectus, "have been chosen from the most romantic and interesting portions of the world," embracing cathedrals, palaces, castles, and abbeys, or mountain, lake, river, and valley, with ports and the seacoast for variety. The text, fluent and un-distinguished, was by Leo de Colange, who had edited *Zell's Popular Encyclopedia and Dictionary*, and who was to handle several other such works for E & L. *The Picturesque World* resembled the many works of this sort turned out in the 1870's, apparently a fertile period for such material, since we have not only the fine series by Appleton but also the handsome large-quarto books, of the same size as E & L's work, on the Rhine, Italy, Venice, Spain, or Switzerland, published by Scribner, Lippincott, Routledge, and others. It brought together from a common pool of such illustrations, one imagines, pictures by Doré, Alphonse de Neuville, Flameng, Giacomelli, Daubigny, Sir Charles Eastlake, Kaulbach, Weber, Hertel, Thomas Moran, Granville Perkins, and others, altogether about thirty artists, with the engraving done by such masters as W. J. Linton, Sidney L. Smith, George Andrew, and a host of French, German, and British craftsmen. Dana Estes, so it was claimed, spent several months in Europe making the arrangements for the plates. The press work was done at the already distinguished University Press in Cambridge, on super-calendered and tinted paper, each part selling for fifty cents, or thirty-nine to forty-four dollars for the whole work, bound in two massive volumes.[47]

Though not quite equal to *Picturesque America,* it was not far below it, particularly in the superb quality of printing and the generally fine pictures. Some of those on Europe and the Orient were new and truly artistic. It was the prosaic text, studded with quotations, that often seemed to drag the work below its proper level.

Other typical subscription books of the mid-seventies were George L. Austin's *History of Massachusetts* and Samuel Adams Drake's *History of Middlesex County, Massachusetts,* both copiously illustrated and reasonably priced. Austin's work, from the landing of the Pilgrims to 1875, emphasized the earlier days and was deemed a fine enough piece of bookmaking to be displayed along with Guizot's *France* and other large sets at the Centennial Exhibition. Drake's *History of Middlesex County,* a subject in which he was an acknowledged expert, was a large two-volume work selling for fifteen dollars (cloth). Along with Drake's general sketch, a very fine one, one found a cluster of town histories, some by their standard historians, and numerous biographical notices. A similar work on Worcester County, by the Reverend A. P. Marvin, had an equal success in that area.[48]

The year 1878 saw the start of several subscription series, including the two county histories mentioned above. There were the first announcements of Rambaud's *Popular History of Russia* and Duruy's *History of Rome,* both important works, along with some volumes of Martin's *Popular History of France,* Edwin Forbes's *Life Studies of the Great Army, Pioneers in the Settlement of America, History of the United States,* and the *Globe Encyclopaedia of Universal Information* with its accompanying *Atlas.* The *Pioneers in the Settlement of America* was a standard subscription work of the lower order, 880 pages with eighty-eight engravings, "the most interesting and indisputably elegant work that has ever been issued in this country," said the prospectus. One can imagine the canvasser going about the country with his sample book or dummy filled with the best pictures and selected fragments of the text of this work, surely an easy one to sell because of its subject alone. The *History of the United States,* in thirty-two parts, had only its illustrations to recommend it, as did another set called *The Living World,* on animals, birds, insects, and fishes, in twenty-four parts. More attractive was Forbes's *Life Studies of the Great Army,* a portfolio of sixty-five etchings of army life during the Civil War. Forbes had been a special artist with the armies and a member of the French Etching Club, so that his record of the war was fresh and yet sophisticated in medium. It was an expensive work, selling either in ten parts at $2.50 each, or in portfolio format, forty plates costing $25 on tinted proof paper or $50 on India proof paper.

As regular subscription publishers it was inevitable that E & L should handle encyclopedias and dictionaries as well as religious works. The latter, it must be admitted, were not numerous, being limited to such works as *Kitto's Family Bible, Pictorial Sunday Reading, Pilgrim's Progress,* and Fleetwood's *Life of Christ,* all in parts and graced with sundry colored plates, steel engravings, and abundant woodcuts. *The Globe Encyclopaedia of Universal Information,* edited by Dr. John M. Ross, formerly assistant editor of *Chambers' Encyclopaedia,* was a good example of the small, popular work available for the home. It sold in forty-eight parts for twenty-four dollars or in six cloth-bound volumes for thirty dollars, then up to forty-five dollars through the range of leather bindings. It was a British or, shall we say, Scotch work, competent, up-to-date, and especially useful, with its many short articles, for the family not equal to the immense and scholarly *Encyclopaedia Britannica,* then appearing volume by volume in its ninth edition. The *Nation* thought it a most useful popular encyclopedia, despite numerous trivial errors.[49] E & L also published the *Globe Atlas,* a companion volume, with maps by W. and A. K. Johnston, the famous Edinburgh cartographers, and the *Globe Dictionary,* a small, illustrated book for students "denied Webster or Worcester."[50] As a cheaper encyclopedia E & L offered *The Student's Encyclopaedia of Universal Knowledge,* also edited by Dr. Ross, which was a less pretentious version of the *Globe Encyclopaedia* and was priced at only twelve dollars. The *Dictionary of Commerce, Manufactures, Commercial Law, Insurance, Patents, Railroads, Maritime Law and an Explanation of Mercantile Terms and Usages,* edited by the omniscient Leo de Colange, is self-revealing in its title.

Before I describe the major historical enterprises, the histories by Rambaud and Duruy, there are several smaller works that deserve mention here. First came Henri Martin's *History of France,* but only that portion of it which served as a continuation of Guizot's

France, which terminated with 1789. The three volumes by Martin brought the account up to the Franco-Prussian War, with major emphasis on French history through 1848. These books, especially designed as a continuation of Guizot, were issued in similar bindings and were adorned by the same wealth of illustration that had made Guizot's so popular. It was an excellent continuation since Martin had even greater narrative power than Guizot, was profoundly religious, relatively conservative, and not too hampered by his theories of the organic development of the nation and the perpetuity of the Celtic spirit, "le génie d'une nation."[51] His prose had greater emotional content than Guizot's, was more "French," therefore, and gave a vivid presentation of the great scenes of the French Revolution and the troubled after years. In the nineteenth century Henri Martin was ranked along with Guizot, Michelet, and Taine, but his reputation has not held up as well as theirs.

In view of the great success of Guizot's *France,* it was only natural that an abridgment should be thought of, and this was prepared by Gustave Masson under the title *Outlines of the History of France* (1880).[52] It was of about the same length as the popular Harper abridgments of famous histories, such as the *Student's Gibbon,* the *Student's Hume* or the *Student's Constitutional History of England* (Hallam's). It was rather cleverly condensed from the English translation of Guizot, and since Guizot had always known what to omit and what to stress, this abridgment retained the merits of the larger work. It also added bibliographical sources, chronological tables, and maps, all necessary to a work designed for students. It was generally praised, though some reviewers wished that Masson had corrected certain deficiencies of the original English translation.[53] C. K. Adams believed it to be the most readable of the smaller histories of France, being dignified yet never dull,[54] and the sales bore out his judgment, for the book reached a second edition in three months. Mining still deeper in Guizot's *France,* Gustave Masson planned "Episodes of French History," a series closely resembling the "Epochs of Modern History," but death cut short his work. Titles such as *Charlemagne and the Carlovingians* and *Louis IX and the Crusades* show the nature of the series. Many of the children's books put out by E & L in this period were historical, such as the numerous "Young Folks' Histories," whether by Charlotte Yonge, Hezekiah Butterworth, or others. The emphasis was always on readability and good illustrations, and their books, deservedly, sold well.

E & L's large historical works of this period, Rambaud's *Popular History of Russia from the Earliest Times to 1880* and Duruy's

History of Rome and of the Roman People from its Origin to the Invasion of the Barbarians, both kept their prestige in the twentieth century, a feat not achieved, among scholars at least, by Guizot's and Martin's histories. Rambaud's *Russia* was first to appear, being published in three volumes (no parts) from 1879 to 1882. The French edition, published in 1878, went only to 1877, but E & L had Nathan Haskell Dole continue the history through the Turko-Russian War of 1877–1878 and up to 1880 as a special feature of their edition. This set was well illustrated with the customary steel engravings, woodcuts, maps, and plans, but, in this instance, the pictures and maps were prepared exclusively by E & L and not adapted from a French edition. The pictures were almost without exception of the authentic variety—landscapes, buildings, works of art, and portraits—and were considerably less glamorous than those in Guizot's histories. The prospectus gave an interesting sales talk for the book:

> The immense popularity of Guizot's *France* is a proof of the fact that the best class of historical works, produced in the highest style of art, are fully appreciated by American book buyers and encourages the publishers to add to the series Rambaud's great work, which has won the unanimous approval of the press in this and all European countries, and has been crowned by the French Academy. A work thus honored by the highest literary authority in the world may safely be accepted by the American public as one which will be acknowledged as the Standard History of Russia. No good history of Russia exists in our language and the present work is offered as the only trustworthy and complete History of Russia in the English language.[55]

This advertisement was not exaggerated, for Alfred Rambaud's work was immediately recognized upon its appearance as the best general history of Russia in a western European language, the work of a great historian, well organized and brilliantly written. It was notable for its balance, its careful research, and its freshness of approach; and the translation, by L. B. Lang, did it justice. Its fairness and generosity of views pleased Russian historians, and its only distinguishable bias was an anti-German tendency, a sort of propaganda for the French alliance with Russia. It gave more space to politics, diplomacy, and military affairs than to literature and art, yet the latter were not neglected. The chapters dealing with recent history were the poorest in the work, but it was superb in its treatment of the main currents of older history, up to the Crimean War. It was one of a series under the general editorship of Victor Duruy, done for the French firm of Hachette.

Victor Duruy's *History of Rome* was the most impressive historical work published by E & L, a truly sumptuous physical production. In the imperial octavo edition, limited to 750 copies, it made a massive set of eight volumes in sixteen, containing four thousand illustrations and one hundred maps and plans. The first printing was from 1883 to 1886, a translation of the French edition, 1879–1885, and E & L made a later printing in 1894, limited to one thousand copies. The translation was admirably carried through by M. M. Ripley and W. S. Clarke, under the editorship of Professor J. P. Mahaffy, the famous classical scholar. The set was magnificent to the eye, with its linen vellum paper, its large, clear type of the prevailing modern face, which was bright and readable, and its profusion of wood engravings crisply printed on the smooth paper. It may seem a little cold to the modern book lover, but it was done to perfection, for its day, by the University Press, who did all of E & L's printing. There were many cuts in the body of the text, frequent full-page plates, and a few chromolithographs, done in France for this edition. The first volume contained forty-three full-page engravings, eight colored lithographs, nine colored maps, and numerous small cuts in the text. These pictures were all genuine—actual landscapes, ruins, works of art, archeological remains, medals, portrait busts, and the like. Only now and then was there an imaginative reconstruction of some building or portion of a city, quite in keeping with the aim of the work.

Victor Duruy was perhaps more noted as a statesman than as a historian, chiefly because of his brilliant work in the reform of the French educational system during the reign of Napoleon III. Befor his stint as Minister of Education he had won repute as a remarkable popular historian, writing, in a warm and lively style, a series of short volumes on Greek and Roman history, surveys of medieval and modern history, and, above all, his justly famous *Histoire de France,* which came out first in 1852 and went through edition after edition in the next forty years. As mentioned earlier, Duruy became the director of historical publications for the great publishing house of Hachette, and had to carry on his own researches while busied with this responsibility.

After the fall of the Second Empire he set out to make a complete revision of his earlier *Histoire des Romains* (1844). Although this was the most scholarly of Duruy's works, he was no Mommsen, and the chief merit of the history was the presentation, in good narrative form, of the scholarly research of his day, with some original material of his own. E & L advertised it as "the most interesting, most valuable and most complete history of Rome ever produced," appealing to the general reader as well as to the classical scholar, but this statement was only partly true. Because of the charm of style in most of the work, it was, as C. K. Adams called it, "the best popular history of Rome."[56] It was, for its day, the only extended history covering both the republic and imperial Rome, and is still the only Roman history with such a wealth of illustration combined with readable text. The work is obviously antiquated now, when one can consult such scholarly triumphs as the *Cambridge Ancient History* and the numerous French series like the "Histoire générale" and the "Evolution de l'humanité," but it is still valuable for classical studies, especially for its admirably chosen pictures, three thousand of which were selected by Duruy for the Hachette edition, and another thousand by Mahaffy for the translation. For this history Duruy was first elected to the Institute and finally, in 1884, to the French Academy, a fitting reward for the public-spirited statesman and scholar.

With these two fine works Dana Estes seemed to have "shot his bolt" in the field of history. There were a few minor new works in the 1880's, but the only famous histories were older classic works, such as Macaulay's, Lingard's, Hume's, Gibbon's, and Hazlitt's, in line with E & L's new emphasis after 1883 on subscription sets of the "standard authors." Rambaud's history of Russia had been fairly expensive to manufacture but it had also sold quite rapidly, since the cheapest edition cost $16.50. Duruy's *History of Rome* was quite a different story for it had been most costly to produce and, by its very nature, was slow-moving, since the cheapest edition sold for $50. Much as he liked the prestige of such big enterprises, Dana Estes had his eye on large profits, and his success with children's books in the early 1880's convinced him that quicker returns could be had from this field than from any other. It was a lot cheaper to publish history in the form of children's series and this was the course E & L pursued. By the time Duruy's history started to appear E & L were selling at least six juvenile series on history: Miss Yonge had started off the series with her "Young Folks' Histories" of England, Rome, Greece, and so forth, to be followed by "Young Folks' Histories" of great cities of the world, "Young Folks' Epochs of History," "Young Folks' Histories" of countries not treated by Miss Yonge, such as Mexico and Russia, with quite a few other historical books not grouped in series, such as *Young People's History of the Reformation.*

Another reason for the shift from large historical works lay in the growing competition from the cheap-reprint publishers. These jackals, as they were viewed by the regular book trade, had the knack of picking up works which had been made successful by skillful and diligent advertising or canvassing and publishing them for a fraction of the trade price, especially when these works were by foreign authors and unprotected by copyright. As early as 1878 John W. Lovell had published a cheap edition of Knight's *Popular History of England,* eight volumes for ten dollars, while E & L had been obliged to ask twenty-five dollars for their edition in 1873. It was a heavier blow when John B. Alden advertised Guizot's *France* in an eight-volume set for only eight dollars, containing the illustrations of the imported edition and the additions made by Mme Guizot de Witt, which E & L did not publish as part of their own set. Thus Alden, in a series of striking advertisements, made it clear that the public could get what E & L would sell for $49.50 at only $8.[57] Although E & L had made substantial profits on Guizot by 1885, it was hard to see them disappear almost entirely, especially since many periodicals, church periodicals among them, celebrated the low price. Of course, the books were not so finely turned out, the paper was woefully cheap and the printing careless, but the Alden set was undoubtedly a bargain. A little later Belford, Clarke and Company, of Chicago, brought out Guizot's *France* at $16. Although some buyers would always prefer the regular edition, the majority would snap up the cheaper sets.

Some publishers brought out cheap editions of their own books, in an attempt to compete with the cheap-reprint publishers, but E & L never did this for any of their large historical sets. They evidently preferred to make what profit they could from continued canvassing of these works, and competed only by publishing cheap editions of Gibbon, Hume, and Macaulay. Their editions were almost as cheap as those of the reprinters and were all bound in cloth; but the paper was execrable, and they were able to sell them at a cheap price only because the plates had already been used for more expensive editions of these authors. In 1886 E & L transferred their historical sets to a subsidiary company, the C. J. Jewett Publishing Company, which E & L wholly controlled, and which had the job of continuing the subscription business in the historical field, while the parent firm concentrated on the many illustrated art books and "standard authors" that began to crowd their list after 1880.[58]

There were a few other historical works of interest and numerous books on travel. Many of the travel books were published chiefly because of their illustrations or because they were the work of artists. *The Beaconsfield Cartoons from Punch* (1878) would qualify as both politics and art, since the cartoonists were such men as Leech, Doyle, and Tenniel. George Rawlinson's *History of Ancient Egypt* (1882) was well written and well illustrated; its publication by E & L was, perhaps, the first evidence of Dana Estes' interest in archeology, an interest that grew immensely after 1890. In 1904 Dana Estes and Company published a *Short History of Ancient Egypt,* just after Estes had returned from an archeological treasure hunt, and the many travel books on Italy in the 1890's testified to his new taste for antiquities. The Reverend A. B. Muzzey's *Reminiscences and Memorials of Men of the Revolution* (1882), a delightful and rather rambling book of memories, mostly of his native town of Lexington, Massachusetts, was almost the only book of this type, so frequently on Boston publishers' lists in this period. With the exception of a few unimportant books on early Massachusetts history, E & L paid no further heed to history, and Dana Estes and Company published very few, mostly popular biographies of such personages as Colonel Hutchinson, Talleyrand, or Lady Castlemaine. One important biography, partly historical, was Laura Richards' *Journals and Letters of Samuel Gridley Howe* (1906–1908), a moving tribute to her father, whose amazing career, whether in the Greek Revolution, working with the blind, or fighting for the abolition of slavery, was fully revealed by his own words, with pertinent comments by both his daughter and his friend, F. B. Sanborn.

The travel books in this early period, up to 1885, are relatively few. (The more numerous titles following 1885 will be described later.) In keeping with E & L's European interests one of their earliest books was Shaw's *Picturesque Tourist Guide to Great Britain and Ireland* (1873), prepared expressly for American travelers, and a few years later they were listing the whole series of Baedeker guides, in common with other American firms. There were the usual imported travel books, *Wanderings from the Alps to Aetna, Meeting the Sun, Roman Legends, Artists and Arabs,* and so on, most of them salable chiefly through their illustrations. The large subscription work, *The Picturesque World,* served exactly the same purpose, and the publication of an old work such as Victor Hugo's *The Rhine,* which had been translated into English in 1843, showed that there was always a market for such fare.[59] New England was not forgotten, and a book by F. E. Clarke, *Our Vacations: How to Go, Where to Go, and How to Enjoy Them* (1874) concentrated on how to travel cheaply, suggesting visits to

the White Mountains for fifteen dollars, and the like. As a loyal
State-of-Mainer, Estes brought out such useful things as a large
map of the *Head-waters of the Aroostook, Penobscot and St. John
Rivers, Maine* (1882), along with some detailed guides by Thomas
S. Steele, *Canoe and Camera, Paddle and Portage,* through the
Maine woods. Even Miss Parloa's *Camp Cookery* would come in
handy.

E & L even made quite a success of Charles Carleton Coffin's
travel book, *Our New Way Round the World* (1880), but this was
merely a new edition of his 1869 volume, with additional illustrations, since his juvenile works were being revived with such profit
that all his other books caught on, too. About the only new travel
book in the early 1880's was Fred Ober's massive *Travels in Mexico
and Life among the Mexicans* (1883), a really good work, which
in its day was hailed as the "largest, freshest and most instructive
work on Mexico."[60] It was finely illustrated, entertaining, even
vivacious, and solid enough in its facts to be useful to anyone wish-
ing accurate, recent data on Mexican life. It was also a fine specimen of bookmaking, in the manner of the eighties.

Thus E & L, after a first try for profits from the vogue for
science in the early seventies, set out to win success through subscription books. That these first successes were gained through historical works was largely coincidental, resulting from getting the
rights to Guizot's histories just as the firm set up in business. Because of the enormous sales of Guizot's *France* it was quite natural
that Dana Estes should calculate on continuing profits from other
historical sets, and some of these profits were realized. By 1880,
however, after exploiting the field of cheap, popular novels for all
it was worth, Estes began to see that immense profits now lay in
children's books and in handsomely illustrated volumes, sets of
classics, art books, and the like, with the result that he gradually
eased away from the historical works that had given E & L its
first true prestige. Although the profits from the newer fields were
undoubtedly greater than from the historical enterprises, probably
the best books on the entire roster of E & L's publications were
Guizot's *France*, Rambaud's *Russia*, and Duruy's *Rome*. It may be
said, of course, that these were not works originated by E & L,
but their presentation of them was far superior to any of the
foreign editions, and they deserved great credit for their devotion
to fine bookmaking, as it was understood in that period, and for
their superlative skill in marketing these large sets, which became
popular successes.

Chapter Four

NOVELS AND VERSE

IT was probably no mere coincidence that E & L's very first announcement of publications, in September, 1872, included the three types of books that Dana Estes planned to promote in the next few years. Like many publishers, he probably hoped to make a fortune in one if not all of these lines: the scientific books were the vogue of the moment; historical works of quality were certain of a good sale; and as for novels, every general publisher counted on them for much of his profits. Some publishers, too, found poetry successful, but except for works by the prime favorites, this was an uncertain field, to be entered upon only by those with unerring taste either for the fine or the very popular. Practically every publisher sold his novels, however, and here the fine work was not necessarily as successful as the sentimental or sensational one, so that the publisher possessed of a sound average taste, or a little below, was more likely to attain a big success than the publisher of more delicate perception.

Because of the variety of novels published by E & L it is a little difficult to generalize about Dana Estes, but it would surely not be unfair to characterize his taste as average. Apparently when he started publishing, he wished to confine himself to serious works of high quality, hence the emphasis on the scientific and historical fields. The need for more rapid turnover than the slow but steady sales in the above-mentioned areas undoubtedly led him to try more novels, especially in a depression period when expensive works could not be sold easily. Everyone read novels because there were many excellent novels to read, and even the poorer works did fairly well in this time of dull sales, if they were properly advertised.

In the first announcement was listed a novel, *Queens,* by Miss E. B. Emery. That Miss Emery was from Gorham, Maine, Estes' home town, is the important fact, not the essential quality of the novel. Miss Emery was not known as a writer, for the "Boston Letter" in the *Publishers' Weekly* remarked on "E. B. Emery, whoever he or she may be,"[1] as the author of a book set up by O. L. Brown's Patent Type Setting Machinery and notable, therefore, as a typographical novelty. The *Literary World* thought well of it: it was obviously the work of an amateur and in no respect great or brilliant, but it reflected the views of a "thoughtful, cultivated and earnest woman," and its pictures of country life were admirable.[2] It was perhaps a bit overladen with discussions of religion and women's rights, but was clearly the "vehicle of much strong and wholesome thought." Many of these feminine and feminist novels were of the same order and few of them achieved any commercial success. Dana Estes had done a favor for a friend, however, and there was nothing cheap about the firm's first offering in fiction.

A little later, in 1873, came the first book of verse, one of the few published by E & L. J. F. Colman's *Poems,* though handsomely printed, was not calculated to oust the New England poets from their pedestals. The major work was a narrative poem in eight cantos, "The Knightly Heart," a tale of Columbus' first voyage, a compound of adventure and broken hearts. "The divine afflatus has not breathed upon his work" was the regretful decision of the *Literary World.*[3] Perhaps Colman was also a friend of Dana Estes. E & L's first holiday gift book was *The Garland of the Year, or the Months, their Poetry and Flowers.* The poetry in this instance was selections from standard British favorites. Along with it was offered a new edition of *Chimes for Childhood, a Collection of Songs for Little Ones,* edited by Dana Estes. Other sure-fire collections, such as Keble's *Christian Year,* were also published in 1873, and were the last volumes of poetry for five years, at least.

After getting his subscription-book business in motion, Estes set out, in 1874, to exploit the novel. His aim was not a lofty one, it was simply to make money with fiction, and he set about it with characteristic thoroughness. He knew that the better American authors were already linked with the older and larger firms, and, whatever his desires may have been, he saw no way of acquiring any of the poorer but profitable authors for his list. The only recourse was to do what so many did, to sign up certain minor British or Continental novelists for new books, and fill out the list with older works that could be printed for a song. For such a plan good selection was imperative, and it is doubtful if Estes had sufficient skill to make a continuing success in this type of fiction. Yet he was nothing if not confident, and, before his interest shifted, he had filled his list with an amazing variety of fiction best described by the hackneyed "good, bad and indifferent."

He began slowly with about ten novels the first year, only a few of them new works. The first was *Elena*, a quiet story of Italian life, by L. N. Comyn, today forgotten, like most of those novelists on E & L's list, but it enjoyed a modest repute in the seventies. Many reviewers liked this book, which was a new publication: the *Nation* termed it a standard love story with almost tragic overtones in its depiction of the Italian struggle for liberty;[4] the *Literary World* called it "singularly sweet and serene."[5] So well was the novel received that Estes decided to revive an earlier tale by the same author, *Atherstone Priory*, dating from 1864. This, too, was noted favorably, "a charmingly-written love story," which the *Publishers' Weekly* recommended for home reading.[6]

These notices encouraged Estes to bring out a group of older books which had had their day of popularity in England and which might go well in America. Most reviewers recognized them for what they were, but a few were taken in and treated them as new books, especially since E & L did not give any indication that they were actually reprints. Such works as F. W. Robinson's *Slaves of the Ring* (1867), Anna Drury's *Deep Waters* (1863), and Albany de Fonblanque's *A Tangled Skein* (1862) mean nothing today and did not mean very much then, but E & L advertised them vigorously. They were all published in neat paper covers at seventy-five cents each, an attempt by E & L to entice buyers who would not sink to the level of the dime novels. Next came novels by authors of somewhat more reputation and with a decidedly different emphasis, *Checkmate* (1871) by J. S. Le Fanu and *Too Much Alone* (1860) by Mrs. J. H. Riddell. With these stories E & L embarked on the stormy sea of the sensational and weird tale, the thriller.

Neither of these novels ranked high among their author's works, but both were typical stories of crime and violence. We think of the literature of the sixties and early seventies in terms of such books as Owen Meredith's *Lucile*, George Eliot's *Silas Marner* and *Romola*, Trollope's *Barchester Towers*, and Louisa

Alcott's *Little Women* or Mark Twain's *The Innocents Abroad*. These
were all successful works, from the publisher's viewpoint as well
as from the public's, but the demand was just as strong in that
period for sensational novels, proving that a solid nucleus of readers would absorb this genre to its limit, then as now. Whether
Dana Estes liked these for his personal reading I do not know, but
he set out to make the most of them for E & L.

Thus the sixties had seen such novels as Wilkie Collins' *The
Woman in White* (1860), followed by *Armadale* and *The Moonstone* (1868). J. Sheridan Le Fanu wrote *The House by the Church-
yard* and *Uncle Silas*, recently restored to favor; Miss Mary
Elizabeth Braddon had demonstrated woman's ability in this vein
with her *Trail of the Serpent* and *Lady Audley's Secret* (1863),
to be matched by Mrs. Henry Wood and Mrs. J. H. Riddell, who
won great notoriety with *George Geith of Fen Court* (1864) and
similar tales of terror. Dickens also supported the sensational demand with *Great Expectations* (1861) and *The Mystery of Edwin
Drood*, left unfinished in 1870.[7] The novels by Wilkie Collins are,
of course, among the masterpieces of this type of fiction, and
Le Fanu was not far behind in at least a few of his works. Mrs.
Riddell is not known today, probably unjustly, but her stories were
great favorites for at least three decades.[8]

Neither Le Fanu's nor Mrs. Riddell's novels were new, but
they were received as new publications on their first appearance
in America. The *Atlantic Monthly* reviewed both novels, showing
that the vogue for such literature was recognized, perhaps tacitly
approved, even though the reviewer had to make some moral stric-
tures. Le Fanu's *Checkmate* provoked the judgment that it was a
commentary on our civilization that for our entertainment we had
to go to records of wickedness.[9] Yet the reviewer gave a good account of the story, whose hero was a murderer trailed by a detective, noting the murderer's disguise by means of facial surgery
quite in the twentieth-century manner. Mrs. Riddell's *Too Much
Alone*, which dated from 1860, was thought to be a new work by
the reviewer, who felt that, in her time, she had written better
stories. This novel, however, like many of her books, dealt with
London business life, usually the seamy side, including all manner
of commercial trickery, the pursuit of a secret formula valuable in
the drug business, with crime to add zest to this lively thriller. The
reviewer didn't like Mrs. Riddell's covert sneers about chemists,
but rated it a thoroughly intriguing story.[10]

The year 1875 saw a fresh group, not all of them thrillers.
Mrs. Riddell's *Above Suspicion* was a new work this time, as were

Victor Cherbuliez's *Miss Rovel* and Florence Maryatt's *Open Sesame*. Older books, such as Elizabeth S. Sheppard's *Charles Auchester* (1853), that curious story of Mendelssohn and musical life in England and Germany, Albany de Fonblanque's *Cut Adrift* (1869), Henry Kingsley's *Stretton* (1869), and Whyte-Melville's *Maud or Nina* (1869), also appeared, but were recognized as reprints rather than new publications. There were two novels by French authors, Cherbuliez and Mme Augustus Craven, both very popular. Henry James reviewed Cherbuliez's *Miss Rovel*, lamenting that Cherbuliez, who had begun so well, was trying so hard to be a Parisian that his stories were ruined by too much wit, cynicism, and extraneous brilliance.[11] It was not, admittedly, Cherbuliez's best, but Cherbuliez was one of the most esteemed novelists in France, so that E & L's contacts with France were bringing them books of high quality, especially when we recall Guizot and Martin. Mme Craven's *Jettatrice* was not quite so good, but this devoted Catholic wrote novels of social life and religious fervor that won a wide circle of readers.[12] Such established writers as Trollope and the Hon. Mrs. Norton made the list, both with older works of no great merit, if we take as an example Trollope's *Sir Harry Hotspur of Humblethwaite* (1870). It is obvious that Dana Estes was trying to provide something for all tastes, hampered as he was by having no first-rate author to vitalize his list.

A new novel by Albany de Fonblanque, who was the British consul at New Orleans, appeared in 1876 "from advanced sheets," but the really important event was a tremendous purchase of stereotype plates at the famous sale of J. R. Osgood's plates and remainders in March, 1876. E & L invested heavily in remainders also, which could be disposed of handily through the bookstore, but the plates included such items as Gail Hamilton's writings and thirty or more titles from "Osgood's Library of Novels," notably stories by Emile Gaboriau and E. Werner. For weeks E & L advertised "great bargains in remainders," such as the Kensington edition of Thackeray, several sets of Dickens, George Eliot, Walter Scott, Jules Verne, and others. The novels purchased would all be reprinted in E & L's own "Octavo Series," at "greatly reduced prices," which meant seventy-five cents instead of one dollar and a half. This purchase from Osgood evidently impelled Dana Estes to make a sensational bid for the market in cheap novels, a move which a few years earlier might have been successful but which coincided in 1876 with the large-scale advent of the cheap paper-covered books selling for ten cents each, such as the Lakeside and the Seaside libraries. One wonders, also, how he dared compete with "Harper's Library of Select Novels," which by 1876 had reached the imposing number of 450 titles, including several of the novelists selected by E & L. These novels were priced, in paper covers, from twenty-five cents to one dollar, and many were by the most famous authors of the day, although a larger number were by mediocrities.

Consequently, E & L advertised, for summer reading in 1876, an imposing list of seventy novels, costing one dollar and a quarter in cloth, or seventy-five cents in paper covers. The novels already mentioned were included, with a most curious medley of new titles, usually of older works. As the *Publishers' Weekly* commented, E & L made an imposing exhibit for summer reading in the advertising pages (by far the largest advertisement) and, if "enterprise will do it, they mean to make their mark and come to the front as publishers of light novels."[13]

Gaboriau's novels, obtained from the Osgood sale, occupied the place of honor, to be followed by the novels of Mrs. Celia V. Hamilton, also purchased from Osgood. Along with the veriest trash appeared J. W. De Forest's *Kate Beaumont* (1872), E. Werner's *Good Luck,* Mrs. Oliphant's *A Rose in June* (1874), George Sand's *Marquis de Villemer,* Octave Feuillet's *The Story of Sibylle,* Besant and Rice's *Ready-money Mortiboy,* Grenville Murray's *The Member for Paris* (1871), and Edmund Yates's *The Yellow Flag* (1872). And one may wonder, if these appeared superior, what the poorer ones were like. Almost all were by British or Continental authors, perhaps not more than five by Americans. They were the same titles to be found in the popular Tauchnitz edition and many of them appeared later in the cheap American libraries at ten or twenty cents, selling in great quantity. Actually, from the publisher's point of view, it was not that Dana Estes' selection was so bad, but that his timing was unlucky. His second advertisement proclaimed "Paper Novels for the Million!" quite in the modern fashion, and his blatant advertising in the following weeks might have succeeded, if other things had been equal.

Estes had been hoping, of course, to sign up a first-rate novelist, and in 1877 his hopes appeared to be realized. In January E & L announced, with much fanfare, a translation of Alphonse Daudet's *Froment jeune et Risler aîné,* to be entitled *Sidonie.* Dana Estes called it the "purest and most successful French novel that has been issued during the Last Quarter of a Century," and perhaps believed this himself.[14] It had been crowned by the French Academy, he noted, and had already sold twenty-five thousand copies in France. A little later came a lush notice by an American critic,

Mrs. Lucy Hamilton Hooper, after sixty thousand copies had been sold in Europe: "The author is gifted with rare and remarkable qualifications, imagination, intelligence, the power of creating character and, above all, with a purity, sweetness and sincerity of nature that lend to his writings a charm exquisite yet indefinable, like the perfume of a flower."[15] E & L announced "unusually heavy" advance orders for *Sidonie,* so heavy, in fact, that they were obliged once again to postpone publication. "Either the business sky is brightening or *Sidonie* is suspected of being an unusually engaging story," said the *Publishers' Weekly.*[16]

Mrs. Hooper's comment on Daudet was not wholly exaggerated: many French critics had already said much the same thing and some American critics were to echo many of these views. *Froment jeune et Risler aîné* was Daudet's first true novel, the first work which gave him major stature in France and elsewhere. He had already published such minor masterpieces as *Lettres de mon moulin, Le Petit Chose,* and *Tartarin de Tarascon,* but none of these fanciful and charming works had captured the entire reading public. Success finally came with *Froment jeune et Risler aîné,* and this success revived interest in the earlier works, themselves valuable. E & L announced in February that they would publish earlier works such as *Robert Helmont, The Lovers,* and *Hortense* along with new books, *Jack* and *The Nabob,* since they had already printed sixty thousand copies of *Sidonie.*

French critics of today are inclined to think *Sidonie,* to give it its English title, one of the most attractive of Daudet's novels. He himself considered it a typical mixture of the real and the fanciful that characterized his work,[17] and it possessed also that keenness of detail, sincerity, and sympathy, which delighted his readers. The story was a huge success in America, five thousand copies being sold the first week of its appearance, and most of the critics were enthusiastic. One writer, in the *Commonwealth,* said of *Sidonie:* "It has all the brilliancy of a French novel, with all the severe morality of a New England romance."[18]

Some soberer critics were not sure of *Sidonie.* T. S. Perry, writing in the *Atlantic Monthly,* thought the book overrated and blamed Daudet for making the heroine too odious, but admitted the lifelike qualities of the story, noting especially its earnestness, which rendered it so impressive to all readers.[19] The *Nation* found somewhat similar faults, blaming the number of unpleasant characters for the somewhat melodramatic touches, but lavished high praise on some of the fanciful characters, such as Delobelle, the broken-down actor, and his lovely daughter, and called the book powerful and tragic.[20] The *Literary World* curiously termed it "one of the most important books in the domain of light literature," though granting it exceptional qualities.[21] The *Publishers' Weekly* considered it "by no means elevating in tone," yet very readable and full of clever character sketches.[22] Nor did the editor think much of the stamping of the cloth binding, which he termed "excessively elaborate and eccentric." The design referred to was a spider's web, wholly appropriate to the theme of the story, and E & L used it as the decorative motif of a new series, the "Cobweb Series."

All critics, without exception, praised the translation by Mary N. Sherwood. T. S. Perry, an expert in such things, rated it "very good," and the *Literary World* said that the translation was so good that the reader could scarcely believe that the book was not before him in its original form. The *New York World* and the *Boston Transcript* offered like tributes, which must have delighted Dana Estes, since most translations were, quite appropriately, picked to pieces by competent reviewers.

Encouraged by this triumph, Estes prepared to translate all of Daudet's novels, which were coming out in rapid succession. Mary N. Sherwood was assigned to translate *Jack*, and Mrs. Hooper would do *The Nabob*. *Jack* had already achieved a sale of forty thousand copies in Europe, and *The Nabob* was being serialized in *Le Temps*. The earlier novels were already under way, and Estes decided to make the "Cobweb Series" (this was a great year for new series in the book trade) a European list to vie with Holt's "Leisure Hour Series." Meanwhile, more light novels were prepared for the "summer trade," and there was a first novel by the famous essayist, Gail Hamilton,[23] to be called *First Love Is Best*, which would appear with a new printing of her earlier works, purchased from Osgood. Since these comprised such sprightly collections as *Country Living, Wool-Gathering*, and *Sermons to the Clergy*, they would be sure of a sale, even as reprints. Some critics were decidedly curious to see what Gail Hamilton's novel would be like, but felt certain that it would be piquant and readable; one prophesied that few of the season's new books would be as pithy and entertaining as the reprints of her eight volumes of essays.[24]

When *First Love Is Best* did come out, it was generally praised. Not a great novel, of course, the critics began, but refreshing to the jaded reader, for the story was told with considerable skill and much humor. This writer, so famed for shrewishness, here manifested her least biting moods and turned out a bright and readable tale, spiced with lovely conversations. Most critics were delighted to find that the story was just what they expected it to be.[25]

By July, three more novels were published, Daudet's *Jack,* E. Werner's *Vineta,* and Mrs. C. V. Hamilton's *My Bonnie Lass. Jack* was much less attractive than *Sidonie* and has never ranked high among Daudet's novels. It was a decidedly painful story of selfishness and suffering, based, like most of the author's tales, on actual happenings but infused with sympathy and with a hatred of evil not visible in real life. As in *Sidonie,* Daudet pursued his evil characters relentlessly, perhaps more than was needed in a story whose pathetic qualities were already clearly marked. There were similar traces of a fantasy and sentimentality which could be called Dickensian, rare traits among the French naturalistic novelists. Many reviewers admitted its power but expressed their dislike, being frequently disturbed by the "hideous ugliness" laid bare so realistically. Again, the character depiction was lauded to the skies, and justly so, but the whole novel left a bitter taste in the mouth.[26] All combined to praise the translation done by Mary N. Sherwood, the translator of *Sidonie.*

E. Werner's *Vineta*[27] was an example of the popular German novel of the time, usually somewhat crudely drawn, heavily splashed with sentiment, with the main characters extremes of good and evil. T. S. Perry thought *Vineta* better than most German novels and believed that few recent German novels had more life in them than this; in fact, he was willing to give a good mention for most of her novels.[28] *My Bonnie Lass* was, for a change, by an American author, Mrs. C. V. Hamilton, whose mediocre writings sold well: her story, *Woven of Many Threads,* published earlier by E & L, had already reached a sale of sixteen thousand copies.[29] The book was advertised as a "quiet story of love and sacrifice, but well written," with a good plot and well-contrasted characters. The title, one suspects, owed something to the great popularity of Frances Hodgson Burnett's *That Lass o' Lowrie's* at the moment, but the story, said the *Nation,* was "more depressing to the spirits than a fortnight's storm."[30] This low was caused not so much by the style, which was slipshod at times, but by the succession of misfortunes and the moisture that accompanied them. Yet the reviewer agreed that it had some good points and was a "great improvement" on Mrs. Hamilton's earlier work.

E & L were not discouraged, however, and went ahead with additions to the "Cobweb Series." Appleton had started a new "Collection of Foreign Authors," which would include novelists from France, Germany, and other European countries; Holt reduced the price of the "Leisure Hour Series" from $1.25 to $1.00, and the cheap libraries had begun to publish some foreign writers too. *Sidonie, Jack, Vineta,* and *My Bonnie Lass* comprised the first four numbers of this series, and F. W. Hackländer's *Forbidden Fruit* was the fifth.[31] Friedrich Wilhelm von Hackländer, the "German Dickens" as E & L recklessly called him, was popular in Germany, fifty thousand copies of this tale having been sold there; the theme of *Forbidden Fruit* could be inferred from the fact that it "ended with three couples married and a fourth in a highly promising state of courtship."[32] More substantial was the sixth number of the series, Daudet's *The Nabob.*

E & L advertised *The Nabob* during the first week of January, 1878. "This work surpasses either *Sidonie* or *Jack* in interest and we believe it will be the great novel of the year. It has run through seventeen editions in as many days in Paris. We have proved our faith in it by the payment of $1,000 for the advance sheets."[33] The advertising of *The Nabob* was more flamboyant than any previous publication by E & L had received, either because Estes really deemed it superior or because he had to implement his investment. He emphasized that the novel dealt with the political life of the Second Empire with startling realism and that Daudet's own post as secretary to the Duc de Morny was mirrored in the story. "His realism, cruel and unfaltering, recalls Balzac's greatest pen-pictures of weak human nature. Intrigue and corruption are the keynotes of the book."[34] E & L were sure that it was Daudet's most powerful work and equally sure that it would be a sensation. The translator, Mrs. Lucy H. Hooper, was praised as rendering "both the spirit and the letter of the work with an ability few translators possess."

Even without the inherent merits of *The Nabob,* which has since been recognized as one of Daudet's finest works, any novel which treated political intrigue and corruption might arouse interest in one of the most troubled decades of American politics. Reviews were obligingly laudatory, practically no one had any fault to find. Almost all agreed that it was the cleverest of the three novels published, and several thought that it stood at the head of the new novels for 1878. The *Literary World* declared: "The author's purpose is distinctly to teach and the teaching is good. As a whole the novel is solid and to mature minds it will bring profit and intellectual pleasure."[35] One critic strangely dubbed Daudet "a French Hawthorne," and another wisely commented that it was called a romance but it was really history.[36] A novel of so many facets could not fail to win a wide circle of readers.[37] The only

blemish anyone noted was not in the novel itself but in the translation, which was called too "sternly literal," indicating that Mrs.
Hooper lacked the felicity of style of Mrs. Sherwood. This series
of three novels by Alphonse Daudet brought to American readers
works of the highest quality, a quality that was recognized by
many critics and by numerous readers, but they were never the
dazzling successes that Dana Estes had hoped for. Any French
novel had to struggle against the imputation of grossness and
immorality, and these novels, even though the wicked were piously
cursed, described more of Parisian life than most American readers
dared absorb. Also, their view of life was sad, even tragic, and
most readers wanted pleasant endings. Henry James wrote excellent critiques on Daudet in the *Atlantic Monthly* and the *Century
Magazine* [38] a few years later, praising his "passionate" observation,
his truly remarkable vision, his keenness of touch, his traits after
Dickens, "an ingenious dilution of the great cockney epic," his
pervasive charm because of the sense of life he brought to his
books. "He is really," he concluded, "a great little novelist."[39]

Estes thought he had another French triumph in Henri
Gréville's *Dosia,* which had been sensationally successful in the
Revue des deux mondes and was making a fine run in book form
in Paris.[40] Henri Gréville was the pseudonym of Alice Fleury
Durand, the wife of a teacher of French literature in St. Petersburg. She had learned Russian and reveled in the gay social life
of the Russian capital, while in her leisure hours she wrote novels
which, her friends told her, were excellent. She returned to France
in 1876 and then began to publish novel after novel from her store
of manuscripts. *Dosia,* her first novel, should be the "literary event
of the season," proclaimed E & L, especially when well translated
by Mary N. Sherwood.

It was next announced that *Dosia* had been awarded the annual
Montyon "prix de vertu" by the French Academy, a prize granted
only to those works having a good moral influence. The *Publishers'
Weekly* thought that if *Dosia* were one half as popular in the
United States as it had been in Paris, E & L should receive a pretty
purseful. It became number seven in the "Cobweb Series," it was
widely advertised, and basically it was a pleasant, bright, and
entertaining story of Russian high society, with clever dialogue
and a thoroughly Russian atmosphere. But the "great prize novel"
was only moderately successful. The reviewers called it cheerful
and facile, a "pretty ordinary story," and that was all it was,
especially as contrasted with Daudet's novels.[41] Estes made no

attempt to buy the rights for Mme Durand's subsequent works, most of which were published by Peterson in Philadelphia.[42]

The "Cobweb Series" was continued with Daudet's *The Little Good-For-Nothing* and E. Werner's *At a High Price*. Daudet's novel, translated by Mrs. Sherwood from *Le Petit chose*, was an earlier work (1868) which won renewed fame after the vogue of *Sidonie*. It is one of his most attractive stories, strongly autobiographical and without the tragic elements that repelled some readers of his later books. "That the story would be entertaining was expected from its authorship," commented the *Nation*,[43] urging those who were quick to label all French people "frivolous" to read this account of strong family attachment and unselfish devotion. Although praising the translation, the critic warned that the title should have been *The Little No-Account* rather than *The Little Good-For-Nothing;* the modern version is still more accurate, being *Little What's-His-Name*, which is the exact equivalent of the French phrase.[44] E. Werner's *At a High Price* brought the "Cobweb Series" to nine, and there it stopped. Perhaps "cobweb" was a rather unfortunate name to give a series.

Estes had begun to see that new novels by foreign authors, especially Continental Europeans, were hazardous in the extreme. Nor were the minor authors from England any safer, now that the cheap-book publishers were attacking all along the line. In May, 1878, most of the cheap novels that were advertised so lavishly two years previously were being reduced from seventy-five cents to forty or fifty cents, in paper covers, and some of the fine historical works were being offered in cheap editions. By the Spring Trade Sale, in 1879, many of the novels "went murderously low," even Daudet's, since the cheap libraries had already begun to publish versions of them at twenty cents.[45] E & L poetry was dumped, as we learn from an anecdote of the Trade Sale: the auctioneer replied to a query from "Bragg," one of the dealers, "What are you selling now?" with the quip *"The Knightly Heart*, but it won't fit you."[46] If E & L's novels were so generally unprofitable, Estes was not going to fight a losing battle, especially since E & L were beginning to see a great future in juveniles and illustrated books. From this time on, the novels were thrust into the background, with one exception, and, until the demise of the company, practically no more adult novels were published.

The one exception was Emile Gaboriau, whose novels could compete, for a time, at least, with the offerings of the cheap-book publishers. Gaboriau, who first achieved fame with the publication of *L'Affaire Lerouge* in 1866—one year before Wilkie Collins'

The Moonstone—was the father of the detective novel, as Poe was that of the detective short story. Gaboriau lived only thirty-eight years and concentrated his output of detective fiction into his last years, from 1866 to 1873. The ten novels he wrote made him famous in both France and England, providing added attractions to those readers who delighted in Wilkie Collins' thrillers. Although America was quick to reprint Collins' tales, Gaboriau's did not begin to appear until the 1870's, and their American popularity came in the 1880's. By the nineties, however, the vogue faded and Monsieur Lecoq, once so highly regarded, gave way to Sherlock Holmes. In 1928, Arnold Bennett proclaimed the merits of Gaboriau and created a brief revival of interest, but the interest could be only historical; Gaboriau could not match some of the modern masters of the genre.

Yet Gaboriau's vogue in the nineteenth century was fully justified. He was a master in the art of storytelling and clearly opened the way for Conan Doyle. His detectives, of whom Lecoq is the more important, were both living figures, amusing, shrewd, logical, and systematic. Lecoq's deductions were similar to Holmes's, lacking only the artistry in telling and the conciseness. Lecoq was a decided realist and a great worker, somewhat in the style of Freeman Wills Crofts's Inspector French. Also, he was a member of the police, with all the resources of the force at his command. Gaboriau's plots were immensely complicated and the action sensational, as in Collins' stories, so that Victorian readers were able to enjoy their characteristic thrillers in a French milieu.

It should be noted immediately that Gaboriau's tales were generally acceptable to Victorian readers on the grounds of morality. Distinctions were carefully drawn by reviewers concerning certain irregularities condoned by the French, but the stories were strongly moralistic and could be read by the "ladies of the family" with relative safety. French manners were vividly portrayed, sometimes with an exaggeration akin to that in Eugène Sue's *Les Mystères de Paris,* yet the sensationalism was secondary to the intellectual satisfaction of working out the puzzle. The modern reader may think that the answer is given away too soon, but the nineteenth-century reader was apparently not so versed in unraveling the tangled skeins of the plot and found little fault with their construction.[47]

Osgood began publishing Gaboriau's stories in 1874 and was the first American publisher to sense their possibilities. Yet when Osgood had to sell his plates in 1876 the six Gaboriau novels went with the rest. Dana Estes displayed real shrewdness in his purchase of the Gaboriau titles; in all probability he enjoyed reading them himself and knew that other novels were still to be translated. Whatever the reason, he set out to make them popular in the United States by energetic advertising coupled with popular prices. Gaboriau's novels were first reduced to fifty cents, in paper covers, in 1878, and were again advertised for "summer reading" in 1879, with new and more attractive covers. E & L claimed that they were selling more rapidly than when they were first issued and were among the most popular paperback novels in the country.[48] It was their popularity that led to the first inroads by the cheap-book publishers, when George Munro began to include Gaboriau's novels, under changed titles, in his "Seaside Library" in 1879.

When Osgood published Gaboriau's *Clique of Gold* in 1874, the *Nation* considered it a dull story. Gaboriau was an industrious workman, not at all a prodigy, and the novel was "very sensational." A few remarks were passed on the "highly spiced" social relations, but the book was classed as clearly a detective story.[49] Although the *Nation* found no fault with the translation, one reader criticized E & L's publication for mistranslations and excessive Americanizing in such matters as "dollars" for "francs" and "Castle of If" for "Château d'If."[50] Few of Gaboriau's novels were reviewed by the better magazines, although the newspapers featured them prominently. By 1880, however, Gaboriau's books had caught on, and *Monsieur Lecoq* received its due when it appeared in May.

In their advertising E & L proclaimed Gaboriau the acknowledged "prince of writers of detective stories," noting that in keen analysis, subtle delineation of character, and dramatic power his skill was unrivaled. They also pointed with pride to the striking paper cover, which would be as "good as a trademark" for their novels.[51] A little later the *Publishers' Weekly* noted that Gaboriau's novels were having quite a run during the summer, suggesting that the novels had force and realism enough to insure their popularity.[52] Some of the reviewers were enthusiastic over *Monsieur Lecoq*. The *Nation* aptly called it "one of the most labyrinthine of detective stories" and prophesied that anyone who began it could never leave it unfinished.[53] The *Literary World* unexpectedly gave it a long review filled with praise, remarking that seldom was a "French novel of such extraordinary power and interest so free from objectionable features."[54] Amusingly, the only adverse criticism was of the cover, which the reviewer called "disreputable": "it is as much as one's good name is worth to be seen in public with such a looking book in his hand."

By 1881 E & L were publishing almost no adult novels, putting all their energy into the highly successful juveniles and sets of standard authors. They were still faithful to Gaboriau, nevertheless, and published *The Count's Secret* in 1881, *The Slaves of Paris* in 1882, and *The Downward Path* in 1883. All were well received, with only occasional notes of disappointment rather than disapproval. The *Literary World,* whose editor had evidently become a Gaboriau admirer, thought *The Count's Secret* "fascinating," showered it with adjectives like "Frenchy," graphic, dramatic, and melodramatic, seasoned with crime and mystery; he obviously enjoyed its glimpses of a gay and naughty world. It was another story not to be put down after being started.[55] The same reviewer liked *The Slaves of Paris,* finding it a highly spiced dish which served to tone up the appetite jaded by the contemporary society novel.[56] Probably the greatest tribute to Gaboriau's increasing reputation was the publication of his novels by the major cheap-book firms, George Munro first, then Lovell, and Street and Smith; Lovell and Munro printed all the Gaboriau novels that E & L had published and some of his lesser works too. Estes, not to be outdone, published the lesser works also through the Aldine Publishing Co., a subsidiary firm started to compete with Lovell, Munro, and others, and finally turned over the whole Gaboriau series, first to the Aldine Publishing Co., then to H. M. Caldwell, in the late nineties, who published by agreement with E & L.[57] The same book was often published under different titles, distressing for the unwary buyer, such as *The Count's Secret* or *The Count's Millions, Chance Marriage, Marriage at a Venture,* or *Promise of Marriage,* yet the price was so low there could be little complaint.[58] E & L could certainly take credit for creating a vogue for Gaboriau, with powerful support from Lovell and his peers.

The year 1882 apparently marks the end of E & L's publishing of new novels. Besides the Gaboriau novel, which was scarcely new, they presented Virginia W. Johnson's humorous story, *An English Daisy Miller,* written as a retort against the sneers of English critics at American girls abroad, and a counterblast to Henry James; by making a loud English girl the heroine it set out to prove that American girls were not the only feminine fools traveling on the Continent. Miss Johnson became one of E & L's valued authors for travel books, a field in which this Brooklyn-born descendant of Judge Sewall was an expert. Another novel seemed an attempt to capitalize on the great popularity of E. P. Roe in this decade: it was *Brought to Bay,* by E. R. Roe. Perhaps people were more discerning in those days, but the intent to deceive appears obvious. After 1882 the only novels published were the already-old tales by

William Ware, *Zenobia, Aurelian,* and *Julian,* which Estes published mainly through his growing interest in history and archeology, in 1892. Of course, Estes was publishing the sets of novelists such as Scott, George Eliot, Dickens, and Thackeray, but the young novelist was given no opportunity.

That there was any poetry at all in this period, considering Dana Estes' absorption in the immediately profitable, is rather surprising. Even more unexpected is the fact that Estes edited an anthology of verse, *The Home Book of Poetry* (1878), adorned with the inevitable steel engravings and priced at six dollars. One suspects that Mrs. Estes may have had a large share in the selection of English and American verse, yet Estes was quite capable of supporting his own tastes. The book was well printed and decorated with attractive headpieces and vignettes, but the four hundred selections evidenced "popular rather than classical taste," in representing considerable newspaper verse and "no clear principle of classification."[59] Significantly, the book was reduced the following year, and by 1882 its price had dropped to two dollars and a half.

It is doubtful whether Estes would have recognized merit among the younger poets; in any event, he published none, only such trivia as Hezekiah Butterworth's *Poems for Christmas, Easter and New Year* or *The Garden of the Heart,* a collection of religious verse, "a choice present from a Sunday-school teacher to his scholars."[60] A novelty was a translation of Virgil's *Aeneid* by the former governor of Massachusetts, John D. Long, which was printed in an edition limited to fifty copies. It is not a work to be undertaken by many governors today, no doubt advisedly, but this translation reflected the scholarly aspirations of many Victorian politicians, notably in England. The last volumes of poetry published by E & L were verse collections by Lloyd Mifflin, in 1897 and 1898, and Dana Estes wisely refrained from any further publishing of verse, except by the truly great.

After Dana Estes and Co. was formed, and Estes was on his own again, he showed willingness to try a new novel now and then. In 1898, probably because he was publishing some of Will Allen Drumgoole's stories for young folks, he was led to publish a book of adult tales by this attractive young woman who deceived many male editors by her mannish name.[61] Most of the novels were mediocre, by such writers as Barry Pain, but in 1905 he brought out a translation of Gustav Frenssen's *Jörn Uhl,* which had achieved a phenomenal success in Germany, selling over two hundred thousand copies, and which he advertised flamboyantly as the "greatest German novel." A tale of Schleswig-Holstein, it was one of the greatest of the *Heimatkunst* school, offering a vivid portrayal of peasant life in a style of mingled poetry and realism. It was a powerful story of tribulation and heroism, with a happy ending, and these elements generated its popularity. One critic remarked that this story had appealed to modern Germany as Dickens appealed to the England of his time.[62] Estes was greatly impressed by the considerable acclaim in America, and in 1906 brought out Frenssen's *Holyland*, "pronounced by competent critics to be the greatest novel of modern times," according to the advertising. But this work was not so successful, and, after publishing *The Three Comrades* in 1907, Estes lost interest.

He published two books by Arthur Machen, *The House of Souls* and *The Hill of Dreams*, but did not care to do more. The novels of this period were chiefly border-line works between the adult and the juvenile, such as Laura Richards' *The Wooing of Calvin Parks* (1908). In 1908, however, Estes published his first modern mystery story, Captain Henry Curties' *The Queen's Gate Mystery*, which was to be followed, several years later, when Estes' sons were running the firm, by novels by J. S. Fletcher, Philip Gibbs, and other writers of mystery and adventure. In 1912 and 1913, novels were more numerous than ever before on the firm's list, but they were mostly English importations of little value, chosen haphazardly. The sons were no more successful than the father in selecting valuable fiction, and they completely eschewed poetry.

In the long history of E & L and Dana Estes and Co., only Daudet's novels were a real contribution to the American public, unless one considers the promotion of Gaboriau and the detective novel worthwhile. Quite evidently, Dana Estes felt no assurance in publishing novels, and his best "finds" were largely a matter of chance, since he never followed them up with the assiduity of true interest.

Chapter Five

JUVENILES AND SUCCESS

IT seems strange, in retrospect, that Dana Estes did not begin by publishing children's books, especially since he made such a great financial success of them later. It was five years, however, before he started any substantial publishing in this area and one can only guess at his reasons for the delay, since he never made any statement in this regard. Possibly he had grown weary of dealing with the great quantities of "juveniles" handled by Lee and Shepard and wished to inaugurate his own firm on a strictly adult level. It is clear that he tried for the best works in 1872, books that reflected the intellectual trends of the day; and the works in science, theology, and history that filled the first few years were proof of his aspirations. The depression that began in 1873 rather dampened his ardor, so that he tried the popular novels as a means of making quicker profits and did well for a time amid those shifting sands. The resolve to turn to children's books was probably coupled with regret that he had not been able to establish E & L as an élite firm for the intelligentsia, but one can imagine that any regrets were quickly assuaged by the golden stream that flooded in from the juveniles. It is very doubtful if Estes had the capacity to run a highly intellectual publishing house, whereas he abundantly demonstrated that he could select, prepare, and sell children's books like an expert.

There were a few books for children scattered through the

years from 1872 to 1877, but they were lost amid the adult books
and were of no importance. The very first title, however, was a compilation by Estes himself, originally published by Lee and Shepard
in 1868 and reissued in the fall of 1872. It was called *Chimes for
Childhood, a Collection of Songs for Little Ones,* with illustrations
by such favorites as Birket Foster and J. E. Millais. There were
about one hundred songs, well selected, and an ample number of
child pictures which critics of the time called "charming." As was
hinted earlier, Mrs. Estes may well have been the moving spirit in
this anthology; in any event, Estes kept it on the list for many
years, making frequent reissues with new bindings and additional
illustrations.[1] Somewhat later came three little books by George
Sand, *The Wings of Courage, The Rose Cloud,* and *Queen Koax,* but
they caused no stir. Estes even tried a few school texts, an elemen-
tary French book and a beginner's history of art, along with Dr.
Lambert Sauveur's *Chats with the Little Ones.* Sauveur was responsible for several books of "chats," notably one popular in
nineteenth-century Latin classes, *Chats with Caesar de Bello Gallico,*
in which the oral method, dear to some modern educators, was
pitilessly employed.

The serious publishing of children's books started with *Chatterbox* in the fall of 1877. The *"Chatterbox* Controversy," which was
to demand so much of E & L's time and money, is described elsewhere as an essential part of the firm's history. This chapter deals
only with its merits as a book for children and its success with its
many readers, with as little mention of the controversy as possible.

Chatterbox had been founded as a weekly magazine in 1866 by
the Reverend J. Erskine Clarke, later a London vicar and Honorary
Canon of Rochester. It was sold at a half-penny an issue, since
Clarke hated to see the errand boys of fourteen or so reading nothing but "blood and thunder" and hoped that this profusely illustrated paper would attract them.[2] Two years before, he had begun
The Children's Prize, another weekly for still younger readers, with
the aim of instilling Christian principles into their minds early in
life. *The Athenaeum* reviewed both these works in a solemnly con-
descending fashion. Of *The Children's Prize* it remarked that the
publication was a "meritorious and useful" one, aimed to please and
benefit the boys and girls in the Sunday schools, and particularly
the members of village clubs "established by benevolent persons interested in the mental culture of the children of agricultural labour-
ers." For its special purpose—the reward and encouragement of industry and intelligence in the classes of schools for poor children—

no better work than this had come to the editor's desk.[3] The judgment of *Chatterbox*, a year later, was much the same. The weekly budget of fiction, essays, poetry, and pictures was for the entertainment of the "less prosperous classes" and the editor deemed the "literary element of the publication" to be, "in some respects, meritorious." He admired the illustrations "of more than average goodness" and recommended the magazine for the "older children of poor families."

Clarke was a decided moralist and he could not forego many anecdotes and scenes prompted by his own experiences in a poor parish. Though his touch was heavy at first, it grew progressively lighter as the years went on, and his own fortune increased. Sometimes the pictures emphasized, in an unnecessarily clumsy and sentimental fashion, certain scenes that were not meant to be the major ones. Ruskin attacked *The Prize* (as *The Children's Prize* was later called) in *Fors Clavigera* for its complete lack of beauty, its bad doggerel, and its mawkish sentiment, and some of the criticism has been attached, unjustly, to *Chatterbox*. Ruskin was annoyed because children were given no lightheartedness, no joy or freedom in these magazines of the pious sort, and there are certainly elements of cheerless moralizing in the earlier years of *Chatterbox*.[4] By the mid-seventies, however, *Chatterbox* came much closer to justifying its title by its exciting serial stories, entertaining bits of natural history, and interesting scraps of history and biography. Barrie had read only "penny dreadfuls" at first but when "that highclass magazine *Chatterbox*" came his way he buried his pirate hoard in the garden.[5]

Probably some American children subscribed to the magazine in weekly form, but most read it as the annual, which established itself in this country as early as 1872. Apparently Americans were not disturbed by the *Athenaeum*'s labeling of it as suitable for poor families; in fact, by 1876, the *Athenaeum* had abandoned its lofty tone and was recommending *Chatterbox* warmly for children of the upper classes. Pott, Young and Co., in New York, first published it in 1872, the American News Co. took it over in 1873, and Appleton published it in 1875. The American News Co. also provided *The Children's Prize* with eight to ten "beautiful engravings" each month, and a "Scripture Lecturette" with a full-page engraving illustrating such themes as "Damsels of the Bible" or the "Life of David." Another work of the same type was *Sunday*, a companion to *Chatterbox*, for Sunday reading: its aim was to make Sunday a bright and happy day as well as a sacred one. In these early years of the seventies, *Chatterbox* had fewer serial stories and more tidbits of biography, anecdotes of heroism or kindness, brief moral tales of frivolity punished and humility rewarded. The pictures were abundant: almost all were full-page woodcuts, often rather coarsely done, certainly not equal to those in American magazines for children, but usually striking and perhaps equally appealing to the children themselves.

In 1876, *Chatterbox* was handled by Thomas Nelson in the United States and the same arrangement was made for 1877. When E & L's order was refused by the London publisher, after they had already offered to supply their customers, Estes "had no recourse" but to reprint the book without the Britisher's permission. Nelson, the authorized American agent, could not prevent it and evidently made no attempt to, such as by advertising their version as the "authorized edition." Estes undoubtedly felt that he could sell *Chatterbox* better in the American market than Nelson had done, else he would scarcely have embarked on the very costly work of copying over two hundred woodcuts. As it was noted in the *Publishers' Weekly* [6] E & L contracted with S. S. Kilburn, the Boston engraving firm, which put nearly forty wood engravers to work, so that in two months' time the woodcuts had been reproduced, plates cast, paper manufactured, and books printed and bound in an edition of twenty thousand copies. Estes was able to sell it for less than the English edition, at $1.50 in "illuminated boards," $2.50 in cloth, with gilt edges. He jubilantly called it "the king of juveniles" and proclaimed the superiority of the American reprint in the quality of the pictures, which was quite true, for the American craftsmen had greatly improved on the English originals. Each issue had a chromolithograph as a frontispiece and this, too, was better than the English counterpart.

So great was the success of E & L's reprint that Estes announced in January, 1878, that *Chatterbox* would definitely be reprinted from the current periodical issues, so that customers would be sure of a supply in the holiday season. The reprint, he asserted, would be "in all respects equal and in some superior to the English copies, and at a lower price."[7] Thus in September the new volumes were offered as exact reprints of the English edition, but more strongly bound and handsomer than the English volumes and this year selling for $1.00 in the illuminated board covers, $1.50 in cloth. The *Publishers' Weekly* had praised *Chatterbox* in 1877: "Estes and Lauriat, with the usual enterprise of their house, present an edition of *Chatterbox*. Almost everybody knows about *Chatterbox*, what bright things and splendid big pictures it is full of, and it is to be found in almost every bookstore the country wide."[8] There was much the same praise in 1878, with wonder that it could be sold so cheaply.[9] By September, at the end of his western trip, Estes had already placed over twenty thousand copies, so that eastern and western sales appeared heartening indeed.[10] As the *Publishers' Weekly* observed, E & L would "especially push their juveniles this season," since this was the first big year of juveniles in E & L's history.

From this time on, thanks largely to Dana Estes' splendid promotion, *Chatterbox* became a striking success in the American market. By 1879 Estes had acquired sole authorization for sales in the United States from the London publisher and was no longer forced to reprint the English magazine without permission. In 1878 Nelson had vainly tried to stem the tide by calling their version the "genuine, English edition," but they cannily arranged with E & L in July to fix a uniform price for *Chatterbox*. The London proprietor evidently felt that E & L would be better American agents than Nelson, judging from the immense sales in 1878, and his expectations were justified, since E & L announced total sales, in juveniles, of over a hundred thousand volumes in 1879, the majority of which were clearly of *Chatterbox*. The *Publishers' Weekly,* in 1879, termed it "this wonderfully popular children's magazine, started purposely to counteract 'the devil's literature.' "[11] In 1880 the *Dial* spoke of the "usual variety of tempting engravings and interesting reading that have long made this work a standard one."[12]

Chatterbox for 1880 provides a fair sample of what the annual was to remain for the next two decades. There were slight changes in price and an increase, in the 1890's, in the number of colored plates, but otherwise the pattern was relatively untouched. In this year there were four different bindings available, priced at $1.25, $1.75, $2.00, and $2.50, the last a binding in green cloth with red panels and lettering, and a black panel on the front cover bearing the figures of a boy giving a puppet show to his dog, brightly emphasized in gilt; both this binding and the illuminated boards made colorful volumes, certain to catch the eye in the days before dust jackets. The chromo frontispiece was not well done, and the register was imperfect in several copies I have seen. The woodcuts, however, about two hundred in number, were all well printed, though many were well below the ordinary American standard. The *Literary World* commented on this fact in the 1881 volume, lamenting that neither in pictures, paper, or typography was the annual up to American standards; Dana Estes had made it a finer work in the two years of pirating, but it was simpler to use English plates now that he had the right to do so.

In this number were four lively serial stories. The first, *Peas-Blossom*, was, under this unlikely title, a story of an English boys' school, with many enticing pictures; the second was by Harry Castlemon, *The Boy Trapper*, which would naturally please English and American readers alike. These were the long stories; the other two, *The Castle Goblin* and *Robert's Turning Point*, were about half as long, the latter being the "moral tale" of the group. A long non-fiction serial was devoted to *Geoffrey Chaucer and His Pilgrims*, with fairly good pictures and excellent summaries of the first portion of the *Canterbury Tales*. There was also *The Thames from Source to Mouth*, probably of most interest to English readers, although the pictures were attractive and the history was well handled. Along with many briefer tales, of perhaps a page or two, were sprinkled *Scraps of Biography*, mostly anecdotal, small bits of scientific lore, such as paragraphs on *Galileo, White Mice, Extinct Animals* (with ferocious drawings of nature "red in tooth and claw"), and brief historical sketches, often illustrated, such as *The Escape of Peter the Great, Donald Cameron of Lochiel,* or *Alexander the Great and the Lion.* All in all, the selection of miscellaneous bits was well done, and very few were tediously moralizing. A boy or girl could find plenty of truly entertaining reading matter in the volume of over four hundred pages, and there was no compulsion to read an anecdote that began too piously. Not only were the pictures a delight to the youthful reader, the text was lightened throughout by fancifully decorated initial letters at the beginning of most new sections and stories. There were verses, too, for those that liked them, although the level of this material was quite low. Whoever read the serials was inevitably led through the pages of miscellany, so that even the reluctant learner might be enticed into reading a paragraph that began with a lively sentence or bore a striking caption.

Although *Chatterbox* is no longer published, the British still turn out books of this sort, and they seem a truly delightful product. Possibly American children are too sophisticated for this kind of book, though I doubt it, but it is no longer the fashion here, in any event. There are American "comic books" which provide a somewhat similar miscellany in the form of annuals, but they are a dismal travesty of the sound entertainment given by these substantial volumes.

There was no doubt that the young readers of the nineteenth century liked *Chatterbox*—the sales alone prove it conclusively. A typical American boy, young Frederic Melcher, looked forward to a visit at his grandmother's, where some books were kept in the cupboard under the best-china closet. "There were usually volumes of *Chatterbox*. There was a special smell of ink on paper in that cupboard that sometimes hits my nostrils again with a twinge of homesickness for that old front room with its deep window seats where I used to curl up for a good read."[13] The critics, too, liked *Chatterbox* and rarely found anything in it to blame. Just to pick a few random judgments, the *Critic*, in 1884, found *Chatterbox* "one of the most substantial of children's miscellanies. For real enjoyment many a child will go to it in preference to the more elaborate holiday books."[14] The *Literary World*, in 1885, noted the "great pictures in English style, filling the whole page," but felt that artistically the book was not up to the standard of the best, though thoroughly wholesome.[15] The next year it reviewed *Chatterbox* and a cheaper version put out by the Aldine Publishing Co., E & L's cheap-book subsidiary. The two volumes were so similar that one might change covers and not know the difference; they were "made for the million," for the paper was cheap and the pictures were coarse in texture though not poor and never vulgar. "These are the oaten-cakes of literature, plain but nourishing."[16] The following year, the reviewer observed that the pictures in *Chatterbox* had a "bigness and boldness all their own," that the reading matter was "unexceptionable," with its stories about animals, its numerous anecdotes of courage and heroism, its abundant history and biography.[17] In 1888 the reviewer did not like some of the stories of the French Revolution, and some pictures of "snakes, dead men and scenes of carnage are enough to set a nervous child wild with terror o' nights." He thought them quite inexcusable in a book of this kind, which should be wholesome and cheerful.[18] It is doubtful that the children complained: such criticisms would seem to indicate that *Chatterbox* was serving children successfully.

Once Dana Estes had secured the American rights to *Chatterbox*, there was a group of lesser holiday books tied to *Chatterbox*, all made up from the magazine, or selected from previous years, to provide picture books for all ages. In 1878 E & L made up a *Chatterbox Gift Book*, which sold for one dollar, then in 1879 came the regular list, the *Original Chatterbox Picture Gallery*, the *Original Chatterbox Album of Animals*, then, a little later, the *Popular Chatterbox Packet*, the *Prize* (for very young children), *Chatterbox Pictures and Prattle*, *My First Book*, and others. The *Album of Animals* contained the full-page plates contributed by Harrison Weir, a favorite English illustrator, while the *Picture Gallery* had a selection of the best pictures from the magazine, especially printed on heavy, toned paper, with a verse for each picture. With such a brood of *Chatterboxes* to make sales, it is no wonder that Estes was ready to fight for the exclusive rights to it!

When E & L first published *Chatterbox* in 1877, it was the only book for children on their list that year. Its phenomenal success led to the preparation of a larger group for 1878, with *Chatterbox* still the leading title, but with a mingling of new and old works to provide a real group of children's books. And, to point up the change in emphasis, the children's books headed the list from this time on! This year, 1878, also marked the first appearance of Laura E. Richards, the most famous writer for children on E & L's list. *Baby's Rhyme-book* contained some original verses by Mrs. Richards plus some rhymes by others, and *Baby's Story-book* was a selection of verses and stories edited by Mrs. Richards, both selling for seventy-five cents. Mrs. Richards was well known already for her delightful nonsense rhymes published in *St. Nicholas*, so that Estes was well-advised in getting her to start off his list of American authors. There were some old favorites, such as Moore's *A Visit of St. Nicholas*, with the Darley illustrations, and the Dalziels' *Pleasant Pages and Bible Pictures*.

More important was the series of "Histories for Young Folks" by Charlotte M. Yonge. Included were brief, illustrated histories of Germany, France, England, Greece, Rome, and the Bible, a series which would be sure to sell because of Miss Yonge's phenomenal prestige. It was also a likely series for E & L because of Estes' interest in history at this time. E & L had no monopoly in publishing these volumes, since D. Lothrop, Henry Holt, and Hitchcock and Walden also published them in an amicable fashion, some volumes using the same plates. It was noted that E & L's books, done at the University Press, were better printed, on better paper, than the rival volumes.[19] All reviewers praised the abundance of good pictures, although the *Nation* thought them rather coarsely engraved.[20] The *Young Folks' History of England* was "without doubt, the best history of England for children that there is," if one could believe the *Nation*.[21] Miss Yonge, thought the reviewer, had every qualification for the work, was thoroughly familiar with the subject, and was famous for her power of narration. She gave children what they wanted, a picturesque view of history along with a portrayal of its great characters. Even though an ardent upholder of church and crown, she was not unfair in depicting events, nor did she write down too much, in a book aimed at young people.[22] It will be noted that Miss Yonge's idea of history coincided closely with Guizot's, a feature which must have weighed heavily with Estes.

The *Young Folks' History of Germany* was not up to the level of the histories of France and England, or of Greece and Rome, for that matter, where she had the subject matter at her fingertips. In the case of Germany, the reviewer in the *Nation* felt that she showed inadequate preparation, noting many trivial slips, but commended her "animated and generally correct style."[23] Although one would have expected her to be an expert in Bible history, she did not satisfy the reviewer of the *Literary World,* who called it "not a book for children, only a childish book," and went on to characterize it as "milk for babes and rather watery milk at that."[24] I can vouch personally for the readability of the histories of England and Rome, which I enjoyed greatly as a child, and I suspect that many children liked them for their liveliness and briefness combined. Robert Morss Lovett spoke of the "lively volumes of prejudice and misinformation supplied by Miss Charlotte M. Yonge," but one suspects that this judgment of his maturity did not hinder his enjoyment of them when a child.[25]

The *Publishers' Weekly* observed that E & L would "especially push their juveniles this season" and this was indeed the beginning of that heavy advertising of their children's books which was to be normal from now on, except when it rose to the spectacular. The *Publishers' Weekly* was obliged to give more and more space to E & L's offerings, particularly in the next decade or so, when good, new books came in almost an avalanche. In the Trade Sales E & L's children's books usually did better than most of their adult books, a fact which must have led Dana Estes to concentrate more and more on juveniles and illustrated holiday books, where profits were reasonably certain.

It was 1879, however, that was the first really big year for children's books. This year saw *Chatterbox* and several of its subsidiaries forming a major section of the list, and the first of a new series, called *Zigzag Journeys in Europe,* by Hezekiah Butterworth. Laura E. Richards had another book, *The Little Tyrant, a Story with a Moral,* and there were several picture books for the tots, like *Little May and Her Lost A,* illustrated by Frolich, *Little Jack's Adventures,* and *Little-folk Songs,* with woodcuts by Addie Ledyard and other favorite illustrators of children's books. By September the *Publishers' Weekly* wrote that E & L were publishing *Chatterbox* "for which they have already orders running up to some fabulous number of thousands and are expecting twice as many more."[26]

A master-stroke in the advertising campaign was the massive notice, circulated widely in magazines and newspapers, entitled "The Survival of the Fittest." It read as follows:

Owing to the unprecedented number of juvenile books published this year it becomes an absolute necessity for all retail booksellers and newsmen to carefully examine all that are offered, and to select only the best. Gaudy covers will no longer suffice to carry off enormous editions of old books with new names, or cheap photoelectrotyped or newspaper cuts, with clap-trap text.

THE PUBLIC WILL DEMAND GOOD BOOKS and retailers who buy worthless ones, simply because they are urged upon them early in the season, will find so much dead stock on their shelves. . . .

While we do not claim that our juvenile books are the only good ones on the market, we ask all retailers to compare them with any others offered them and judge for themselves, letting each stand or fall on its own merits.

Next followed paragraphs lauding *Chatterbox*, though cautioning the public against buying imitations, and also the *Zigzag Journeys in Europe*, "which is pronounced the handsomest and most entertaining juvenile book ever issued from the American press."

The specific object of this announcement is to request all retail booksellers and others to see our juvenile books before making their holiday selections. As several large jobbers have refused to have them represented in their stocks, because we will not send them 'on sale,' or exchange them for inferior books of the same class, or other unsalable stock, we are obliged to ask dealers who cannot find them at one jobber's to go to another.[27]

Let the Fittest Survive!

This advertisement appeared in early October, 1879, prompted by the fact that several of E & L's books were not yet ready. It was a clever advertisement, however, which exuded so much confidence in the firm's new books that most dealers were intrigued enough to examine and stock them when they did appear. Since their books were indeed good, and they knew how to advertise them, it is small wonder that in January, 1880, they could boastfully repeat their slogan, "Survival of the Fittest," with the following notice:

Events have justified our announcement. We sold over
100,000 VOLUMES
and we believe this sale unprecedented in the annals of this class of books. *Zigzag Journeys in Europe* proved the most popular new book of the season. Over 8,000 copies were sold, and we were unable to supply the de-

DANA ESTES

CHARLES E. LAURIAT

Charles E. Lauriat

THE SEVEN LITTLE TIGERS
AND THE AGED COOK

Seven little Tigers they sat them in a row,
Their seven little dinners for to eat,
And each of the troop had a little plate of soup,
The effect of which was singularly neat.

ILLUSTRATION FROM MRS. RICHARDS'

Sketches & Scraps

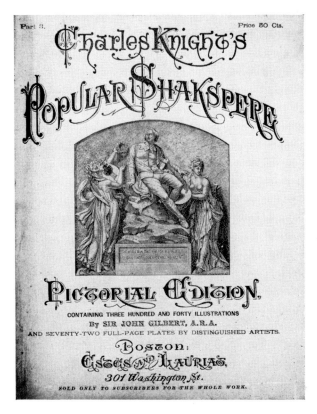

COVER OF CHARLES KNIGHT'S *Shakspere*

BINDING OF *Zigzag Journeys in Europe*

If check'd in soaring from the plain,
Darken to fogs and sink again,
But if they once triumphant spread
Their wings above the mountain-head,
Become enthroned in upper air,
And the sun-bright glories there!

And who is he that leads the might
Of freedom on the Green Sea brink,
Before whose sabre's dazzling light
The eyes of Yemen's warriors wink!
Who comes embower'd in the spears
Of Kerman's hardy mountaineers,—
Those mountaineers that truest, last
Cling to their country's ancient rites,
As if that God, whose eyelids cast
Their closing gleams on Iran's heights,
Among her snowy mountains threw
The last light of his worship too!

'T is Hafed,—name of fear, whose sound
Chills like the muttering of a charm,—
Shout but that awful name around,
And palsy shakes the manliest arm.

'T is Hafed, most accurst and dire
(So rank'd by Moslem hate and ire)
Of all the rebel Sons of Fire!
Of whose malign, tremendous power
The Arabs, at their mid-watch hour,
Such tales of fearful wonder tell,
That each affrighted sentinel
Pulls down his cowl upon his eyes,
Lest Hafed in the midst should rise!
A man, they say, of monstrous birth,
A mingled race of flame and earth,
Sprung from those old, enchanted kings,
Who, in their fairy helms, of yore,
A feather from the mystic wings
Of the Simurgh resistless wore;

And gifted by the Fiends of Fire,
Who ground to see their shrines expire,
With charms that, all in vain withstood,
Would drown the Koran's light in blood!

Such were the tales that won belief,
And such the coloring fancy gave
To a young, warm, and dauntless Chief,—
One who, no more than mortal brave,
Fought for the land his soul adored,
For happy homes, and altars free,—
His only talisman, the sword;
His only spell-word, Liberty!
One of that ancient hero line,
Along whose glorious current shine
Names that have sanctified their blood;
As Lebanon's small mountain flood
Is render'd holy by the ranks
Of sainted cedars on its banks!

FACING PAGES FROM MOORE'S *Lalla Rookh*

mand for several thousand more for which we received orders late in the season. A new edition is in preparation; we shall receive orders at the special holiday discount up to Feb. 1, after which the discount will be reduced.[28]

Let the Fittest Survive!

It is now time to consider Butterworth's *Zigzag Journeys in Europe,* one of the most successful juveniles that E & L ever published. Americans had always been fond of travel books, for Americans had the spirit of travel in their veins, and Bostonians, like most Easterners, enjoyed books of European travel. The popular magazines, both for children and adults, contained countless articles on faraway places, not by any means forgetting the beauty spots of America. But the glamor, naturally, lay more in the Old World, and the constant reading of English literature and history made the readers long for a visit to the historic shrines, the London streets or the old castles, Edinburgh, the Highlands, the galaxy of English landmarks. The more sophisticated yearned for Paris, Normandy, Florence, all the wonders of Italy or romantic Germany. Many an adult had first acquired this yearning for travel by reading Peter Parley or the Rollo books, in the earlier years of the century.[29] The Rollo books, in particular, were favorites throughout the nineteenth century. They were not over-didactic, they were certainly entertaining, and were written in a style that was easy to read, with just the right amount of information sweetened by childish pranks and adventures. The grown-ups in these books, such as Uncle George, were not boring and were models of taste and decorum; Barrett Wendell, in *A Literary History of America,* felt that, with their unconscious humor and art, they gave admirable pictures of Yankee interest about 1840, and that however limited Rollo's world was, it possessed "a refinement which amounts almost to distinction."[30] Wendell was a bit too concerned about refinement, but the later travel books for children were often judged by this yardstick, and those most correct and wholesome were accordingly prized by fond parents.

Jacob Abbott's last Rollo book was published in 1858, and until 1875 there is a gap, so far as series are concerned, although Oliver Optic did his "Young America Abroad" in this period.[31] Horace Scudder's "Bodley Books" brought the Rollo method up to date, with infinitely more literary grace and suavity as well as skill in drawing living characters. The Bodleys, however, did their traveling in America, at least up to 1880, and then took up the European journeys, which competing series had made the vogue. Many children, like young Robert Lovett, looked forward to a new Bodley book at Christmas: they were not didactic, they were not even exciting; their major appeal was to the "domestic affections," the pleasures of family jaunts and activities and they were "as wholesome as oatmeal and yet how entertaining!"[32] When the author started the Bodleys on foreign trips, young Lovett resented it, good as the stories were, because this field was already occupied by the "Zigzag" books.

It was undoubtedly the success of the "Bodley Books," two of which were published before 1879, as well as the announcement of a forthcoming book by Colonel Thomas W. Knox, the *Boy Travellers in the Far East,* to be published by the Harpers, which led Dana Estes, with his keen sense of the market, to search for a rival series and cash in on this vogue for child travelers. How he became acquainted with the writings of Rodolphe Töpffer, whose *Voyages en Zigzag* had long been a European schoolboy classic, is not known, but he had hit on a fascinating title and a fertile idea. Töpffer had begun life as an artist but lack of sufficient talent led him to become a schoolmaster, and here he was a great success. During each vacation he took a group of his boys on "zigzag" trips through Switzerland, always starting from the school in Geneva, trips which became more extensive as years passed, so that the band finally covered much of northern Italy as well. Töpffer's account of these journeys was published in large, album-like volumes embellished with his own sketches as sole illustrations.[33] The accounts are gay, very lively, with excellent depiction of the idiosyncrasies of his own pupils and the travelers and "natives" met on the way; Pierre Loti called him "le seul véritable poète des écoliers," a statement likely to puzzle the average American, since Töpffer seems to excel by his wit and high spirits. All admitted that the *Voyages en Zigzag* were amazingly clever, with as much appeal to adults as to children.

It was this book that Dana Estes brought to Hezekiah Butterworth, to see if it would serve as a model for a new series. To quote from Ralph Davol's article on Butterworth, in the *New England Magazine*:

" 'How would a zigzag journey through Europe do?' The author paced to and fro in his bachelor study. 'Why, of course it will do. The whole human family have been doing things just waiting for me to gather them into holiday dress and pass them out to Young America.'

"So the next day he gathered about him an imaginary class of boys, and, assuming the title of 'Master Lewis,' set out—for the

Public Library, and soon produced the first of the famous 'Zigzag Journeys' . . ."³⁴

Hezekiah Butterworth, born in Rhode Island, was from an old New England family. Like many country boys, he had been brought up on local history and local legends and his love of such tales remained constant throughout his life. Even as a small boy he planned to be a "great writer" and financed his brief stay at Brown University by selling to religious papers the ghost stories his Aunt 'Liza Ann had told him. Going up to Boston, he went to church, like a good Baptist, and met D. S. Ford, a brother Baptist, who was editor of the *Youth's Companion*. Butterworth started working in the office of the magazine and soon became its associate editor. From 1877 to 1887, when Butterworth was most influential in magazine policies, the circulation jumped from a hundred and forty thousand to four hundred thousand.³⁵ Mark Antony De Wolfe Howe thought him "the very embodiment of the sentimentality which doubtless contributed a potent element to the building up of the paper."³⁶ It was not only sentimentality he contributed but a sound awareness of what boys and girls liked to read, and his skill in gauging this imponderable must have recommended him particularly to Estes, who was ever on the watch for authors in touch with the times. Butterworth's own contributions to the magazine carried his name everywhere, and he spent much of his time searching out new talent. He received many writers at his Boston office, entertaining them handsomely, and even getting a surprise now and then, as when a favorite contributor, Will Allen Drumgoole, turned out to be a young lady.³⁷

Deeply religious, Butterworth was proudest of some of his books in this field, such as the *Story of the Hymns*, which received the Wood Medal, the most cherished of his treasures. His *Poems for Christmas, Easter and New Year's* was later published by E & L and most favorably received. It was natural, therefore, that he would feel moral responsibility in writing for young people; as he wrote in his journal in 1885, "It is my purpose to give my whole heart and thought to my work with the pen and to write only that which will tend to make my readers better in heart and life, and richer in spiritual knowledge."³⁸ Thus he was not so much artistic as persevering and direct; he knew enough, however, not to make his moralizing obtrusive, and his deep sympathy for children and his ability to sense their desires kept his work always on a very sane, readable level.

The idea of a schoolmaster making trips with his students he got from Töpffer, as well as the all-important title, "Zigzag Journeys," but some of the elements which contributed most to the books' success were his own. Töpffer had taken very short trips, afoot ordinarily, and had not thought it necessary to tell much about the history or literature of the places visited; his books, in fact, are filled with the minor happenings on the way, getting soaked in a shower, the good things to eat at a certain inn, boys' mishaps or humorous adventures. They were strictly about schoolboy life and interests, with comments on beautiful scenery and the mechanics of travel. Butterworth, in most instances, took long trips with his imaginary school; he brought in much schoolboy conversation, seemingly with success, and told of pranks and adventures now and then. But the books were filled with stories, some of them straight out of history, others famous legends, fairy tales, fragments of epics, or other literature. It was these, with scores of pictures to illustrate them, that made the great appeal of the "Zigzag Journeys." Of course, there were the customary trips to famous towns, castles, museums, as were found in all the travel books, and sometimes the group would be conducted through a building, such as the Tower of London, with comments by the boys and by Master Lewis on the historical significance of what they saw. These passages were quite readable, rarely dull, and never lengthy, since a story would be introduced to lighten the historical burden.

As Butterworth said in the Preface: "The aim of the publishers and writer, in preparing this volume for young people, is to give a view of the principal places in England and France where the most interesting events have occurred; and, by a free use of pictures and illustrative stories, to present historic views of the two countries in an entertaining and attractive manner. . . . The illustrations of history, both by pencil and pen, are given in the disconnected way that a traveller would find them in his journeys; but they may be easily combined by memory in their chronological order. . . . That the volume may amuse and entertain the young reader, and awaken in him a greater love of books of history, biography, and travel, is the hope of the publishers and the author."

Zigzag Journeys in Europe had 128 illustrations, all woodcuts. A few, depicting Master Lewis and his boys, were obviously done specifically for this book. Probably the most amusing portrait of them is found on the "illuminated board" cover, where a very quaint group appears, admirably setting the tone of the work. Some of these are fairly rough sketches, others are highly finished in the best American manner. The great bulk of the pictures came from E & L's own stock of wood blocks and electrotypes, notably from the pictures used in Guizot's histories of France and England.

There were some, in this volume, from Charlotte Yonge's "Young Folks' Histories," some from Darley's *Sketches Abroad with Pen and Pencil,* and others from the many picture books on England and France put out by firms such as Cassell and Routledge. The pictures were well chosen, a few being decidedly handsome; there were frequent maps and decorative map end-papers. These pictures are still delightful to those who like woodcuts and wood engravings, but the suspicion arises, on turning the pages, that the zigzagging of the group depended, to a certain degree, on the availability of illustrations. Of course, in the instance of England, so many pictures were available that there would be almost no restriction, but in more remote lands the problem was different. Assuredly, youthful readers were not disturbed by such problems, and enjoyed the clever mingling of history, story, and picture, as the author intended. E & L were delighted, naturally, to cut down on the enormous expense of illustration by using their own stock as much as possible.

The book was vigorously advertised by E & L, during the fall of 1879, as "one of the handsomest and most instructive juvenile books ever issued in America."[39] The *Publishers' Weekly* thought that if the book had half the charm of Töpffer's classic it would be a decided addition to juvenile literature.[40] When it did appear, in mid-October, the same periodical declared that "it is all that was promised, rich in illustrations, excellent in its mechanical parts";[41] the handsome covers were praised, the book was "exceedingly delightful, a capital thing to put into the hands of children." Every reviewer concurred: the *Nation* liked the plan of the book, selected several stories, such as *The White Ship, Joan of Arc,* the *Wise Men of Gotham* for particular mention, and thought the whole volume both entertaining and instructive; that this book, like some others, featured "elegantly illustrated tales from history" was a gratifying sign of the times.[42] The *Literary World* called it an extension of the "Bodley Books" to England and France, but noted Butterworth's own qualifications for a book of this sort and called his pages "bright as well as instructive." The reviewer spotted an error in the labeling of Henry VIII's Chapel, but declared that the book was deservedly one of the half-dozen most popular books of the season.[43]

We have already seen that *Zigzag Journeys in Europe* sold over eight thousand copies during the holiday season, and two thousand more were sold in January. Butterworth was everywhere acclaimed, and received a special biographical notice in the *Literary World* in March, 1880. Thanks to the juveniles, E & L reported

80 per cent improvement in sales over the previous January and enlarged their store. With *Chatterbox* so successful, it was inevitable that the "Zigzag" formula would be exploited too, for all it was worth, in the hope of making it equally salable as a series.

Since there were seventeen "Zigzag Journeys" in all, I can only list them, with a few comments on certain volumes and their reception as the years passed. They are: *Zigzag Journeys in Europe* (1879), *Zigzag Journeys in Classic Lands* (1880), *Zigzag Journeys in the Orient* (1881), *Zigzag Journeys in the Occident* (1882), *Zigzag Journeys in Northern Lands* (1883), *Zigzag Journeys in Acadia and New France* (1884), *Zigzag Journeys in the Levant, with a Talmudist Story-teller* (1885), *Zigzag Journeys in the Sunny South* (1886), *Zigzag Journeys in India* (1887), *Zigzag Journeys in the Antipodes* (1888), *Zigzag Journeys in the British Isles* (1889), *Zigzag Journeys in the Great Northwest* (1890), *Zigzag Journeys in Australia* (1891), *Zigzag Journeys on the Mississippi* (1892), *Zigzag Journeys on the Mediterranean* (1893), *Zigzag Journeys in the White City* (1894), and *Zigzag Journeys around the World* (1895).[44] For the first eight volumes the pattern consisted of the travels of Master Lewis and his boys from the Academy of Yule, somewhere near the Blue Hills in Massachusetts.[45] Later on, as in *Zigzag Journeys in India*, the boys' club was omitted and the book became a delightful collection of folklore, animal stories, and historical fragments. This element of folklore was abundant in all the books because of Butterworth's own interest, and his taste was usually excellent. The stories were almost always retold in simple, rapid prose, and many poems were introduced, some of them admirable for youngsters. It was their constant change of pace, as mentioned before, the shift from history to poem to legend to descriptions of landscapes or buildings, that kept the reader's interest alive. Butterworth haunted the Boston Public Library to good purpose, and some of the freshness of his early morning labors—he always rose between five and six to write for two hours before breakfast—comes over into his writing.

The Preface of *Zigzag Journeys in Classic Lands* noted that "the warm reception which the public gave to *Zigzag Journeys in Europe* and its large sale and continued success have led the publishers and the writer to plan a series of entertaining and instructive books. . . ." Since the previous volume found so much favor as a gift book, Butterworth introduced a special Christmas chapter in this book, describing an entertainment of the Zigzag Club and printing some of its stories. This journey, which arose out of

Master Lewis' ill health, covered Portugal, Spain, Marseilles, Genoa, Milan, Venice, Parnassus, Rome, and other side trips in Greece and Italy. The pictures were of the same type: some few done expressly for the book, the majority from standard travel books, notably Doré's illustrations of Spanish scenes, with more from Darley and from Miss Yonge's histories. The *Literary World* spoke of it as an "American book written to fit English pictures,"[46] which was only partially true, but a shrewd criticism none the less. Although most reviewers found it as good as the first volume, the *Nation's* critic thought it disjointed, being especially annoyed at the intrusion of some American tales, such as a possum hunt, while the group was engaged in European travel. "Mr. Butterworth threatens to go on, but there are still some corners of the earth which ought to be spared this treatment." He admitted, however, that the work contained a great amount of information and entertainment.[47]

In 1881 came *Zigzag Journeys in the Orient,* but the Orient here meant simply eastern Europe, from the Adriatic to the Baltic, Vienna to the Golden Horn, Moscow, and St. Petersburg. It was an attempt to explain the "Eastern Question" to young people, and incidentally to cover a region less well supplied with picture books. E & L's edition of Rambaud's *Popular History of Russia* was obviously of great use at this juncture, but the quality of the pictures, in general, was lower. In this book Butterworth sought a collaborator in Miss Edna Dean Proctor, who had already written articles for the magazines on her stay in Russia. The journeys in Europe and in Classic Lands had sold nearly fifty thousand copies! The *Dial,* remarking on the large sale of these books, thought their popularity well deserved, the next best thing to a view of the countries themselves.[48] The *Critic* was equally laudatory: the "encyclopaedic gentlemen were no less entertaining and instructive than in the earlier volumes"; they elucidated the intricate political question admirably. The pictures, though, were old friends, some appearing elsewhere in E & L's publications; a sort of metempsychosis or transmigration was sometimes visible, as when a picture called "Allegorical Picture of Charlemagne" became "Allegorical Picture of the Tzar."[49]

The series continued with *Zigzag Journeys in the Occident,* in this instance the United States, a trip from the Atlantic to the Pacific. Its aim was to describe homesteading and to celebrate the resources of the great Northwest. By this time, 1882, the sales had reached nearly a hundred thousand volumes, which meant that the earlier books were still selling in quantity. The Preface indicated that these books had become popular in schools as collateral reading. The pictures and maps were excellent, a return to better quality. This volume centered on cities, such western, perennially favorite themes as Mormonism, and the great wheat lands.

Zigzag Journeys in Northern Lands returned to Europe, mostly Germany, with a brief excursion to Scandinavia. The same purposes stated for the earlier volumes were reaffirmed: the books were intended to stimulate the love of history and to suggest the best historical reading. "Popular stories and pictures are freely used to adapt useful information to the tastes of the young. But in every page, story and picture, right education and right influence are kept in view." Thus, many German legends and fairy tales were brought in, but "they are so introduced and guarded as not to leave a wrong impression upon the minds of the young and immature." As Robert Lovett recalled, the books were "agreeably written and incredibly wholesome."[50]

There followed journeys to Acadia, the Levant, the Sunny South, and then India, in 1887. This book was almost entirely stories, so arranged as to give a view of the history of India and its conditions and progress in the 1880's. Virginia Haviland recalls that Frederic Melcher's lasting interest in India grew from poring over the engravings and folk tales of this book.[51] In the Preface Butterworth remarked that he had not intended to go beyond eight volumes, but a quarter of a million copies had been sold, and the books were still so greatly sought in families and schools as helps to the education and training of the young that he began a new series.

The remaining volumes were much the same. Only *Zigzag Journeys in the White City* departed from the established pattern by emphasizing folk lore societies and the Folk Lore Congress at the Columbian Exposition. The volume was filled with American tales "of service to patriotic American holidays, Village Improvement Societies and to social life." Half-tone pictures appeared in this book as a concession to modernity.

Although the early volumes were clearly the best, the later ones did not show too much falling-off, and children who had started reading them waited eagerly for every new title. May Lamberton Becker remembered the "series of Christmas trees, growing taller as I grew, and in the pile of presents a copy of Hezekiah Butterworth's *Zigzag Journeys in Europe* or one of its successors. . . . Always I asked for it and got it."[52] "There must have been many other readers of these series, for they sold by the 100,000, but I never found any boy or girl to share my enthusiasm for them," said Robert Lovett.[53] Books which sold about half a million copies were surely popular with young readers, even if parents frequently bought them because they were safe reading for the young hopefuls. Butterworth had "the distinction of being a literary millionaire," from the profits of these and his other books, totaling sixty volumes.[54]

As the years passed, the reviewers sometimes grew weary of the pattern, although they rarely omitted a review, since the demand appeared "unappeasable," as one said. It was the miscellany that shocked many: "As miscellaneous as the contents of a monthly magazine, but none the less entertaining."[55] The artificiality in *Zigzag Journeys in the Occident* might tempt a critic to sarcasm, but the reading public would probably overlook it, said one reviewer glumly.[56] The *Dial* liked every volume it reviewed, but the critics in the *Nation* alternately raged and relented: of the volume on Northern Lands, one said, "the mixture of colors on the outside typifies the confusion of topics within," but he admitted that there were many interesting pages and pictures and the book ought to find favor "with those who like a little of everything at the same time."[57] The *Critic* was almost always favorable; its reviewers seemed to know that the books had stories children liked to hear or read, and were certain that they "snared the hearts of young and old alike."[58]

Only the *Nation,* in fact, was ever caustic, and its reviewers seemed frequently more bilious and arrogant than anything else. One of their critics preferred Knox's series of *Boy Travellers* and automatically damned all the "Zigzag Books." Another pounced on Butterworth's device of using many stories strung on a thin thread of narrative, especially his remark that although such methods were open to criticism, they had not proved unpopular, judging by sales of a hundred thousand volumes, at that time.[59] This was a question, sneered the critic, for a dime-novelist rather than a maker of holiday books; the pictures were shoveled in rather than inserted, and such slovenly bookmaking was "ruinous to the literary taste of the young."[60] This criticism was silly, for the books were always finely made and the pictures invariably attractive. It was when they blamed the books for being "written for the pictures" and commented on certain pictures as being "veterans bearing the scars of service" that these critics performed a useful function.

As Virginia Haviland suggests, "whatever weaknesses the series had, the 'Zigzag Journeys' must be acknowledged as a chapter in American children's literature and some considerable influence in the firm establishment of this new 'style' of books for young people."[61] The publishers also deserve a great deal of the credit, for the consistently handsome dress of these books, their delightful pictures, and their crisp printing were features supervised by Dana Estes and his helpers. The covers of these books were just as gay and colorful as many of today's children's books; they lacked only the profusion of colored plates within, which that period of printing could not adequately supply. That many children would read them today is most unlikely, even supposing a batch of them was resurrected from the attic, but the older person may not disdain to give them a glance, for old time's sake, and even find a laugh over Master Lewis and his boys.

It is time now to return to the burgeoning list and sales of children's books in 1880. In July, the "Survival of the Fittest" was proclaimed once more: "our juvenile books are among the very best offered and we desire to inform the trade that we have new books in press that are unequalled by any heretofore published."[62] The new *Zigzag Journeys in Classic Lands* led the fall list, with a "prodigious sale" anticipated. Laura E. Richards had a new book, *Five Mice in a Mouse-trap,* and there were several varieties of *Chatterbox,* a group of baby-books, *Our Baby's Primer, Little May, Little Jack's Adventures* and the like, and some new editions of books by Charles Carleton Coffin, *Winning His Way, Following the Flag, My Days and Nights on the Battle-field,* and *Our New Way Round the World.* A series, the "Young Ladies' Library," made its brief appearance, including such titles as Sarah Tytler's *Papers for Thoughtful Girls* and the Reverend Daniel Eddy's *Christian Heroines, The Young Woman's Friend,* and *The Angel Whispers.* These old-timers had sold by the hundred thousand before but were now on their way out. More lively was "The New Adventure Library," with such titles as *Rocky Mountain Life, Perilous Adventures in the Far West, Jack in the Forecastle,* and *Rovings on Land and Sea.* Many of these were trivial, but the list was larger than ever before and there were some real favorites on it. In October E & L were proclaiming that the thirty thousand printing of "Zigzag Journeys" was exhausted and dealers were urged to get their orders in for the next printing; the "Zigzag Journeys," E & L reminded them, would sell at all seasons of the year, as they did in the usually dull winter months of early 1880.

A few weeks later a boastful advertisement summarized E & L's satisfaction with business: "Three years ago we published no juvenile books. We now claim that we publish the best and most popular line in the country. Daniel Webster said that in his profession 'there was always room at the top.' In juvenile publishing we aim at the top!"[63] The *Literary World* noted that E & L were preparing editions of 50,000, 70,000, 80,000 for three forthcoming juveniles, and 100,000 for a fourth (presumably *Chatterbox*), with the regret that this was not 20,000 larger.[64] Yet just at this moment, as business was booming, began the long controversy over the reprinting of *Chatterbox* by other American publishers, which is described in full later. Nevertheless, E & L announced that sales of the two Zigzag books, in fourteen months, had reached thirty-six thousand volumes: "unparalleled in the history of the book trade."[65]

For 1881 the list was even better. Three new series were begun, all of them good, besides a fine new book by Laura Richards, *Sketches and Scraps*. E & L's fall list was the largest ever, in all subjects, but the juveniles more than held their own for quality and for sales; in fact, juveniles made up half the list in number of titles. In December E & L again affirmed, in a massive advertisement:

> *There is Nothing So Successful as Success*
> *The Survival of the Fittest*
>
> Among the shoals of new juvenile books there are a large number of imitations of our famous *Zigzag Books*. No greater compliment to our enterprise and taste could be paid us by our rivals. It is admitted on all sides that the publication of these world-renowned books formed an epoch in the annals of juvenile publishing. Their success was unprecedented and no rival can hope to repeat it.[66]

The three series included the first volume in C. A. Stephens' "Knockabout Club Series," "The Young Folks' Histories—Second Series," and "Great Cities of the World." The last of these was also a history series, the first volume of which was Butterworth's *Young Folks' History of Boston*. Butterworth also turned out a *Young Folks' History of America* early in 1881 and his third Zigzag book, the Orient, in the fall, a pace not conducive to the best literary accomplishment. His *Young Folks' History of Boston* was one of three juveniles on Boston appearing in the fall of 1881, the others being Samuel Adams Drake's *Around the Hub* and Horace Scudder's *Boston Town*. Most people thought Drake's book, published by Roberts Brothers, the best in all-around quality, and ranked Butterworth's volume third. The *Nation* pointed out its weaknesses of style and its inaccuracy, but noted that it offered the most for the money, was the most up-to-date, and the best illustrated, with an abundance of good anecdotes.[67] It obviously reflected the library in its encyclopedic approach and thus appealed to those who wanted information.[68] The second book in the series was a history of London by W. H. Rideing, a Britisher who settled in America and finally became an editor of the *Youth's Companion*. It was highly commended when it appeared, in 1884, for its attractive style and excellent illustrations; it was actually as much guide book as history, somewhat in the "Zigzag" manner.[69] The third was a history of Edinburgh by Frederick H. Allen, E & L's art editor, who was to do another work on the Reformation.

The second series of "Young Folks' Histories"—Miss Yonge's being the first—was uniformly good and received as much praise as hers. The first in time, but not in quality, was Butterworth's *Young Folks' History of America,* published in June, 1881. Because of his phenomenal success in the "Zigzag Journeys," everyone expected a masterpiece; E & L had such large advance orders they were forced to delay publication. Yet the book was a disappointment: instead of being wholly original it utilized a British work as the thread of the historical narrative and strung the tales along it in a way which ruined its consecutive flow; the style was poor, and there were small mistakes.[70] "Not a good work," commented the *Literary World,* echoing disappointment more than anything else.[71] Yet some thought it readable and entertaining, and Butterworth's name as author made it sell year after year.

The other volumes in the series were excellent, among the best that E & L published in the area of history for young people. Alexander Young, a Boston journalist, wrote the *Young Folks' History of the Netherlands* (1881). It was largely a condensation of Motley and managed to retain some of the flavor of that brilliant stylist, without certain of his prejudices. Nathan Haskell Dole's *Young Folks' History of Russia* (1881) was an immediate success: "Interesting from beginning to end" was the *Nation*'s verdict [72] and the *Critic* considered it "entertaining as any romance." [73] All agreed that it was both compact and trustworthy, it had good maps and illustrations, with such conveniences as marginal dates throughout. Frederick Ober's account of Mexico (1882) received like praise: "welcome and timely"; profusely illustrated and well written; done with great industry and patience.[74] One reviewer felt Ober was a bit harsh in terming Philip II an "incarnate demon," but had no other criticism.[75]

Another series, though not so called, was the group of books by Charles Carleton Coffin, known everywhere as "Carleton" from the pen name he chose while winning fame as a Civil War correspondent for the *Boston Journal*. His early books on the war were read everywhere, but his great popularity came with the splendid

The Boys of '76, which Harper published in the centennial year. After this came a long series done for Harper, on which he continued work until his death in 1896. Dana Estes cleverly arranged with Coffin to reprint his earlier books and capitalize on his present vogue, hence the appearance in 1880 of the three books: *Winning His Way,* a novel originally published in 1866, which was "transformed by printer's magic into a quarto fitted out with a new stock of pictures and dressed up in a most gorgeous cover";[76] *Following the Flag* (1865), and *My Days and Nights upon the Battle-field* (1864). The last two were products of his reporting and were unusually vivid and colorful, among the best eye-witness accounts of the conflict. They too received a glamorous new attire and a new supply of pictures.

In 1866 Coffin wrote a single-volume history of the war called *Four Years of Fighting,* a considerable success at the time, which E & L chose to revive under the salable title, *Boys of '61.* The book had long been out of print and many who had read it before were glad to see it again. The *Literary World* remarked on the anticipation for Carleton's *Boys of '61*[77] and the volume was no disappointment when it arrived in a brightly martial illuminated cover, celebrating army and navy alike. A thick book of 558 pages, it was profusely illustrated, mostly with full-page plates, and had handsome endpapers of zouaves and cavalrymen. This was another instance of Estes' skill in exploiting current vogues for all they were worth, since this was the time of a fresh wave of interest in the war, with numerous articles in the magazines, to be followed by *Battles and Leaders of the Civil War,* that classic of war history. To this group by Coffin E & L joined his *Our New Way Round the World,* the narrative of a trip made first to Europe for the *Boston Journal,* which turned into a sixteen-month journey after his reports proved popular. This, too, was entertaining, especially the bits on Asia and his return by way of California.

All of these books sold amazingly well, as Estes had hoped they would, and E & L were even led to reissue a story, *Caleb Krinkle* (1875), as *Dan of Millbrook,* in 1895, but this was not a success. Estes was quite an admirer of "Carleton" and was, no doubt, somewhat disappointed that "Carleton" did not let E & L publish his later books. After Coffin's death, the Reverend W. E. Griffis, a close friend, prepared a biography, which E & L published in 1898. It was the only one ever published and is quite lengthy, over three hundred pages. It was intended as a tribute to this distinguished and beloved Bostonian, and, incidentally, it was a tribute by the pastor of Coffin's church to a most loyal member. Coffin was really an excellent writer for young people and the Harpers had profited from his tremendous and deserved popularity. Many a boy got his first notions of the Revolution from *The Boys of '76* and went on to read *Boys of '61*.

The last and most important of the new series in 1881 was Charles Asbury Stephens' "Knockabout Club Series." Stephens was an associate of Butterworth's on the *Youth's Companion* and one of the chief reasons for its popularity. Samuel Hopkins Adams is sure that the *Companion* had its golden age in the 1880's, when he and his cousins read it, and this was in the period when Stephens was at his best.[78] The boys had outgrown *Chatterbox* and were a bit fearful of some of the moral poems in the *Companion,* read to them as proof of its worth, but soon discovered that it was full of capital stories. Lovell Thompson, who edited the treasury of the *Youth's Companion* in 1954,[79] is convinced that no other contributor to the paper did so much to fix its tone; again, he asserts, it is hard to think of any writer who continued to appeal to generation after generation of young readers and yet was curiously unknown except to *Companion* subscribers.[80] Here he is wrong, for Stephens was very well known by his books, which had been published since the early seventies and had won a host of readers before E & L took him over. Thompson thought that his writing had been a perceptible force in the shaping of American character, and was certainly for the best. When one realizes that this stint of writing lasted for more than sixty years, to the tune of three thousand short stories and one hundred serial stories, one can only be amazed at his stamina.

Stephens wrote for a world that he believed in, about a world he loved, says Thompson. "He probably thought more of his readers than he did of his reputation. That makes him a hack and an old pro."[81] The tributes to Stephens in the treasury are quite warming, especially from the 1950's, and if a reader tackled one of his many books he might find it thoroughly readable because of its gusto and life, its unstilted prose and rapid movement. It must have required almost limitless energy to keep up this manner in book after book, for he wrote with unbelievable rapidity: by 1873 he was writing the series "Young Yachters" and "Camping Out Series" in such quick succession that the *Literary World* said that he promised to rival Lope de Vega, since within a few months he had turned out half a dozen books, remarkably good in quality.[82] In 1872 he wrote one of his best works, *On the Amazons,* a book of delightful adventures, exotic scenery, and really living people, both adults and young folks, with plenty of real humor. In this book also was described as in many of his stories, his plan for a floating college, which would restore life to education and create young cosmopolitans. This excellent idea has been revived every now and then, but never with any success; Stephens pressed it with might and main, and for a time he aroused interest, only to see it wane at last. This was his one crusade, however, for the books were otherwise superb stories with no preaching.

Stephens contributed three volumes to the "Knockabout Club Series": *The Knockabout Club in the Woods* (1881), *The Knockabout Club Alongshore* (1882), *The Knockabout Club in the Tropics* (1883). The first of these told of hunting and fishing in Maine and Canada, the Rangeley Lakes, Moosehead, the St. Lawrence, and the Saguenay. The *Critic* called it "a bright and breezy chronicle of youths afflicted with rich parents."[83] The bear and fish stories were "tall tales" of the American variety, but well written and with good pictures. The *Literary World* even thought it instructive and considered that Stephens' taste was "improving," but stressed its interest for boys.[84] The second book took the club to Labrador, was equally lively and adventurous and was, in the opinion of the average boy, "a regular stunner."[85] The reviewer in the *Nation,* none the less, was much annoyed at Stephens' scheme for a floating college and condemned him as a "radical" for his insidious undermining of traditional education.[86] This may have been an unconscious tribute to Stephens, but it was undeniably silly. The third book took the boys to New Mexico, Mexico, and Central America; there was the same mingling of stories, adventures, lively chatter, all brightened with many pictures. The *Nation* still had a grudge against Stephens, rating his style "at once coarse and inane," yet couldn't but admit the vigor of the narrative and the charm of the spirited tales.[87]

In 1882 Stephens turned out another story, *The Young Moose Hunters,* about northern Maine. This was generally praised as delightful, full of the real spirit of youth. The stories might sound overdrawn, but anyone who knew Maine would not think so.[88] Apparently Stephens had time for no more full-length stories and henceforth confined himself to the *Youth's Companion.* But the idea of the "Knockabout Club" was too good to disappear, and Dana Estes finally settled on Frederick Albion Ober as a likely man to continue the series.

Ober, another New Englander, had already proved his skill as a writer: E & L had published his books on Mexico and Lee and Shepard had brought out, in 1880, his *Camps in the Caribbees,* which recounted the adventures of a naturalist with notebook and camera. He lacked Stephens' *élan,* but he was adequate, and had the advantage of actually knowing the scenes he described, since he was an inveterate traveler. Being interested in early Spanish exploration, he visited Spain as well as the Antilles, Florida, Mexico, and Central America. His books remind one more of the "Zigzag Journeys" in their encyclopedic approach: there were the serious, studious youths, the "Historian," the "Antiquarian," and the "Doctor," who were responsible for the history, the stories, and the scientific background. Generally, Ober wrote to instruct, though he did his best to gild the pill and built the framework of many of the stories well enough to keep the readers' interest despite the dry passages, which were not so frequent as some have asserted.[89]

Ober contributed six stories to the "Knockabout Club Series": *The Knockabout Club in the Everglades* (1887), *The Knockabout Club in the Antilles* (1888), *The Knockabout Club in Spain* (1889), *The Knockabout Club in North Africa* (1890), *The Knockabout Club on the Spanish Main* (1891), and *The Knockabout Club in Search of Treasure* (1892). It is truly amusing to see how these volumes were received by the critics. If one read only the *Nation*, whose reviewer still saw red at the very title, "Knockabout Club," one would have concluded that the stories were incredibly dull, hard reading, poorly illustrated, and painfully humorous.[90] Speaking of the Antilles volume, the reviewer said that Ober should have omitted the humorous passages with which he vainly tried to lighten the monotony of the narrative.[91] Just to prove that the New York air did not necessarily create hostility to books from Boston, the *Critic*, from the first, was friendly. *The Knockabout Club in the Everglades*, the reviewer said, was a bit clumsy in its construction, with the material presented in crude masses, but it was lively reading, the illustrations of bears, panthers, rattlesnakes, and Seminoles were fine; it would surely attract all lovers of adventure.[92] The book on the Antilles was full of enthusiasm, the descriptions were easy, and the local color was indeed authentic.[93] The *Literary World* agreed concerning both books: the first had exciting incidents and good pictures; the second was most attractive, with its good illustrations by Champney, Taylor, and other American artists, its stories and historical anecdotes, its fine descriptions, its spirited style.[94] There was similar commendation for later volumes. The *Critic* was positively rhapsodical in its praise of the *Knockabout Club in Spain*: the reviewer felt that Ober was particularly fitted to handle this subject, liked his good quotes from Prescott and Irving and also the Doré illustrations that were employed.[95] It was the same with the volumes on North Africa, good from its cover, "as gay as an Oriental bazaar," to the end of its text, in which Ober served as the "natty and chatty American guide," with tales of horsemanship,

history, and good descriptions. "The last page comes too soon!"[96]
With similar enthusiasm for the Spanish Main, the *Critic* noted
that Ober had a youthful clientele that increased annually, and that
parents who wanted entertaining and instructive reading for their
offspring should take notice.[97] It would seem that Ober was almost
as successful as Stephens, in a quieter fashion.

With good travel books for boys appearing every year, it was
only right, morally and commercially, that there should be a series
for girls. Dana Estes showed publishing acumen in selecting Elizabeth Williams Champney, the wife of J. Wells Champney, who did
so many illustrations for E & L's books, as the writer of the "Three
Vassar Girls Series." Virginia Haviland, in her articles on the
travelogue story books, is most enthusiastic about Mrs. Champney
and gives ample details about her background and accomplish-
ments.[98] Suffice it to say that Elizabeth Champney was, inevitably, a
Vassar graduate (who married her instructor in art), and that she
spent the early years of her married life traveling about Europe.
She began writing for *St. Nicholas* in 1873, but her work also attracted notice by adults when she wrote articles on her journeys
for *Harper's* and the *Century*. She had written books for children,
among others *All Around a Palette* (1877), illustrated, as always,
by her husband, which had been highly praised. Estes made no mistake in picking this husband-wife team, both very well known, for
a girls' series, and the results certainly proved his wisdom. In fact,
after the first of the series appeared, she had to devote all her time
to the Vassar girls and a later series, "Witch Winnie," published
by Dodd, Mead in New York after 1891.

The "Vassar Girls" did not continue the same characters
throughout the series: new ones would be invited to go on the trip,
some got married, with changes a matter of course. Some girls were
spoiled daughters of the rich, others the strong-minded, moral type,
who might become missionaries, musicians, or doctors. Thus there
were always implicit lessons in high thinking and unselfish conduct.
Mrs. Champney naturally concentrated upon things artistic, and
did it very well. She was also a finished storyteller: her lively dialogue, exciting incidents—some of them based on actual history—
her occasional melodrama, all served to make these books the equal
of any the boys were reading. Possibly some degenerate males even
read these tales, but history would scarcely record this fact. Her
stories strove particularly to overcome prejudice, prejudices
against nations, such as England, or against the Jews; several international marriages helped to underline her arguments. She was
naturally at her best in scenes with which she was herself familiar.

Virginia Haviland points out that the Champneys were not tourists, in the ordinary sense, but cosmopolitans living abroad, so that her accounts of trips through the Alps or down the Rhine were sure to be colorful and convincing.[99] But even her stories dealing with South America or Russia were delightful and sought after by her readers, so that E & L found in her a gold mine.

There were eleven volumes in the "Three Vassar Girls Series," from 1882 to 1892. They had the same bright covers as the "Zigzag Journeys," the endpaper maps, and the profusion of pictures by "Champ" and "other distinguished artists." The author signed herself Lizzie W. Champney, to give a more youthful touch, supposedly. The titles of the volumes were: *Three Vassar Girls Abroad, Rambles of Three College Girls on a Vacation Trip through France and Spain for Amusement and Instruction, With Their Haps and Mishaps* (1882), *Three Vassar Girls in England* (1883), *Three Vassar Girls in South America* (1884), *Three Vassar Girls in Italy* (1885), *Three Vassar Girls on the Rhine* (1886), *Three Vassar Girls at Home* (1887), *Three Vassar Girls in France* (1888), *Three Vassar Girls in Russia and Turkey* (1889), *Three Vassar Girls in Switzerland* (1890), *Three Vassar Girls in the Tyrol* (1891), *Three Vassar Girls in the Holy Land* (1892). Although "Champ" contributed numerous pictures for each volume, most of the illustrations were from E & L's own stock, now well supplied for European scenes by the Zigzag books and the histories. Nevertheless, many of the pictures were newly selected, and the general effect was as successful as in the "Zigzag Journeys."

The diversity of critical appraisal of these books reaches extremes that are often amusing and certainly revealing. Almost all critics deplored the mingling of old pictures with Champ's illustrations: although they were introduced to increase the interest of the book, they actually cheapened it, said one critic of *Three Vassar Girls Abroad.*[100] The "other distinguished artists" were often of ancient vintage and some hostile souls declared that the cuts lent a "helping hand to the poverty of the text."[101] What is surprising is the rather shocked tone pervading some of the reviews, doubtless an unconscious tribute to the basic sprightliness of the narrative. The *Nation* was especially sour: "Their sayings and doings afford the reader but little entertainment." The heroines had not even attained to mastery of correct English, "nor is the strong, pronounced type to which they belong consonant with that finer culture and higher breeding which Vassar graduates ought to show and which sensitive criticism demands."[102] Speaking of *Three Vassar Girls in South America*, the reviewer admitted that it was a lively story, but the style remained without charm and the heroines were "singularly unattractive."[103]

The *Literary World* was almost always favorable: *Three Vassar Girls Abroad* was hailed as a good, lively story, as was the volume on England, and *Three Vassar Girls in South America* was called unusually fine, with Champ's fresh and spirited pictures. The heroines were "sprightly and girlish, not frivolous."[104] *Three Vassar Girls in Italy* was also praised, notably for its art criticism and pictures, but the reviewer had to say: "The 'Vassar type' does not stand, to our mind, as the highest type of American girlhood, but Mrs. Champney has toned down the type somewhat and a dialogue which might be offensively loud is subordinated to descriptions which are pleasantly quiet."[105] Later volumes were uniformly admired, however, with only a weary comment, at times, on the use of well-worn pictures; *Three Vassar Girls in France* was "bright and vivid," as was *Three Vassar Girls in Switzerland,* a few years later.[106] The *Dial* was laudatory from the start. The book on South America was written "with a dashing and confident hand," though careless of syntax occasionally; it was a "gay and sprightly" work that would find plenty of admirers.[107] The *Critic* was also friendly throughout, and the remark about *Three Vassar Girls in the Tyrol* sums up their attitude fairly: the reviewer described the "merry peripatetic trio of sweet girl graduates," who had been going abroad for ten years by 1891. Like all such heroines, they were "perennially youthful, keen-eyed and vivacious," and the love story that was brought in made the book "as good as a novel." This reviewer even praised the illustrations, as some others had done, so it is obvious that they did not displease everyone.[108] The sales alone would have corroborated the popularity of this series, and they were formidable, but it is good to observe that most of the reviewers saw in them the qualities that made them favorites. The "Three Vassar Girls" were favorites for another decade, but by 1909, when Dana Estes died, they had gone out of print.

In the next few years two more historical series were initiated, the "Young Folks' Epochs of History" and the "Library of Entertaining History." The "Young Folks' Epochs," in direct imitation of the highly successful "Epochs of Modern History," which E & L had been publishing since 1874, was itself of value and was usually welcomed by reviewers. The first in the series, the *Young Folks' History of the Queens of England,* was based on Agnes Strickland's famous work, in this instance condensed by Rosalie Kaufman. The *Nation* thought it an excellent abridgment and lauded it as interesting and useful reading, in which the *Literary World* con-

curred.[109] Only the *Critic* believed it "superfluous," giving superfluous information.[110] Mrs. C. E. Cheney's *Young Folks' History of
the Civil War* found favor with all: "seldom better told," declared
the *Critic*, and the *Nation* recommended it heartily, praising its objectivity and avoidance of tiresome minutiae.[111] Frederick H. Allen
wrote a history of the Reformation that evoked little comment.

The "Library of Entertaining History" was of no great importance, brief works, largely anecdotal and oversimplified, with
old pictures. Mrs. Clara E. Clement, later to be a regular on E & L's
staff, wrote a history of Egypt, and there were histories of India,
Spain, Switzerland, and the American people. A series of biographies was planned but only one volume—E. E. Brown's *Young
Folks' Life of Washington,* a handsomely illustrated quarto—was
published.

Outside of *Chatterbox* and the many series already discussed,
there were not large numbers of juveniles, and very few worthy of
separate mention. As in most of E & L's books, the illustrations
were always a strong point and the quality of paper and printing
was above average. Fannie B. Irving's *Six Girls,* whose illustrations by F. T. Merrill were the chief merit of the book, remained
on E & L's list to the end, proving that a very average book could
subsist on pictorial appeal.[112] More important was *Page, Squire
and Knight,* a free adaptation by W. Davenport Adams of Mme
Colomb's *Franchise.* This was a story with real flavor, showing both
the flowery and thorny sides of French feudalism; the young hero
observed the showy pomp of chivalry and the harsh lot of the
peasants in a tale full of realistic adventure.[113] It was one of the
best historical novels E & L published and still is found in the L. C.
Page catalogue under the title *The Days of Chivalry.* Its French
illustrations were clear, vivid, and artistic, doing much to explain
the spirited text. "Just the book," remarked a reviewer in the
Publishers' Weekly, "to make a boy manly and brave."[114] Of the
total number of books published in 1882, seventeen were juveniles,
twenty-six were for adults, which shows the important place the
juveniles now occupied in E & L's output.

Walter Montgomery's *Boys of the Sierras,* a lively tale of the
gold miners of 1849, was featured in 1883, and became the key
work, in later years, of a series of adventure stories, none closely
related but all dealing with far-away places and events. The next
year E & L acquired for their list an annual edited by one of the
most popular names in American juvenile literature, William T.
Adams, whom boys knew as Oliver Optic. It was called *Our Little
Ones and The Nursery,* and, in earlier years, had been published by

Lee and Shepard as an annual, while another firm put out the magazine. This volume, closely resembling *Chatterbox* but intended for a slightly younger group, had been more popular as an annual than as a magazine largely because of the editorial skill of Oliver Optic and because of its superior illustrations. E & L set out to give it even better printing and pictures, with immediate public favor as a response. It was noted that the wood engravings, when it was published by Lee and Shepard, were the equal of the best turned out in America, such as were found in *Harper's* and the *Century* magazines.[115] In the 1884 issue there were 370 illustrations, by many artists of repute, engraved by the master craftsman, George T. Andrew. Each year the major reviewing periodicals sang its praise, usually preferring it to *Chatterbox* in quality of illustrations and printing. Thus the *Literary World*, in 1884, called it superior in text, typography, and illustrations,[116] and noted, the following year, that it was a "handsome and refined book, an education in the things that are pure and lovely and of good report."[117] Each year the reviewers for this magazine praised the excellent wood engravings, of the "best American grade," its admirable collection of good advice, stories, songs, and poems, concluding that the editor's share was vital in its excellence. The *Critic* declared: "Adams is the prince of editors for children's books," and knew that youngsters would find it fascinating from the first page to the last.[118] The *Critic*'s reviewers felt the same as the years went on, praising the fine printing, attractive toned paper, its generous size, its bright covers, and its splendid selection of reading matter.[119] Both the *Nation* and the *Dial* liked it and frequently preferred it to *Chatterbox* for its quality of pictures. It should be noted that *Our Little Ones* sold for $1.75 as compared to $1.25 for *Chatterbox*, but most reviewers thought it well worth the difference. While *Our Little Ones* was popular until the very end, in 1896—Oliver Optic died in 1897—it never achieved the phenomenal sales of *Chatterbox* because it catered only to younger readers and therefore did not have the broad age appeal of the rival annual.

Now and then an isolated work would catch the reviewers' eyes, as did a little book called *Pictures of Other Folks at Home*, in 1884. It was another variant on the travel theme so well exploited by E & L, a series of letters in verse describing a family trip through Europe; it was adorned with twelve colored pictures, each having a postage stamp of one country, with its flag, coat of arms, map, costumes, and sports depicted around the stamp. The pictures pleased all the critics; the rhymes were gay and "good information was sifted in with the sugar."[120] A practical little book, declared the *Literary World,* "its tone is refined and cultivated."[121] Most of the many titles published during these years were trivial, even though a book by a popular author like Sophie May might appear now and then. The bulk of the juveniles was always found in the many *Chatterbox* volumes and the travel series; the lesser books never received major advertising, were always treated as minor padding for the list. The tremendous battle over *Chatterbox* absorbed so much of the firm's energies during the years from 1883 to 1887 that it is surprising that there were so many good books on the yearly lists.

After the final victory in 1887, when *Chatterbox* became a treasure for E & L exclusively, the list of juveniles improved again. Two historical novels by Professor James Russell Soley, of the Naval Academy, *The Boys of 1812* and *The Sailor Boys of '61,* were great favorites. Soley had already written histories of the navy's part in the Civil War and his works had the advantage of being stirring as well as accurate. The *Critic* thought him too severe on the English in the first work, but had nothing but praise for the second: "it will help recruit candidates for Annapolis."[122] The pictures were especially good and the stories were magnificent: "Feed your boys such diet!" The *Nation* thought the second book so fair that it could be read by Southerners without offense, and approved of its simple, straightforward style.[123] Rival books by a certain Willis J. Abbot, called *Blue Jackets of '61* and *Blue Jackets of '76,* may have inspired the writing of these books by Soley, and, no doubt, helped the others' sales. These books are still on L. C. Page's list, with the claim that they have sold sixteen and eleven thousand, respectively.

The tireless Lizzie Champney also provided a short series which began, in 1887, with *Great-Grandmother's Girls in New France.* This was the story of a Deerfield minister's six-year-old daughter carried into captivity by the Indians in 1704; a really charming story, written in the dignified style appropriate for Puritan maidens, and handsomely illustrated by Champ.[124] The fiction was deftly interwoven with fact and, in this instance, Mrs. Champney did not have to worry about Vassar-style sprightliness. The next year saw *Great-Grandmother's Girls in New Mexico,* commended again as an "interesting and wholesome story," of praiseworthy accuracy, especially since the author had traveled through the region.[125] This was more of a holiday book, in the style of the "Zigzag Journeys," and one reviewer lamented the fact, since it made the book heavy to hold.[126] Both books were enjoyed by adults, who regretted that the series was not continued.

The other writer of importance in this rich period of the eighties was Laura E. Richards, who had several good books in this decade and who was to dominate the following years. There is considerable literature about the importance of Mrs. Richards as a writer for children: the warmth of the tributes to her evokes constantly the pleasure children felt in reading her books as well as the delight of adults who read her books to their children.[127] Particularly fine is her autobiography, *Stepping Westward,* where her refreshing individualism is amply revealed; it has the same tricks of style as her stories, and is just as readable.[128] When she died, in 1943, the obituary notices recalled that she had written about eighty books, many of them still read and enjoyed as widely as when they were first written. Most of her books during these fruitful years after she went to live in Gardiner, Maine, were published by E & L, though a few went elsewhere, such as those published by Roberts Brothers in the eighties.

In the seventies she had written constantly for *St. Nicholas.* She had been brought up by Julia Ward Howe on a generous diet of verse, and the kind she liked best was "the ringing kind 'with bells and trumpets.' "[129] As she herself puts it: "ballads and songs and the like, early assimilated, had given me a good ear for metre and rhythm (say *jingle,* woman, and have done with it!)."[130] With her first children came a "prodigious welling up of rhymes," with tunes to accompany them; she tells how the first baby was "plump and placid, with a broad, smooth back which made an excellent writing desk." In her autobiography she speaks of her first book as appearing in 1880, but she had apparently forgotten the little holiday books of rhymes and stories, the first of which came out in 1878: *Baby's Rhyme-book* and *Baby's Story-book* I have already noted, as well as *The Little Tyrant,* of 1879.

Five Little Mice in a Mouse-trap (1880) was probably her first distinctive book. Mrs. Richards was glad that children were still reading it in 1930.[131] There were illustrations by Addie Ledyard, but the pictures by Kate Greenaway were simply borrowed and were not done expressly for this volume. It was fanciful, the Man in the Moon's words were translated from the "lunacular" into the vernacular, with many echoes from her own children's sayings and even her own remembered words and ways of twenty years before. It was fairly well received: the *Literary World* called it "imaginative," but thought that the quantity of baby talk limited it to young minds;[132] the *Nation's* reviewer was puzzled by it, rated it a voluble and slightly bewildering performance, "utterly formless."[133] "We cannot congratulate the child set to read it," he added.

Though *Five Little Mice* was a puzzle, *Sketches and Scraps by Papa and Mamma* was a delight to all. The text, of course, was by mamma and the pictures by papa, Henry Richards. "A brilliant book for a young child," said the *Critic*.[134] There was an amateurish flavor of the best sort in her jingles and in the bright-colored prints by her husband: the result was something entirely new and fresh. There was also praise for the decorative details, such as borders, head and tail pieces. Evidently they were supremely satisfying to children, and Mrs. Richards voiced her regret at having allowed the plates to be destroyed.[135] Most reviewers had their favorite verses: the *Literary World* quoted "Phil's Secret" in its entirety, and liked "Seven Little Tigers and the Aged Cook," "The Little Cossack," and "The Frog of Lake Okifinokee" just about as well.[136]

Anne Eaton writes in the *Critical History of Children's Literature:* "*The Seven Little Tigers and the Aged Cook, Skinny Mrs. Simpkin and Fat Mrs. Wobblechin* and *The Frog of Lake Okifinokee* are ineradicable memories to those who were children in the eighties."[137] Edmund L. Pearson is even more rhapsodic. He recalled Mrs. Richards for her humorous poetry, "which like all really good work in this field, may be enjoyed by the children's parents without loss of self-respect."[138] He didn't think that Mrs. Richards had a successor in the twentieth century, and noted, as many did, her points of likeness with Edward Lear. He could still remember the details of Henry Richards' drawings, from the heavily dyed beard on the servitor of Bobbily Boo to the monocle of the Fourth Turk. He, too, was enraptured by the "Seven Little Tigers," the frog who lived in a bog and the "Little Cossack," which he considered the chef-d'oeuvre. It was really a huge success, and it is indeed curious that L. C. Page, which kept so many of Mrs. Richards' books in print, should have dropped this one.

Next came *Four Feet, Two Feet and No Feet* (1885), "a venture into the realm of natural history, where I did not really belong."[139] In 1885, perhaps, she did not feel this way, and the reviewers outdid themselves in lauding it. "Most delightful," "one of the most attractive books for children ever to come to our notice," "happy the child who receives this book," "quite unsurpassed" were a few of the phrases showered upon it.[140] It was a fine piece of bookmaking: paper, print, and illustrations were superior to those in the ordinary children's book. The illustrations, according to the *Nation,* were remarkable for truthfulness and beauty, and the stories were not only charmingly told but completely original. All praised the liveliness, the human interest on each page, the appeal to adults as well as to children. Another unquestioned success! In this same year she wrote the *Joyous Story of Toto* and, in 1886, *Toto's Merry Winter*, both published by Roberts Brothers, and both highly successful. These books were written during the period of grief following the death of her little girl, Maud, when she had to write happy tales to keep up her courage.

E & L had no more books from Laura Richards for several years, but kept advertising *Five Mice* each season, as well as the others. Then, early in 1889, began one of her most successful series, the "Hildegarde-Margaret Series," perhaps her outstanding achievement. They were published from 1889 to 1904, and are still listed in the catalogue of L. C. Page: *Queen Hildegarde* (1889), *Hildegarde's Holiday* (1891), *Hildegarde's Home* (1892), *Hildegarde's Neighbors* (1895), *Hildegarde's Harvest* (1896), *Three Margarets* (1897), *Margaret Montfort* (1898), *Peggy* (1899), *Rita* (1900), *Fernley House* (1901), and *The Merryweathers* (1904). Just how much they are read today is difficult to say, although they are still borrowed from public libraries which stock them. Dorothy Dix wrote of them: "Since the days of 'Little Women,' nobody has written so delightfully and so sanely and humanly of girl life as she does. Her girls are real girls, full of fun and frolic, and growing up into beautiful womanhood."[141] My daughter began to read them at age thirteen and enjoyed them, but her judgment was most positive that the "Margaret books" were the best, that the Hildegarde stories were almost too "goody-goody."

Almost all the stories were well received. *Queen Hildegarde* (1889) was praised as a sweet and wholesome tale, purposeful but without distinct preaching. It was never forced, the character development was, for the most part, probable, though the transformation from the spoiled rich girl to the self-sacrificing saint is a bit sudden. There was humor, graceful narration, adventures, and surprises, enough to entice readers for years to come.[142] There was certainly a large share of personal reminiscences in all these stories, details drawn from the happy summer days spent at the Howes' summer home at Newport, in Lawson's Valley. The characters in the stories were largely drawn from life, as were the incidents and anecdotes.

It is unnecessary to give more than a few excerpts from reviews to show how the books were welcomed. Only the *Nation* disagreed with the general chorus of praise: *Hildegarde's Home* provoked the comment that one needed a robust constitution to follow

the heroine through a third volume, for the story showed her as
"tiresomely vivacious" as ever; "she runs, jumps, exclaims, and
claps her hands almost without relief, except when she is 'crying
quietly.' "[143] The usual reaction was quite different: the *Critic*
spoke in 1895 of the "excellent Hildegarde Series" and of Hildegarde's innumerable girl friends in real life.[144] The *Literary World*
was delighted with each new volume, commented on Mrs. Richards'
lively style, her sympathy with children, her entertaining plots,
and her living characters.[145] The *Dial* was equally enthusiastic, especially about *Three Margarets* and *Margaret Montfort,* and the
author's skill in character drawing, in spite of melodramatic
touches.[146]

Mrs. Richards commented that she had "nothing special" to
say about this series. "The later ones are better written than the
earlier ones; if I were twenty years younger I would write *Queen
Hildegarde* over again."[147] There is a heart-warming critique of
these stories in the *Critical History of Children's Literature.*[148]
Elizabeth Nesbitt writes nostalgically that rereading these books
as an adult recaptures much of the impression made on the child,
not so much in the details of the stories but the remembrance of
"halcyon days in the country, the delights of wood and stream and
planted fields, of a barn with 'dusty, golden cobwebby sunbeams
slanting down through the little windows.' " The characters were
simple, virtuous men and women; there was the "fun and frolic of
a large family, each an individual"; there was also the joy of good
talk, discussion of good books, all spiced with enthusiasm and sincerity. Perhaps it was life surrounded by a golden haze, yet it en-
compassed the sorrows as well as the joys of life. Many in our time
characterize Hildegarde's day as sentimental and excessively romantic, even in its realism, she continues; this is superficiality
(based almost invariably upon ignorance, may I add) and the present fashion of cynicism leads people to label as sentimental anything less than cynical.

Mrs. Richards was still composing rhymes and jingles, sometimes inspired by the misery of influenza, which prompted her
verses on the Hottentot, but more often inspired by the joy of living.[149] In 1890 these rhymes of the eighties, along with the early
ones from *St. Nicholas* and *Sketches and Scraps,* were collected
under the title *In My Nursery.* Roberts Brothers published this
work, not E & L, perhaps an indication of Estes' indifference to
poetry. Theodore Roosevelt liked it very much, as he tells us in his
Autobiography.[150] Speaking of the "nursery rhymes," he notes:
"My own children loved them dearly, and their mother and I loved

them almost equally; the delightfully light-hearted 'Man from New Mexico Who Lost His Grandmother out in the Snow,' the adventures of 'The Owl, the Eel, and the Warming-Pan,' and the extraordinary genealogy of the kangaroo whose 'father was a whale with a feather in his tail who lived in the Greenland sea,' while 'his mother was a shark who kept very dark in the Gulf of Caribee.'" Such tributes help to establish Mrs. Richards as an unexcelled nonsense-rhymester for her contemporaries, at least.[151]

In 1890 also appeared what is probably Mrs. Richards' most famous work, *Captain January*. She tells in her autobiography how, during a visit to Bar Harbor, she looked out over the sea to a distant lighthouse and began dreaming and wondering what life might be in such a place. The theme of the story came to her and she wrote it quickly, this tale of the rough old lighthouse captain who brings up a little girl on the bleak islet, reading Shakespeare and the Bible to her and telling his vivid stories of sea life and shipwrecks. When she took the story to E & L, they refused it: it was too short for a long story, too long for a short story. She sent the story to "every reputable publisher, or to all I knew about, in this country, and to several in England."[152] None wanted it, so she put the manuscript away in a drawer. A year or so later she chanced to meet Dana Estes, who was a personal friend, and he asked her what she had been writing: "Nothing except the little story that you refused." And then, "perhaps seeing some interest or sympathy in his kind face, I said: 'Mr. Estes, would you be willing to read that little story yourself, and give me your personal opinion of it?' It was much to ask of a publisher, but he kindly consented. That was forty years ago, and *Captain January* still heads my list of sales."

It was advertised, in the fall of 1890, as "a very striking story, written in an original manner, full of spirit and thoroughly interesting." The reviewers agreed: all praised the graceful and sympathetic handling of a theme that could have been trite. The *Nation* was particularly impressed by the fine depiction of the old man, the pathos of his unselfish devotion, his shrewd common sense, his homely maxims.[153] The *Literary World* celebrated its freshness, its originality, its picturesqueness.[154] All critics praised the atmosphere of the tale; as one of them said, "one feels the breath of the sea and the roar of the breakers in this story."[155] Fifteen editions were issued in the next two years, and a new edition, with illustrations by Frank T. Merrill, came out in 1892. It soon became the key title in a series of short tales of New England life, but always remained the prime favorite. By 1950 it had sold 288,000 copies and is still selling. Alexander Woollcott had bestowed his blessing on it by saying: "Captain January is truly a masterpiece and deserves, as it will, to live forever."[156] Such fulsome praise might ruin it for some people, but sentimental or not, it is a thoroughly good story and deserves its success with readers young and old.

During these years Mrs. Richards had also written short stories for *St. Nicholas* and her "good friend of many years," the *Youth's Companion.* These were brought together, in 1895, under the title *Five Minute Stories.* They were followed by *More Five Minute Stories,* in 1903, and finally by *Three Minute Stories* (1914). These collections intended for very young children were popular, the *Five Minute Stories* reaching a sale of thirty-seven thousand copies, and all of them are found in the L. C. Page catalogue.

Stimulated by the success of *Captain January,* Mrs. Richards embarked on a series of stories of approximately the same length, long short stories, that is, dealing with New England life. The first of these was *Melody* (1893), "a highly sentimental little tale" as Mrs. Richards herself terms it, relating the adventures of a blind orphan girl and an old fiddler. "Sweet and simple" was the verdict of most of the reviewers; "the author has created a starry soul," commented the *Dial.*[157] This tale, like *Captain January,* was intended more for adults than for children, and was almost as successful. By 1950 it had sold 102,000 copies; as one reviewer put it, "if there had been no *Captain January, Melody* would take first place." It appeared in illustrated holiday editions, with designs by F. T. Merrill, and became one of the "Captain January Series." *Marie* came next, in 1894, the story of a little French girl and her precious violin, in the strange environment of a typical New England town. It was given a warm welcome, but never achieved the same popularity as *Melody. Narcissa* was published the same year, with its companion work, *In Verona;* these were both stories of New England life, unrelated to the previous tales. Mrs. Richards' books were becoming a mainstay of E & L during these years; listing those already published, E & L proclaimed: "Every live bookseller in the country will keep *all* of the above mentioned books constantly in stock. Their sale, already enormous, is steadily on the increase."[158]

Nautilus and *Isla Heron,* more New England tales, were published in 1895. *Nautilus* was adjudged charming, but lacking the fine simplicity of *Captain January.* The *Nation* thought that the "excessive exuberance that marked Mrs. Richards' former stories" had broken out on the cover of this volume: a black and white schooner was driven across a white and yellow sea by a wind as violent as the brilliant chrome sky. Fortunately, concluded the critic, the superfluous color stayed on the cover.[159] *Isla Heron* told of child life on a lonely island off the Maine coast.[160] *Some Say,* a humorous story featuring two village gossips, followed *Jim of Hellas* and other minor bits.[161] The "Hildegarde" and "Margaret Series" were both appearing during these years of the nineties and many felt that they ranked next to Louisa May Alcott's famous "Little Women Series"; "no books in recent times can be more safely put into the hands of a bright, intelligent girl than these," said E & L. *Rosin the Beau* and *Love and Rocks* were issued in 1898, the first a sequel to *Melody* and *Marie,* the second a love story on one of the Maine islands. Most of these have now dropped out of sight, for all were of little consequence. The series sold well, however, for, by 1898, 250,000 of the group, including *Captain January,* of course, had been marketed.

Some other books by Mrs. Richards, not in series, are worth noting, especially the delightful papers about her childhood, *When I Was Your Age* (1893). These articles had first appeared in *St. Nicholas* and were only slightly changed in book form. The *Literary World* deemed it a fault that there were no more chapters, for nothing was more captivating than these accounts of life in the Howe family circle, which included the famous Dr. Samuel Gridley Howe and his even more famous wife, Julia Ward Howe.[162] The papers gave the records of the doings and sayings, the pranks and the mischief of this very unusual group of children. The pages rippled with fun, and there were excellent pictures of "Green Peace," the family home in South Boston, the parents, and the three daughters, Julia Romana, Laura, and Maud. Many children reading the book wished that they could have had playmates like the Howe girls! There was also an historical book, *Glimpses of the French Court,* intended to appeal to the "lovers of the picturesque in history," in this instance, France in the seventeenth century.[163]

Since Mrs. Richards' later books were published by Dana Estes and Company, they will be discussed in subsequent pages, under that firm. It remains only to mention a few of the other juveniles issued by E & L in the nineties. The other author of juveniles to share honors with Mrs. Richards was James Otis Kaler, who used the pen name James Otis. Kaler had made a name for himself when he wrote *Toby Tyler, or Ten Weeks at a Circus* (1881), a story still read and enjoyed. He had published numerous stories in the eighties and, in the next decade, came to E & L, for Estes seemed to have a natural affinity for writers born in Maine, having already won Stephens and now Otis, and Mrs. Richards who, living in Gardiner, was as good as a native. Otis' stories in the eighties had been mostly of New York life and he made his start with E & L in the same vein. *Jenny Wren's Boarding-House* (1893) told of a house for newsboys run by Jenny, aged fifteen. It was a trite, absurdly sentimental story of a baby, found and adopted by the houseful of adolescents. Yet Otis knew how to avoid bathos and keep his story moving, so that the book prompted a whole series aptly termed the "Jenny Wren Series." Some reviewers felt that these stories, which were realistic enough, were possibly disturbing for children to read, but the *Literary World* concluded that well-to-do children would see from the life of bootblacks and newsboys that street children were not so unlike them in thought and nature as they might fancy.[164]

More palatable to most reviewers, though not necessarily to the children, were Otis' "Stories of American History." These began in 1895 with a group of four and continued through the nineties. The list included: *The Boys of 1745 at the Capture of Louisbourg, An Island Refuge: Casco Bay in 1676, Neal the Miller: a Son of Liberty, Ezra Jordan's Escape from the Massacre at Fort Loyall, Under the Liberty Tree; a Story of the Boston Massacre, The Boys of Fort Schuyler, The Signal Boys of '75; a Tale of the Siege of Boston,* and *When Israel Putnam Served the King.* The series was continued by Dana Estes and Co. with the following titles: *Defending the Island; a Story of Bar Harbor in 1758, When We Destroyed the Gaspee, Boston Boys of 1775, When Dewey Came to Manila,* and *Off Santiago with Sampson.* Most of the stories were very readable, if undistinguished in style; "they have the right patriotic ring," said the *Critic.*[165] Some gave them credit for a sort of "Colonial dignity" that accorded well with the stirring events recalled. They were books by a good workman, and thoroughly delightful to boys, as I remember from my own reading of several of them.

There was a great vogue for books on American history, especially toward 1898, and Otis wrote some other stories, *The Boy Captain* (1896), and the like, which found favor. Particularly enjoyable was *The Cruise of the Comet,* which was to start a new series, the "Privateers of 1812 Series"; this was an exciting tale of a privateer in the War of 1812, filled with hairbreadth escapes relished by boys everywhere.[166]

For the patriotic fervor of 1898 E & L revived again the books by Charles Carleton Coffin, which had renewed success and are still to be found on the L. C. Page list, with sales running to eighty-three thousand for the *Boys of '61* by 1950, and in the thirty thousand range for the other two dealing with the Civil War. Most of the other series were minor: "Christmas in Many Lands" was made up of dainty little books, each containing a story of Christmas in a foreign country, with colored illustrations; "College Life in All

Countries" was somewhat more ambitious, being a series translated from the French of André Laurie, and was fairly successful,
though some reviewers doubted if the author had ever set foot in
some of the countries he described, such as Russia.[167] The "Ruby
and Ruthy Series" ran to only four titles, fortunately, and the adventures of *Cricket,* by Elizabeth W. Timlow, with its sequal *Cricket
at the Seashore,* gave all that was needful about a little girl whom
the reviewers found "sweet."

E & L, always on the alert for business, shrewdly lumped
many older titles into two long, disconnected series, changed the
bindings to make them uniform, and started selling them again.
Under the heading "Boys of the Sierras Series" were grouped such
works as *Page, Squire and Knight, Hunting in the Jungle, Land
of the Incas, Young Moose Hunters,* and the *Schoolboys of Rookes-
bury.* Some of these isolated works have not been mentioned before, because they were minor, but they did well in the series. Another series, "Stories of Adventure," brought in Coffin's *Our New
Way Round the World,* Ober's *Travels in Mexico, Sailor Boys of
'61,* Dickens' *Child's History of England,* and *Pioneer Life!* A third
series, the "Young of Heart Series," had twelve titles, most of them
trivial short stories by such authors as Will Allen Drumgoole and
Mary Sheldon, but there were also some by Juliana H. Ewing, Edward Everett Hale, and Rudyard Kipling. Most of these, however,
appeared under the imprint of Dana Estes and Co.

Although Dana Estes and Co. published many children's books,
they were almost invariably continuations of lines already established by E & L. A large portion—and the best—of the Dana Estes
list was made up of older books which had won success under E & L's
imprint. Estes showed little originality in this field, perhaps because his own interests were centered more on history, travel, and
sets of standard authors. There were many series, and some of them
will be listed as examples of the diversity of Dana Estes' catalogue,
but none of the new ones were comparable to the "Zigzag Series" or
the "Three Vassar Girls." The mainstay for children's books was,
as in the nineties, Laura E. Richards, yet even she wrote more
for adults than for children in this period. It was only natural for
Estes to exploit his back list as much as possible, and the new material, that was so similar to the old, did well too, though never with
the startling sales achieved under E & L. Children's books under
Dana Estes and Co. represent, then, a distinct tapering off in quality, and it is not necessary to give them lengthy treatment.

Mrs. Richards had really done most of her best books for
children under E & L, although the "Three Margarets Series" was
not concluded until 1904 with *The Merryweathers.* The "Captain

January Series," mentioned before, was having wonderful sales all through this period; *Captain January* was even published in a French edition, a somewhat unexpected sign of cosmopolitanism. There were more volumes of nonsense rhymes and jingles, *The Hurdy-Gurdy* (1902) and its companion volume, *The Piccolo;* there were "little stories" for "little folks," *Jolly Jingles* and *A Happy Little Time,* and a few of the sort suitable for children and adults, such as *The Little Master, Snow-White,* and *For Tommy.* Most of these were unimportant, though the nonsense verses were still clever.

Mrs. Richards' major works under Dana Estes and Co. were adult novels, although most of them were like *Captain January* in that they would appeal to adolescents. She evidently felt that to keep her material always on the children's level was too narrowing, especially since she delighted in the many curious bits of life she observed every day in a Maine community. "I overflowed my banks!" she remarks, and attributed it to her love of that racy dialect and dry humor so characteristic of the Maine Yankee. *Geoffrey Strong* (1901) started a series of New England tales and romances, most of them pretty good, but hardly in the same class with Sarah Orne Jewett's masterpieces. Geoffrey Strong was a young physician in a Maine village, and from this tale came the two stories about Mrs. Marcia Tree, the most successful of the whole group. *Mrs. Tree* came out in 1902 and a sequel, *Mrs. Tree's Will,* in 1905. Both were highly praised, the latter called a "gem in its own way." They were humorous and lively, for Mrs. Richards always knew how to keep a story moving. Dana Estes touted Mrs. Richards as a major American novelist, since he was inclined to judge literary eminence by sales, a not unknown criterion among publishers; by 1905, Mrs. Richards' books had sold 600,000 copies (for thirty-five titles) and Estes declared that *Mrs. Tree's Will* could "hardly fail to establish the author's place in the upper rank of American novelists."

Other New England tales followed and were generally well received. *The Wooing of Calvin Parks, Up to Calvin's,* and *On Board the Mary Sands* all dealt with a master mariner full of homely humor; none of them had much plot, they were studies of quaint characters, like those Joseph Lincoln was to do for Cape Cod some years later. They were for specialists in New England character, with distinctly local interest. There were some collections of short stories too, such as *Miss Jimmy,* which carried on the same sentimental themes and gave further pleasure to her considerable band of admirers.

More solid were the works about her distinguished parents. As early as 1876 she had planned to edit and publish her father's letters and journals, but the great quantity of stories and verses that followed that date, plus her difficulties in deciphering her father's crabbed handwriting, delayed the publication until 1906–1909.[168] They finally appeared in two volumes, edited by Laura E. Richards and annotated by F. B. Sanborn, who had known Mr. Howe in the abolition days. The second volume she was able to present to her mother just before her death, in 1910. In 1911 she brought out *Two Noble Lives,* brief biographies of her father and mother, written for both children and adults; the *Outlook* thought that no better book could be given school children to read than this simple story of the victories of these true heroes of peace.[169] Her biography of her mother was started after 1910, and would undoubtedly have been published by Dana Estes and Co. if the firm had continued until 1915. *Two Noble Lives,* adapted for school use, is still found in the L. C. Page list.

Mrs. Richards' books were undoubtedly one of the major financial supports for the firm in the new century, but there were many new series to help out. James Otis continued to turn out books until his death in 1912. We have already observed the extent of his "Stories of American History Series," some of which were written after 1898. Another series, entitled "Our Boys Library," incorporated more books by Otis, notably *The Boys of '98* in obvious imitation of Coffin's *Boys of '76* and *Boys of '61;* the Boer War suggested another book, *Fighting for the Empire.* Then there was the "Minute Boys Series," eleven in all, of which nine were written by Otis and two by Edward Stratemeyer. The Minute Boys served at the Battle of Lexington, at Long Island, Wyoming Valley, Philadelphia, Yorktown, and in the Green Mountains. They were good boys' stories, no more, but certainly equal to much of the same sort turned out in later decades. Still another group, "Business Venture Series," brought in the sea, with such titles as *The Cruise of the Phoebe,* and *An Island Secret,* with Otis responsible for half the series.

The "Zigzag Journeys" were still popular, and Hezekiah Butterworth even added three similar works, *Travel Tales of South Africa,* also of China and of Central America, and other authors followed the pattern for the Hawaiian Islands and the Philippines, F. A. Ober writing the one for the West Indies. An omnium-gatherum of old and new was the "Boys' Own Authors Series," attractively and colorfully bound, including many titles from E & L's list, some of which had appeared in smaller series previously, such as André Laurie's "College Life in All Countries" or "Privateers of 1812

Series," by James Otis. There were forty-two books in the set, most of them old, but it included a few by Harry Castlemon, C. C. Coffin, F. H. Costello, Stephens, and Ober to give the list vitality.

For girls, there were all the old successes by Laura Richards, the "Cricket Series" and the like, and a few new ones. "Amy Blanchard's Books for Girls" were stories of life on Maryland's Eastern Shore, typically Southern to offset slightly the preponderance of New England material. There was also the "Girls' Own Authors Series," with but eighteen titles, some of them by Laura Richards. A set of cookbooks was deemed attractive for girls, though, in all probability, it was bought by the parents and not at the girls' request. "Famous Children of Literature" was suitable for boys and girls, and included such adaptations as *Little Paul,* by Charles Dickens, *Little Eva,* by Harriet Beecher Stowe, and *Little Peter,* by Captain Marryat.

The remaining books were mostly for young children, such series as "Natural History Stories," "Animal Stories for Little Folks," "Rebus Books for Little Folks," "The New Little People's Series" (for children from seven to ten) and the many "Chatterbox Picture Books," which now comprised the *Chatterbox Book of Soldiers and Sailors* as well as books of *Horses, Cats and Dogs, Birds,* and *Wild Animals.* There were, of course, individual stories which did not fit any series, but not many, for the series urge seemed inescapable. After Dana Estes' death, in 1909, the number of new children's books dropped sharply, and in the last year of the firm there were almost none.

In twenty-five years, Dana Estes had published a thoroughly respectable list of children's books, beginning with Hezekiah Butterworth's "Zigzag Journeys" and ending with Mrs. Richards' "Three Margarets Series," and extending even a bit later, if one includes the many books by James Otis Kaler. These were almost without exception by American authors, and, whether they dealt with American scenes or not, they were clearly American in flavor. The few European works were minor, with the exception of *Chatterbox,* which Estes made a sensational American success by his advertising plus its own merits. He was never lucky enough to attract a really great writer for children to his list, although he probably thought that Mrs. Richards was one; he deserves much credit for making the most of the lesser writers he did get, especially in furthering the wholly admirable taste for popular, well-written history and travel for young people, a field in which he exerted real influence on American children's literature.

Chapter Six

ILLUSTRATED GIFT BOOKS
AND STANDARD AUTHORS
BY THE FOOT

ALMOST all the books published by Estes and Lauriat were profusely illustrated. As a matter of fact, it is difficult to recall any
books of theirs without illustrations, except the novels, and even
some of them had pictures. If one could scan the total output of
E & L and Dana Estes and Company, he would soon conclude that
the unillustrated works were the exception that proved the rule,
since most of these firms' books were not only illustrated but profusely illustrated, possibly overillustrated. The taste or, better, the
fashion of this generation is averse to illustrations in most adult
books, unless in books of art or travel. Without attempting to explain, defend, or decry the current practice, let me say only that it
is rather agreeable to turn the pages of most of E & L's books because of their illustrations; the books are usually more cheerful and
enticing with pictures, even if the text is not always on the same
level. No one should interpret this remark as a blanket recommendation of all illustrated works published by the two firms; it merely
stresses the generally brighter appearance of their books as contrasted with the chaste and often beautifully printed books of today, which are obliged, ordinarily because of cost, to do without
pictures. It is a relief to admit that children's books are still
favored, as sumptuously as of old, with gay illustrations; the adult
must ordinarily patronize limited editions, or the like, with their

somewhat precious designs, to get his illustrated novels, poems, or plays.

E & L were but following the custom of their day in turning out illustrated books, yet their reluctance to turn out any other kind reveals their constant search for popular approval. Many books published by other firms during this same period were not illustrated: they were the serious works, not only scholarly treatises but lengthy histories, collections of essays, poems, and short stories, and many novels. After Estes decided to give up the struggle for new novels, he concentrated on those types of books which lent themselves best to illustration and published nothing else. Such a decision involved no sacrifice, since he realized that his ventures in fiction were not bolstered by any sure taste and had not been uniformly successful, whereas his pictorial works had brought him both prestige and dollars. Thus he could devote his energies—and they were considerable—to books for children, to pictorial gift books of all sorts, and to sumptuously illustrated sets of famous authors. Here a refined taste, though desirable, was not so essential as a shrewd insight into popular desires, and Estes, with his co-workers, seemed able to gauge popular taste with marvelous skill. In one sense he was too successful: almost all the books are of their time only, except for the already famous authors whose works he published in lush volumes. Possibly he thought that some of his publications were deathless—I suppose all publishers do— but it is more likely that he had few illusions in this regard, being grateful for his good luck in his own day.

One of the staples of the successful publisher was the holiday gift book, usually a familiar classic with abundant pictures, sometimes a luxurious book of travels or reproductions of paintings. We still have them today, many of them handsome volumes indeed, though we are happily spared some of the typical gift books of the nineteenth century, those poems illustrated line by line, in some instances with designs by several artists, which resulted in a complete lack of unity and, often enough, a woeful matching of picture and text. Yet the appetite for those hybrid works was immense: scores of them appeared every fall, frequently the same poems had competing editions in one season, or in following years. Some, of course, were carefully and tastefully done, and display their quiet charm even to the critical eyes of a twentieth-century reader; but most were of dubious value and were commonly sneered at by the more discerning book buyers of the day. As one would expect, E & L turned out holiday gift books in ever-increasing quantities, some of them good, some of them bad, almost all of them successful.

Merely to examine their variety gives one a good notion of the popular taste of these decades, and a few of them deserve some attention in their own right. The illustrated sets of standard authors were, naturally, more important, and constituted one of E & L's major contributions to publishing. These works, along with books for children, were the main emphasis of E & L and Dana Estes and Co. after 1880 and consequently represent most of the publications which brought the two firms their distinguished reputations.

E & L set up business too late in 1872 to have a holiday book, but 1873 saw their first venture, a thoroughly mediocre volume entitled *The Garland of the Year, or the Months, Their Poetry and Flowers*. This was all too characteristic of the lesser species of gift book, with its selections from standard British poets and its colored lithographs. Actually, finer holiday books were the early parts of Guizot's *Popular History of France*, with stirring pictures, although these were sold only by subscription. In the following year E & L published a minor novelty, Frederick B. Allen's *Leaves from a Summer Sketchbook*, a portfolio of photographs made of drawings done originally in West Campton, New Hampshire, and on Mount Desert, in Maine. Moritz Retzsch, who had already done several books for Roberts Brothers and other American firms, provided the two specifically holiday books for 1876, *Retzsch's Illustrations of Goethe's Faust*, with extracts from Bayard Taylor's translation, and *Retzsch's Illustrations to Schiller's Fridolin and the Fight with the Dragon*. In this instance the pictures were steel engravings made from plates imported from Germany, each volume having twenty-six illustrations.[1] Except for the pictures by Allen, all were standard works of their class, displaying no originality or even luxury.

Also in 1876 appeared the first of the sets of famous authors. This work, Charles Knight's *Popular Shakspere, Pictorial Edition*, was sold only in parts, by subscription. The "conditions of publication" declared that the work would be published in *exactly* thirty-six semimonthly parts, at fifty cents per part—"no matter how much material it may be necessary to put into the last part to complete the work within the stated number."[2] It contained 340 woodcuts and thirty-six full-page plates by Sir John Gilbert, together with steel engravings from pictures by C. W. Cope, W. P. Frith, Leslie Maclise, E. M. Ward, C. Clint, H. S. Marks, W. Q. Orchardson, and others. Gilbert's pictures, engraved by the Dalziels, had been greatly admired ever since they appeared in the English edition of Staunton's *Shakespeare* in 1858–1860. Joseph Pennell thought his series of Shakespeare illustrations still unsurpassed and Weitenkampf remarks on their robustness, their "roast beef of Old England" sturdiness.[3] The text was that edited by Charles Knight in 1839–1841, with some later revisions, as well as his notes for each play. The size of the page, royal octavo, gave space for the pictures but made the two-volume set not a work for reading but "a handsome addition to books for the drawing-room table."

Though the printing was done at the "renowned University Press of Cambridge" on "superfine, tinted and extra calendered paper, made expressly for the work," the letterpress seems drab, yet the illustrations retain much of their effect. To pay sixteen dollars in 1876, in the midst of a depression, for the thirty-six parts, in paper, seems rather steep even today, although the two bound volumes cost twenty dollars a few years later. They were sold by determined agents, who undoubtedly hammered home the theme that "no home, where the English language is spoken, can be said to be furnished in its truest sense without a copy of Shakspere on its shelves."[4] It can at least be said that purchasers were not wholly defrauded.

Another subscription set of 1876, Owen Jones's celebrated *Grammar of Ornament* (1856), which had been hailed as "beautiful enough to be the hornbook of angels," was sold in twenty-eight monthly parts at one dollar and fifty cents each. This work testifies to the interest always shown by E & L in art books. English and French imports were naturally found in a bookstore such as E & L's, and, from the beginning of the firm, many of these works appeared in their trade lists. At the Trade Sales these volumes fared well or ill, according to the temper and finances of the crowd, but usually did better than the ordinary stock. At their first Trade Sale a handsome edition of Hogarth sold rather well, while other books lacked buyers. Many of E & L's advertisements in the 1870's listed distinguished imports, such as Pugin's *Glossary of Ecclesiastical Ornament and Costume,* at sixty dollars, and similar works on architecture, painting, and sculpture.[5] Later on the imports were listed in the bookstore's catalogues rather than in the trade lists, but the interest in art books was undiminished. In the next year, for example, E & L turned out an American replica of Benjamin Haydon's *Correspondence and Table Talk,* a handsome work in two volumes, adorned with facsimiles of his drawings and pages from his journal, selling at six dollars a volume.

The year 1878 was a banner one. The firm was publishing novels, scientific books, subscription works, children's books, and holiday books, practically every publishing line they ever attempted. Their leading gift book, *French Pictures with Pencil and Pen,* was their first original picture book of high quality. A large quarto of portfolio dimensions, it was "showy in a good sense."[6] Treating first Paris, its streets, palaces, parks, and suburbs, it went on to the provinces, centering on picturesque châteaux, quaint city streets, and mountain landscapes. The text was by Dr. Leo de Colange, whose work in E & L's subscription sets I have already mentioned; the illustrations comprised ten full-page steel engravings and one hundred wood engravings, most of them large size, by such artists as Doré, Alphonse de Neuville, Giacomelli, Daubigny, Delaroche, Anastasi, and Schoff. That some of these had already done service in illustrating Guizot's *Popular History of France* was not to their discredit. If the text was average—and most reviewers praised Colange—the pictures were superior, and the total effect of fine pictures, paper, printing, and particularly rich binding was "stunning."[7]

The same year brought also the *Beaconsfield Cartoons from Punch,* timed to celebrate his return to the post of Prime Minister; it was a collection of 104 full-page drawings by Leech, Doyle, and Tenniel.[8] Also Edwin Forbes's *Life Studies of the Great Army,* a portfolio of sixty-five etchings; Dana Estes' *Home Book of Poetry,* with twenty steel engravings, and his *Chimes for Childhood,* amply illustrated; *Edwin Booth in Twelve Dramatic Characters,* another portfolio of portraits engraved by the famous W. J. Linton; Sylvester Crosby's *The Early Coins of America;* and F. O. C. Darley's *Sketches Abroad,* originally published in 1868, whose plates were purchased at the Osgood sale in March, 1876. And this was in addition to the fine scientific books on ferns by Emerton and Robinson, both beautifully illustrated, which were certainly holiday books.

H. N. Hudson's edition of Shakespeare was the first trade set made available by E & L, since all the previous works of this type were sold only by subscription. It was a modest beginning for the immense business in sets that was to engross the firm's later years. Characteristically, E & L bought the plates from another Boston house, Lockwood, Brooks and Co., then turned out a variety of editions, either in six or twelve volumes, with bindings in cloth, calf, or morocco. The "University Edition," in six volumes, was priced ten dollars, "the best cheap edition in the world."[9] Hudson's edition was, of course, an old favorite and remained on E & L's list until the end; its notes and editing won praise from Edward Dowden, H. H. Furness, and F. J. Furnival, three great Shakespeareans. In later years, many illustrations were added to make up de luxe editions, but the basic text retained its popularity through all costume changes, and was published by several other houses in the United

States. E & L had imported many sets from England, the standard Waverley novels, Dickens, Thackeray, or Ainsworth, and had bought a mass of set remainders at the Osgood sale, but Hudson's *Shakespeare* was the first trade set under their own label.

E & L published two major works in 1879, both distinctly art books of the highest quality. In the first, the *American Art Review,* Dana Estes paid his highest tribute to art. Although the magazine lasted only two years, from 1879 to 1881, it won the plaudits of all the critics and failed only of enough public response to keep it alive. The first number was issued in November, 1879, with considerable fanfare. Its subtitle designated it as "A Journal Devoted to the Practice, Theory, History and Archaeology of Art." Its managing editor was S. R. Koehler, a German-born writer on art topics, who became editor of Cassell's *Magazine of Art* and did editing and translating for E & L for many years. Associate editors were William C. Prime, a New York journalist and later professor of art history at Princeton, and Charles C. Perkins, one of Boston's most distinguished art critics and connoisseurs. The prospectus informed the public that this monthly magazine would embrace contemporary as well as older art, with particular emphasis on the history and archeology of American art. A special feature was to be a series of original etchings by American artists, but there were to be many contributions by European celebrities. The aim of the publisher was to make it equal in quality to the best European publications of a similar nature and to have it serve as a truly representative American art magazine. Each monthly number would contain three full-page plates and about forty-eight pages of text; in size it was a generous quarto ($9\frac{1}{4}$ x $12\frac{1}{4}$) and the subscription was twelve dollars a year.

Appended to the prospectus was a list of thirty-six contributors, comprising both serious and popular writers on art. Such names as Charles Eliot Norton, W. J. Linton, John La Farge, W. I. Stillman, T. G. Appleton and S. G. W. Benjamin reveal its strength, while some of the popularizers, such as Mrs. Clara Erskine Clement and Mrs. Margaret Junkin Preston, were very well known in their domain.[10]

The magazine set out to cover archeology, painting, sculpture, architecture, industrial arts, public and private collections in the United States, exhibitions, and new publications. In each issue was a long section entitled "American Art Chronicle," which listed art news of clubs and societies, lectures, exhibitions and sales, acquisitions of museums, and necrology. Much the same was done for foreign art, though in less detail. The bibliography section was unusually full, and there were some lengthy reviews.

The *Literary World* hailed this new periodical as a sign of the revival of arts and letters in the United States. It pointed out that, except for the *Aldine,* there was no purely American art periodical, although there were journals on technical art; three British journals held the field, Cassell's *Magazine of Art,* itself started only the year before, the famous *Art Journal,* and P. G. Hamerton's fine magazine, the *Portfolio.* Obviously it was a bold venture to compete with these, and although the price, twelve dollars, seemed high, it could scarcely be lower for a publication with such lofty standards.[11]

The first number brought a succession of laudatory notices and good wishes for the future. The *Literary World* found the contents "strong and good," noted the tasteful design, the many vignettes and ornamental capitals as well as the luxurious plates and wood engravings. The cover, too, was of "rich and appropriate design." All in all, it was most handsome and obviously represented "no small outlay and difficulty."[12] The *Nation,* inclined at first to be cautious, soon declared that the magazine was equal to the *Portfolio,* the best of the British journals, and praised both the text and illustrations, reserving highest commendation for the etchings. The critic liked the "solid information" provided in the second number, with its basic articles on the researches and discoveries at Olympia and the reminiscences of William Morris Hunt.[13] The *Publishers' Weekly,* after the first seven numbers had appeared, declared the work a credit to both editors and publishers for the taste displayed in text and illustrations alike; all that practical knowledge and money could do had been expended in making the *American Art Review* the leading art periodical of the United States.[14]

The *Literary World* continued to review almost every issue of the magazine, celebrating especially its fine articles on American artists, such as William Morris Hunt, Elihu Vedder, John La Farge and William Rimmer, and its papers on American etchers, with generous examples of their work.[15] Koehler wrote the articles on American etchers, W. J. Linton contributed a history of wood engraving in America, S. G. W. Benjamin wrote on many exhibitions in New York and Philadelphia. The *Nation* continued its favorable mention, as did several other periodicals, but critical acclaim was not sufficient. The first number had sold very well—five thousand copies went almost immediately—but this was probably because of its novelty.[16] In its Holiday Number for 1880 the *Publishers' Weekly* urged a subscription to "that prince of art journals, the *American*

Art Review" as a suitable Christmas gift.[17] But at the end of the second year, in November, 1881, E & L announced the cessation of the magazine on which they had spent so much. The *Literary World*, which had been first to praise, led the mourners. E & L, said the editor, have done all that publishers could to make the magazine worthy of its place and name. "The price was high and the constituency small. Never mind. A brave good work is never wasted."[18] S. G. W. Benjamin noted in his memoirs: "I had numerous articles to write for that stately art magazine, the *American Art Review*, edited by Mr. S. R. Koehler, a periodical for which our public was still hardly ripe. . . . "[19] It was a sumptuous periodical, well edited and beautifully printed, and it certainly deserved a better fate.[20] Even though short-lived it did much to foster etchings as illustrations in American books, and in this movement E & L took a leading part. Unfortunately, it convinced Estes that art work of this caliber was wasted on the American public, with the result that he gave up any attempts to lead and sought only for popular favor in the field of conventional and sentimentalized art. One element, however, he did not abandon, and that was the constant striving for the resplendent and showy in art books.

The other major work of 1879 was Maxime Lalanne's *Treatise on Etching*, translated from the French by S. R. Koehler, himself an etcher. Hamerton had proclaimed Lalanne the best French etcher of the day, and his treatise was very influential in the revival of the art in France. Seymour Haden and Hamerton had fostered the revival in England and there was a small band of enthusiasts in America who were beginning to call attention to the merits of etching, quoting Haden's remark that the comparison of the etching-needle with the engraver's tool is "the comparison of the pen with the plough."[21] Lalanne was a master of landscape, brilliant in the essentials of the art, and almost irritatingly sure of himself.[22] His treatise reflected these traits, probably claimed too much for the art of etching, yet it was clearly stimulating and authoritative. All praised Koehler's translation and particularly a small additional chapter by him on the "Technical Elements of Etching," which some considered even clearer than Lalanne's own pages.[23] The book itself was finely printed, having ten etchings by Lalanne as examples of the art, and was published in two editions, the trade version selling at three dollars and a half, as well as a limited edition (one hundred copies) on India proof paper, at six dollars. It received almost universal praise and was acclaimed as evidence of superior taste in publishing.[24]

Though on a lower level, the other art works of 1879 were

quite respectable, featuring such items as M. M. Ripley's *The World's Worship in Stone, Temple, Cathedral and Mosque,* impressively illustrated with 150 full-page engravings; *Selected Pictures from Great Artists,* composed of fifty steel engravings from the London *Art Journal,* grouped in three portfolios; the start of Rambaud's *Popular History of Russia;* Leo de Colange's compilation, Zell's *Dictionary of Commerce,* filled with plates and woodcuts;[25] and finally, among the most attractive, the first volume of the "Zigzag Series," *Zigzag Journeys in Europe,* which was crammed with delightful woodcuts. The rich abundance of these two years was not easily repeated.

There were almost no gift books in 1880, since much of the firm's energies had gone into their editions of Charles Dickens' works, the first of their series of modern authors to appear in sets. E & L had been importing and selling British editions of Dickens and decided to make a play for American buyers with three types of sets, to suit all pocketbooks. The People's Edition, the cheapest of the three, was printed in "long primer, leaded and spaced, making it equal to small pica set solid." Including the authorized works, it laid claim to three thousand more pages than the "best editions heretofore offered in the same number of volumes." It was on the number of illustrations that it banked most heavily, since there were over two hundred, mostly woodcuts, by Cruikshank, Phiz, Darley, Barnard, and others. The fifteen-volume set, a large duodecimo in size, was printed at the University Press in Cambridge on "fine tinted and super calendered paper." In a black cloth binding, decorated in red and gold, the set sold for $22.50, or separately at $1.50 per volume. A few years later (1884) the set was reduced to $18.75, with higher prices for calf or morocco bindings, which were usually $40.00.

The University Edition, only slightly more expensive, printed on fine white paper, cost $25 for fifteen volumes bound in maroon cloth, $50 bound in half calf. It was the Cambridge Edition that was intended to attract the wealthy buyer. This was advertised as the "best and most profusely illustrated American edition yet offered."[26] It consisted of thirty volumes, in crown octavo (really the same size as duodecimo), adorned with 650 steel plates and woodcuts, including all the artists previously named and a group of French illustrators too, such as Alphonse de Neuville, Bayard, and others; many of the pictures had appeared in no previous British or American edition. Bound in cloth, the thirty volumes sold at $45, and $100 was demanded for calf or morocco bindings.

Thus was begun the long sequence of sets, soon to embrace

cheaper editions than the People's Edition and more luxurious versions than the Cambridge Edition. The three basic types, however, lasted for fifteen years or more, undergoing various transmigrations from lower to higher levels, dressing the original text in many curious garbs. Dickens, by 1884, was also published in a Handy Large Type Edition, still in fifteen volumes but reduced in size to sextodecimo; with its two hundred illustrations it sold, in a cloth binding, for only $11.25. By 1892, after other changes, the same set was priced at $7.50, such had been the competition. Yet, although E & L continued to sell their cheap editions until 1898, they were always more interested in the sumptuous editions, and on these they lavished their funds year after year, striving for more luxurious and ever more limited editions.

Once the set was completed it was easy enough to single out a popular title for extra illustration as a holiday book. Hence Dickens' *Child's History of England* was offered in 1880 with a hundred illustrations, mostly by French illustrators, at $2.50 in cloth, $6.00 in morocco. Another fertile device was to make etchings of some of the new illustrations prepared for the set and sell them in a portfolio. Fred Barnard's designs were, consequently, reproduced as etchings, which sold for $3.50 in portfolio. Modern publishers are not averse to such multiplications (and these are not wholly worthless, either) ; E & L, however, exploited these methods with tireless pertinacity.

It was probably inevitable that Thackeray should follow Dickens in 1881. Here again were the three basic sets, the People's, the University, and the Cambridge editions, the cheaper versions in ten volumes, the Cambridge in twenty; the People's Edition, priced at fifteen dollars in cloth, was the only one sold both in sets and single volumes. All three editions, this time, claimed over three hundred illustrations, by Thackeray and others, and differed chiefly in quality of paper and binding, the Cambridge Edition selling for thirty dollars, bound in dark green cloth, with gilt tops.[27] There was also a limited edition of 250 numbered copies, in which nearly all the illustrations were proof impressions from the original wood blocks; this set of twenty volumes sold for forty-five dollars, in cloth. E & L asserted that this was the first fine edition printed in America, a claim not ungrounded since none of the previous American editions were so profusely illustrated.

There were also new editions of Macaulay's *History of England* and his *Essays and Poems,* the more expensive ones with woodcuts and steel engravings. The advertising declared that these were the only illustrated editions of Macaulay on the market,[28] and, for both

Thackeray and Macaulay, "the best editions for the money ever published." Despite the exaggeration they were good, readable editions for both authors, with attractive illustrations. In the case of Macaulay, however, the illustrations had already given service in Guizot's two histories and in the volumes of the "Zigzag Series" for young readers.

With the sets well and expensively launched and the children's books selling in thousands, Estes invested in several distinctly holiday items, some good, some no more than average. The book given greatest advertising, naturally enough, was *Nature and Art,* compiled by Dana's wife, Louise Reid Estes. It had been announced in March that a certain Charles A. Nelson, who hailed from Calais, Maine, and was employed with E & L, was to prepare a new selection of poetry for an illustrated work to be entitled "Nature in Art and Poetry." By September Mrs. Estes appeared as the compiler, and Mr. Nelson went to the Astor Library as cataloguer. Whatever the reason for the change, it apparently worked out well, since the book was generally praised. In most respects it was all too typical of the gift books of the day, with its sixty poems provided with pictures that matched them as well as could be expected. In fact, one critic thought some pictures were "amazingly fitted for the verses."[29] The novelty lay in presenting a gift book with etchings along with the expected wood engravings. The etchings were done by such contemporary notables as Rajon, Moran, Forberg, Gifford, Farrar, and Smillie, fourteen in all, and the wood engravings were by W. J. Linton, George Andrew, and other experts. E & L proclaimed it the first gift book with etchings by celebrated artists to be issued in America and thought it would help to popularize "this most beautiful form of art."[30] The vogue for etchings was really beginning, as shown by Osgood's publication of *Poets and Etchers* this same season, and, from this time on, both standard sets and gift books employed etchings as expensive novelties. It was fortunate that the book had such a friendly reception, since Mrs. Estes died in August, 1883.

The other works of 1881 were two quarto volumes, *Beautiful Wild Flowers of America* and *Beautiful Ferns of America,* with colored plates after original drawings by Isaac Sprague and other artists, and Tennyson's *Song of the Brook,* the first of a brief series called "Songs of the Great Poets." The first titles won praise for their realistic colors and fine drawings, the *Beautiful Wild Flowers* attracting particular attention for its cover, embossed with a spray of clematis, in white and gold, with the letters of the title braided through the flowers![31] The *Song of the Brook,* with twenty-one illustrations, followed the usual practice of stringing out the poem, a few lines being faced by a full-page plate, until the poem was mercifully terminated. Almost invariably the verses were infinitely superior to the pictures, but our ancestors demanded their pictures regardless of quality. This volume was on the same level as other holiday books of the year, and the fact that such works were sought after convinced E & L of their wisdom in producing them.[32]

If 1881 had marked the start of the descent from the heights of 1878, 1879, and 1880, the year 1882 decisively confirmed the downward trend, even though a few superior books were listed. The specific gift books showed little originality: one was a poem by Elizabeth Akers Allen, *Rock Me To Sleep, Mother,* suitably adorned with infants and rocking chairs; another was Schiller's *Song of the Bell* (second in E & L's series), a poem which had already suffered from too much illustrating. Schiller's work was advertised as illustrated by E. H. Garrett and A. L. Mayer, two favorites of the day, but, in reality, they did only six pictures and the remaining twenty were borrowed from earlier books. E & L were not the only ones guilty of this practice, and they had become so used to juggling old pictures with new that it had become a habit with them. Yet the *Literary World*'s critic was annoyed: "We do not like this way of offering old work for new."[33] There were also *Flowers of the Field and Forest,* with colored plates after Isaac Sprague and text by the Reverend A. B. Hervey, who wrote with the "accuracy of a botanist and the feeling of a poet,"[34] and two "elegant folios" called *Picturesque American Scenery* and *Picturesque European Scenery,* each a hodgepodge of plates from E & L's now voluminous archives. Evidently the pictures determined the make-up of the volumes, and Leo de Colange was obliged to manufacture a sprightly text for the European volume and compile a potpourri of prose and verse on American scenes.[35] These books were not bad or crude; they were, in fact, considerably better printed than many rival works, but they revealed a mediocrity of taste that the firm apparently approved.

On the other side of the ledger, speaking artistically and perhaps financially, stood W. J. Linton's *History of Wood-engraving in America.* This fine book, which had appeared in the *American Art Review* originally, was here expanded by a concluding chapter and several additional illustrations, making about a hundred in all. E & L published it in a limited edition, a thousand numbered and twenty-six lettered copies, each signed by the author. Some regretted the limited edition, but, in a work where the beauty of the plates was so important, the restriction was probably wise. All the critics agreed that the book was an art treasure, excellent in its typography and its beautifully printed illustrations. Most agreed on its critical and historical value, hailing its authoritative presentation, its stimulating approach, its independence and vigor. Linton made a fiery onslaught against what was called the "new school" of engraving and was scarcely polite to many contemporaries. Most reviewers seemed to favor his attack and felt that his criticisms had the weight of expertness, but one, at least, the reviewer for the *Critic,* complained of his harshness and thought that he gave too much space to his attacks in a work which should have been wholly historical.[36] To anyone today still interested in nineteenth-century wood engraving this volume is indeed a delight, for it includes some of the finest work done in that amazing period, much of it in full-page plates. The text, too, is valuable, written by one of the masters of the American school who gives us contemporary opinion on this brilliant era.

Some of the other illustrated works, W. L. Gage's *Palestine, Historical and Descriptive,* Fergusson's famous *History of Architecture,* and Fred Allen's *Glimpses of Parisian Art,* were better than average both in text and pictures. There was also a set of Goethe's principal works, which E & L termed the first American collected edition, in one uniform series. It was edited from standard English versions by the well-known scholars, Thomas Henry Hedge and Leopold Noa, and contained critical introductions, notes, and a variety of translations, such as Hayward's prose version of *Faust* along with Anna Swanwick's metrical rendering, and similar variety for the lesser dramas. This set was published in the three styles, People's, University, and Cambridge editions, well printed and bound, but—a strange thing for E & L—without illustrations.[37] The firm had printed Heinrich Düntzer's *Life of Goethe* in 1880, which undoubtedly inspired the preparation of the collected works. A natural companion to the Goethe was a set of Schiller's writings, also in the three styles and edited from Coleridge's and others' translations by the same scholars. A fancy edition of John Forster's *Life of Dickens* served as an admirable pendant to the set of Dickens, being printed and bound in the more expensive styles.

Of less artistic interest, but useful in the light of publishing history, was the first of the cheap "Boston Editions," intended as a counterattack on the cheap-book publishers such as Alden and Belford, Clarke and Co. Hume's *History of England,* published as six volumes bound in three, and printed on cheap paper, sold for $3.75. Soon afterward, in 1883 and 1884, came cheap sets of Macaulay's *History of England,* Addison's works, Plutarch's *Lives,* Hazlitt's *Life of Napoleon* and *Miscellaneous Works,* and Gibbon's *Decline and Fall,* all moderately priced, some even with steel engravings as frontispieces. After 1885 these sets were also distributed by an E & L affiliate, the Aldine Publishing Co., for even wider subscription sale throughout the country. All of the early "Boston Editions" were printed on atrociously poor paper, with the result that copies now on library shelves are practically worthless. Yet they did help to stem the tide of the "pirates," however slightly, and many persons were able to put bound volumes, with illustrations, on their shelves at bargain prices. Another bargain was E & L's single-volume edition of Knight's *Pictorial Shakspere,* 1,120 pages with 350 illustrations, for only three dollars.[38]

E & L's fall announcement for 1883 was longer than those of the big New York publishers and reflected their activities in every field. These years in the eighties were years of vigorous experimentation and bustling activity, so that a large measure of both wheat and chaff appeared under the firm's imprint. The gift books again were decidedly popular in tone, even hackneyed, with such ancients as Gray's *Elegy,* Coleridge's *Ancient Mariner,* and *Songs and Scenes from Faust* heading the list. As if by intuition, three publishers chose Gray's *Elegy* this season, thereby causing much debate by critics and buyers alike: Lippincott's was the largest and most expensive, Roberts Brothers' and E & L's cheaper and less pretentious. Most critical votes went to Roberts Brothers' edition, illustrated by Harry Fenn, but E & L's received favorable mention, with its designs by Birket Foster, W. L. Taylor, and others. The *Ancient Mariner* had chiefly Doré engravings and appeared in a variety of styles, such as bindings of full tree calf, illuminated and fringed covers, or decorated satin and fringed covers. These elaborate bindings were the vogue, destined to endure for several years: The *Bookbuyer,* in 1884, called them "things that occupy the borderline between letters and stationery—the upholstery of literature."[39] But few critics dared scorn them openly at that time. The *Songs and Scenes from Faust,* illustrated by A. L. Mayer and A. Lalauze, was generally praised and was featured in the holiday number of the *Publishers' Weekly.*[40] There were also new volumes manufactured around a series of engravings, *The Heart of Europe from the Rhine to the Danube* and *Mountain, Lake and River,* devoted to American scenery; sumptuous books, they undoubtedly gave great pleasure to many readers and are still pleasant to leaf through today, for the pictures if not for the text.

There were better works, however, such as the magnificent subscription edition of Duruy's *Rome,* and a new limited edition of Lingard's *History of England,* only three hundred copies for the

United States, with a special, large-paper edition of one hundred copies, uncut, for those seeking a truly luxurious edition. Fred A. Ober's *Travels in Mexico*, a lavishly illustrated book of 672 pages, was widely acclaimed as one of the largest, freshest, and most instructive works on Mexico.[41] The *Nation* commended its accuracy, its striking descriptions, and its pictures; the new ones were all good, said the reviewer, and the old had at least the charm of old friends.[42] And Hezekiah Butterworth, whose reputation was at its height because of his "Zigzag Series," turned out a beautifully illustrated anthology, *Poems for Christmas, Easter and New Year*, called "admirable" by the *Nation*, which ordinarily was hard to please.[43]

There were also *éditions de luxe*—a term not discredited in the 1880's—of Thackeray and Carlyle, although the Carlyle was not actually ready until early in 1884. Such editions had been published for several years in England, with varying degrees of success. Houghton, Mifflin had produced splendid sets of Hawthorne and Emerson, both limited to five hundred copies, and announced that they had been subscribed immediately; contemporaries rated them perfect in form, material, and workmanship. In 1883 Lippincott was doing an edition of Prescott, limited to 250 copies; Dodd, Mead presented Sheridan, limited to three hundred copies; Cassell had *Original Etchings by American Artists*, two hundred copies on Japan and India paper, signed by the artists, with a "super de luxe" version of only three copies. The *Dial* thought this trend to fine editions of standard authors a good one, for these books were more lasting than the usual holiday book, yet equally handsome. Disagreeing with those who deemed them expensive, the *Dial* saw no reason why persons desiring their favorite authors in elegant editions, with rich paper and perfect print, should not be afforded the opportunity to own them.[44]

E & L's Thackeray was apparently modeled on Houghton, Mifflin's two sets of American authors; in fact, in their advertising they called it "uniform" with the recent edition of Emerson. It was limited to 250 numbered copies, manufactured at the University Press on fine tinted paper, nearly all the illustrations being proof impressions from the original wood blocks on India paper; there were also India proof impressions of twenty original etchings and two etched portraits found in no other edition of Thackeray. Sold in complete sets only, the twenty volumes, in cloth, were priced at $45. The Carlyle was described as the first complete, uniform edition of the author produced in America. It was printed on parchment linen drawing paper, with a profusion of India proof impressions

of etchings, steel engravings, and photogravures. It was absolutely
limited to 375 copies, numbered and registered, and sold only in sets
of twenty volumes, at $3.50 a volume. It was called the Parchment
Edition, since most of the copies were bound in this material, but a
few were available in dark calf or vellum cloth; the parchment volumes had illuminated stamps and gilt tops, with the customary
uncut edges.

Early in February, 1884, all but twenty sets were subscribed
for, and the remainder were disposed of by threatening to raise the
price from $70 to $80 by the end of March. The two other forms of
binding cost the subscriber from $100 to $150, and these were sold
too. Most reviewers did not have a chance to see this set, but the
Nation praised a sample volume.[45]

In London, meanwhile, George Smalley, correspondent for the
New York Tribune, had noted that de luxe editions were a drug on
the market and declared that many were obtainable at half price.
After this remark was quoted in the *Critic,* Dana Estes sent in an
immediate reply, for he had undoubtedly assured his buyers that
de luxe subscription sets would increase in value with the years.
Estes wrote that he would be glad to find some of these half-cost
sets of Dickens, Thackeray, George Eliot, and the rest, for he
could make a real profit on them. He, for one, knew that American
éditions de luxe were not suffering such blows, whatever might be
true in England, and he knew that many American sets were now
worth 50 to 100 per cent more than their retail price and were
widely sought after, as, for example, Hawthorne's *Works,* Emerson's *Works,* Irving's *Life of Washington,* Burton's *Book Hunter*
and Walton's *Angler.* E & L's new edition of Carlyle was now fully
subscribed and was even advertised for in advance of the publication
date.[46]

At least one subscriber—and probably many more, if the firm's
correspondence files had only survived to show it—was not entirely
satisfied with his set of Thackeray. An anonymous letter from New
York to the *Critic,* in the same issue as Estes' letter,[47] is worth
quoting almost entirely.

> I was glad to see that Messrs Estes and Lauriat take an
> optimistic view of *éditions de luxe.* They must set a high
> value on their luxurious edition of Thackeray's *Complete
> Works.* This edition was begun— if it is not a rehash of an
> old one—some fifteen months ago or more and was to be
> complete in 20 volumes. On account, probably, of the great
> care spent on the 'novel cuts from original plates and
> blocks' only 16 volumes have as yet appeared. As a sub-

scriber and the fortunate possessor of these treasures, let me call your attention to four out of the seven illustrations in the volume of *Miscellanies:* View from Richmond Hill, Last Speech of Chatham, Hôtel de Ville, Brussels and Hôtel de Ville, Ghent. These, I venture to say, come out of some books of travel for boys. However, let us be thankful for such works of art. There are seven valuable illustrations to the *Roundabout Papers*. Five are: Guizot, Dôme des Invalides, Thiers, Murat and Napoleon's Funeral. I wonder if these come from some history of France? In the *Four Georges* you will observe with interest a Naval Battle. But it is in the *English Humorists* that the real humor of the Boston publishers bubbles out. Here you see portraits of the well-known comic poet Milton and of that other delightful English humorist, 'King James at the Battle of the Boyne.' Buying an American *édition de luxe* is interesting—because you never know what you are to get. In justice, I should say that in other respects the edition is satisfactory. But these later 'novel cuts'—*horresco referens!*[48]

This amusing correspondent put his finger on the exact weakness of E & L's methods of illustrating. Naturally, it was a temptation to draw from their archives of wood blocks and electrotypes for some of these sets where a picture could be dragged in on a slim pretext. Probably most subscribers never knew the difference or would not have cared very much, even though it was unethical to advertise "original blocks and plates" so blatantly. Other firms did it too, which was always an excuse, but E & L were far too prone to keep shuffling their enormous variety of pictures throughout any new books they published. Many of the pictures were really good, and, from this distance, it is rather amusing to observe the odd juxtapositions of old favorites, but subscribers to limited editions surely had a right to be annoyed, if they knew enough.

Great preparations were made for the holiday season of 1884, for business had never been better. There was trouble ahead, however, in the increasing competition of the cheap-book publishers. John B. Alden had started to print sets of several authors on E & L's list, especially Guizot, and, now that E & L brought out their three regular trade editions of Carlyle, Alden responded with a set at one fourth the price. E & L could only stress the superior merits of their editions as regarded paper, printing, and illustrations and apparently had no great trouble finding buyers who preferred attractive books to merely cheap ones. As for the sumptuous gift books and limited editions, they were perfectly safe from Alden and his fellows and were worth exploiting to the limit.

There were the usual trivial items, such as Dickens' *The Ivy Green,* with colored print and plates; *The Last Rose of Summer; Great Events of the World;* Kate Sanborn's *Cupid's Calendar,* "a heart-shaped novelty"; and the *Garden of the Heart,* made up of twenty-five heart-shaped leaflets, each with a text from the Bible and a bit of verse. The *Critic* thought well of this last novelty, praising the selections and agreeing with the publishers that it made "a choice present from a Sunday-school teacher to his scholars."[49] The richer items were quite pretentious: Moore's *Lalla Rookh,* to be sold only by subscription, was embellished with colored photogravures and cost from $35 to $50, in a satin portfolio. This book will be described later, since it was, perhaps, the most ambitious single volume E & L ever attempted. Fred H. Allen, who was E & L's art editor, prepared *Masterpieces of Modern German Art* by visiting more than one hundred German and Austrian artists and obtaining reproductions of some of their favorite works. Especially mentioned were J. G. Meyer (Meyer von Bremen), Franz von Defregger, Anton Alexander von Werner, Victor Müller, and Adolf Menzel; all of these were well known in the 1880's but Menzel was incomparably the greatest. There were one hundred photogravure plates (some colored) and thirteen etchings, as well as a woodcut portrait of each artist. The work was a folio (12 x 17) sold only by subscription in twenty-five parts, each costing one dollar.[50] E & L claimed the exclusive right to make photogravures in the United States and used it lavishly in this volume and the *Lalla Rookh.*[51] These were indeed desirable books for the center-table, as one advertisement put it. For those who wished something less expensive there was Alexander Young's handsome *Concise History of the Netherlands* or W. H. Davenport Adams' *The Land of the Incas and the City of the Sun.*

Another set appeared in 1885—this time the works of Samuel Richardson, limited to 250 copies and costing $2.50 for each of the twelve volumes. There were several unfavorable comments on limited editions this year, though not directed specifically at any one firm. The *Art Age* felt that the device had been carried to excess and was in danger of annihilation because of corrupt practices.[52] This prophecy was merely twenty-five years too early. Apropos of J. R. Osgood's failure, in May, 1885, George A. Townsend, writing in the *Boston Globe,* condemned "sensuousness" in book publishing: there were too many decorated books, too many sumptuous illustrated sets but not enough strong meat for the mind.[53] Undeterred, naturally, E & L prepared another elegant display for the fall season and won even more acclaim than in previous years.

There were first the old stand-bys, suitably adorned, this time *Lenore* and *The Eve of St. Agnes.* These were offered in limited editions of 280 copies, large paper, India proof impressions, at $10 a copy; for the mob there were trade editions at $1.50 and $2.50. *Lenore* was illustrated by Henry Sandham, *The Eve of St. Agnes* by the popular Edmund H. Garrett. Sandham's designs were somewhat uneven, though better than average, but Garrett's pictures won general praise. The *Critic,* calling it "always a welcome gift book," considered it "unusually attractive." Garrett was a talented and versatile artist, excelling both in landscape and in figures, thought the reviewer, and he was remarkably successful in decorative details, Oriental luxuries, and the like.[54] Also on the conventional side was a volume called *Picturesque Russia,* with text by the omniscient Leo de Colange and pictures by French artists. Why Russia? Simply because E & L had just published Rambaud's *Popular History of Russia* and had a lot of plates at their disposal.

The remaining works were more distinctive and quite delighted the critics of the day, although some of them seem mildly amusing at present. The gayest was entitled *The Modern Cupid,* a translation of Mounet-Sully's little poem *En Chemin de Fer.* Done entirely in colored photogravure, with the text in italic, this imposing trifle of fifteen stanzas was, as the *Literary World* said, a "dish of whipped cream."[55] Printed on loose sheets, with cupid borders and immense margins, it was characteristically French, dainty and frivolous, yet perfectly tasteful. The loose sheets were placed in a gray cloth-covered portfolio with purple decorations and tied with purple silk. The *Literary World* thought it reached the "most exquisite degree of book art; nothing could be more refined and beautiful." Just to demonstrate the craze for limited editions, this trifle was limited to 370 copies, of which five were printed on parchment, fifteen on satin, thirty-five on Japan paper, sixty-five on India paper and 250 on vellum paper. The prices ranged from $7.50 to $50, and the books sold so rapidly that by December 1 E & L were able to raise the price on the few remaining copies, making the vellum copies $10 and the satin $35.[56]

American Etchings, a thoroughly serious production, was a resurrection of the *American Art Review.* This was in no way a disparagement, commented the *Literary World,* since the *American Art Review* was too good—not to live—but to die and the public ought to be grateful for every revival from its precious ashes.[57] This was another portfolio (12 x 18) containing twenty original etchings by such artists as James D. Smillie, Thomas Moran, Edmund Garrett, Parrish, and Ferris, with text by S. R. Koehler, former editor of the magazine. It was handsomely printed in red and black, with very wide margins, and the etchings all had mats. The portfolio itself was thought worthy of praise and the pictures were generally admired, only the text being thought a bit too uncritical.[58]

Although this work was much above the average for holiday books, it still is difficult to realize the intensity of the vogue for limited editions without noting the details for this one. The portfolio was strictly limited to 350 copies, in the following styles: five copies, proofs on genuine parchment, text on vellum paper, in parchment portfolio, $150; fifteen copies, proofs on satin, vellum paper text, in satin portfolio, $75; forty copies, proofs on India paper, vellum paper text, vellum cloth portfolio, $35; forty copies, proofs on Japan paper, usual text, parchment portfolio, $35; 250 copies, proofs on Holland paper, usual text, cloth portfolio, $15. And, in this instance also, by December 1 E & L raised the price of the remaining seventy copies on Holland paper to $17.50! If, in the instance of *The Modern Cupid,* we may congratulate ourselves that, whatever the deficiencies in our taste, we do not fall for that sort of thing today, we can only feel amazement that people would and could pay $150 for *American Etchings,* even though it was reasonably attractive.

I have left *Lalla Rookh* to the last since this is indeed the *pièce de résistance.* In many respects, it is the best book that E & L designed, original and with a high quality of artistic work. It also reflected popular taste amazingly well, probably because it was a wholly American production, both in general design and in the collaborating artists. Reviewers unhesitatingly called it one of the finest and most luxurious holiday books in years; some thought it really unique. It first appeared in 1884, in a small limited edition, ranging from $35 to $50; this year it was made available more extensively, though still in limited editions of 275 copies on vellum paper, five hundred copies on Japan paper, priced at $15 and $17.50, respectively. It was offered in a diamond-papered box: the book had a loose cover of light brown linen, tied with satin ribbons of deep seal brown; the book itself was bound in parchment, with end papers of watered silk. The printing was crisp and clear; the photogravures, 140 of them, were colored in shades of gray, blue, green, and sepia, many of them twined about the text and a few printed directly on it, with occasional obscuring of the letters here and there. The *Critic* felt it deserved respectful admiration as an example of American bookmaking and the *Literary World* called it "a first-class art book" which scored another high mark for American taste and skill.[59]

The general design was by Fred H. Allen, the printing was supervised by Joseph H. Wheeler, and both were commended by reviewers. Not only was the format generous (9 x 12½) but the 140 illustrations were amazingly good, considering that a score of artists contributed. They were among the most prominent illustrators of the day, including such names as J. W. Champney, W. B. Closson, E. H. Garrett, Henry Sandham, F. T. Merrill, W. L. Taylor, S. G. McCutcheon, Walter Satterlee, W. St. John Harper, Kenyon Cox, F. S. Church, W. J. Mozart, J. A. Fraser, and W. H. Low. Some few pictures were taken directly from Persian sources and are not the least attractive of the group. That there was any unity at all, with so many artists, is somewhat of a miracle, and may properly be credited to the good taste of Allen, who also contributed a few designs. The photogravures, although one may shudder slightly now at the tints, were rather appropriate for the atmosphere of the tale, with soft, velvety effects mingled with Oriental luxuriance, scenes of action mingled with landscapes or fantasy designs. To contemporaries it did have a tone of Eastern splendor, presented in luxurious and even exotic style; in fact, it probably had more appeal because it was an American realization of Oriental life than it would have had if it used only authentic Oriental motifs.

Amid the general praise for the work as a whole, the *Critic* singled out three artists for particular mention. W. St. John Harper's work was really distinguished, especially his portrayal of elaborate Eastern pageants; Kenyon Cox bore off the palm for finely executed compositions, superb as decorations; and Will H. Low's decorative borders were among the very best plates. The book, said the reviewer, gave genuine artistic pleasure.[60] No verbal picture of it is adequate: it is a book that must be seen, and it is not easily found any longer.[61] It is an excellent sample of what one of the foremost purveyors of illustrated books considered a supreme treat for the American public, and, judging from its favorable reception, the public heartily agreed. Thus, in many respects, it is a better exhibit of the average taste of the 1880's than the works by more distinguished artists, which sometimes found favor in that period, but only among the few.

The remaining years of the 1880's follow much the same pattern—sumptuous editions of standard authors and a miscellany of specific gift books, some very expensive and others moderately priced. It is difficult to keep track of the many activities of E & L,

since, at this time, they were publishing through subsidiary firms
such as the C. J. Jewett Co., which handled their historical sets
after 1886, the Aldine Publishing Co., which sold very cheap editions of standard authors, and finally the Fine Art Publishing Co.,
which offered somewhat different titles from those in E & L's list.
This firm, located at the general headquarters on Washington Street,
put out some truly beautiful works, limited de luxe editions that
were very costly and yet tasteful. As an example, Carl von Lützow's
Art Treasures of Italy, translated by Susan Thayer Hooper and
edited by Mrs. Clara Erskine Clement, who was soon to become a
regular on E & L's list, was an impressive portfolio containing one
hundred full-page etchings, photogravures, and steel plates, of royal
folio size, plus forty-seven full-page wood engravings and three hundred smaller engravings scattered throughout the text. It was splen-
didly printed, many pages having Renaissance borders and decorated initials, with a text that made up two generous volumes. It
was, of course, unwieldy to read but delightful to pore over.

There were so many attractive works turned out in the eighties
and early nineties that one is tempted to dwell on them at greater
length than is desirable. I have given details primarily to emphasize
E & L's concern for fine illustrated books and their success in the
field, since their reputation steadily increased. It was expected, as a
normal event, that E & L's holiday list would be "sumptuous," and
their own success urged them to even greater endeavors. Such a succession of lush works may seem monotonous, but satiety did not appear to bother them for many years to come, and one must also remember that these luxurious books were balanced by a host of excellent juveniles, many of them attractively illustrated too, but at
reasonable prices.

For 1886 there were two sets, Shelley's *Complete Poetical
Works* and an *édition de luxe* of George Eliot. Shelley was limited
to fifty copies, the set of George Eliot to five hundred. A long list of
artists, including many of those who worked on *Lalla Rookh,* did
the fifty India proof impressions of etchings and photogravures,
both of which were now deemed necessary for a de luxe edition.
There was also a concise biography by the Reverend George Willis
Cooke, Emerson's friend, and the twelve volumes, in cloth, sold for
$72, the highest price yet. The gift books included two picture col-
lections: *Recent German Art,* with text by Fred H. Allen, a folio
volume containing seventeen photogravures; and *Foreign Etchings,*
another folio with twenty original etchings made by French and
German artists from paintings by Rembrandt, Titian, Palma Vec-
chio, Munkácsy, and Bonnat. This hybrid form was evidently popu-

lar and was sold in the usual exaggeratedly limited edition of five copies on parchment, at $150, then working down to 250 copies on Holland paper at $15.

The illustrated editions of the "old chestnuts" brought the usual acclaim. The *Literary World* gave due praise to *Foreign Etchings,* noting that it too came largely from the *American Art Review,*[62] but reserved their gushing tribute for Owen Meredith's *The Earl's Return,* whose illustrations were done by W. L. Taylor. It was a mingling of tinted photogravures, colored etchings, and wood engravings with tinted margins.[63] No reviewer criticized these monstrosities; they clearly represented the taste of the day. Only the *Critic* was disappointed in the mechanical execution of certain of the photogravures,[64] but agreed that the book showed "manifold evidences of loving thought and patient work," and the *Dial* thought it "uncommonly meritorious."[65] Thomas Hood's *Fair Ines* was also approved, though the *Critic* ventured to suggest that it was hardly sensible to depict Ines as a damsel in Elizabethan dress in one picture, and as an American girl, successively of the Southern and Northern varieties, in the other plates.[66]

It is painful to report that the quarto gift books for 1886 and a selection of those from past seasons were offered in three new "ornamental" bindings, if desired: Burmese plush, wild rose, and peach blow, which cost $1.50 more than the standard binding.

Dana Estes, speaking for international copyright before the Senate Committee on Patents, gave some idea of the money tied up in illustrated editions.[67] He announced that his firm emitted about a million dollars' worth of books yearly, but that he was obliged to refuse many American manuscripts because it was impossible to make the books of most American authors pay unless they were first published in magazines. Since English authors were protected by international copyright, Estes could accept the manuscript of a British author because he could arrange with the British publisher to share the enormous expense of illustrations, which must be borne before the work was produced at all. He said that he was then producing a book the original outlay upon which was more than a hundred thousand dollars "for the plant," an expense he was able to share with the English publisher. Although Estes did not elucidate, one may suspect that he was referring to the edition of George Eliot.

Plainly, the publishing of these pictorial works was costly but, once started, so insidious that it became almost a disease. If one didn't succeed this year, the next year would see the luck change. The mistakes made this year could be avoided: the book came out too late, or the competition was too strong or the theme was not popular enough. Thus the victim always deluded himself with excuses and explanations. The senior partner of a well-known firm said to his younger partners, as reported by O. B. Bunce in the *Critic*: "I hope I shall never see another Christmas book published by us. After I am dead, do as you please, but while I live please make no more books for the holidays."[68]

Bunce pointed out that the increasingly large consumption of "choice standard editions" of famous authors might run the ordinary gift book out of the market, a fate which, to him, did not seem overly harsh.

According to the usual practice, the sumptuous edition of George Eliot having served its purpose, it was reduced to cheaper versions, the Handy Volume Edition and the Sterling Edition. The Handy Volume Edition was limited to one thousand copies, but the twelve volumes could be purchased, in cloth, for only $18; it was stressed that these were the first thousand copies printed after the de luxe edition, that the sets were printed on ivory-finish paper, with sixty original woodcuts on Japan paper. There was also the Cabinet Edition of Hudson's *Shakespeare,* twelve volumes for $15, and the Boston Edition, six volumes for $9, and the Boston Edition of Macaulay, Gibbon, Scott, Hume, and others, so cheap editions were more numerous in 1887.

The *Düsseldorf Gallery,* with twenty etchings and descriptive text, provided the sumptuous gift book, again ranging from $150 to $15. The etchings were by minor Germans, Ernst Bosch, Carl Irmer, Volkhart, Meissner, Grotiohann, Kroener, and Leisten, but they were etchings, and etchings were the rage.[69] *Recent French Art,* with photogravures after Dupré, Meissonier, Breton, and others, was not so dear, only $7.50. It was called a "superb gift book in royal folio," with gold and colored stamping of the French arms on the cover. Charles Kingsley's *Song of the River,* limited to five hundred copies, won praise from the *Literary World,*[70] and there was a new edition, with many new pictures, of Mrs. Estes' *Nature and Art.* The vogue for photogravures led to the unnecessary stuffing of Starr King's delightful book, *The White Hills,* originally issued in 1859, with plates that were decidedly inferior to the original woodcuts, which were retained. Another book, called *Flower Idylls,* with tags of verses illustrated by tinted photogravures of flowers, seemed to strike the rock bottom of popular taste with dreadful precision.

If there had been a slight slackening in luxuriousness in 1887, the holiday books for 1888 aimed to remedy that deficiency. A new version of the George Eliot set appeared, called this time the Illustrated Library Edition; it was between the de luxe edition and the Handy Volume, rearranged in fifteen volumes priced at $37.50 in cloth, and including most of the pictures in the original de luxe edition. But the star of E & L's books was Keats's *Endymion*, illustrated by W. St. John Harper with forty-eight tinted photogravures, on imperial Japan paper. The reviewer in the *Publishers' Weekly*, who had lush praise for E & L's books this season, purred happily over *Endymion*, with its yellow satin cover lettered in gold;[71] "nothing excelling it has passed through our hands this season." It sold for $15, not a limited edition this time. Other reviewers also liked Tennyson's *Fairy Lilian* and *Bugle Song*. The *Fairy Lilian*, in the eyes of the *Literary World*, was clearly one of the most sumptuous books of the season. This attractive large quarto (10 x 12) was illustrated by the usual team, Taylor, Harper, Church, Garrett, and a few others; each page had ornamental borders, "printed in a delicate tint."[72] The *Critic* liked it too, pictures, borders, vignettes, everything![73] *Bugle Song* was equally successful, judging from an almost unanimous chorus of praise.[74]

But the reviewer in the *Nation*, with fine critical perversity, had nothing but scorn for these favorites. *Fairy Lilian* provoked a sneer that the "very genius of higgeldy-piggeldy presided at the construction of this volume."[75] Here were fourteen artists whose drawings had no relation to each other and very little to the text. In fact, plenty of cleverness and ability had been wasted for want of intelligent direction; the illustrations were like the pictures at an exhibition, each swearing at its neighbors. Also, there was not a picture in the book printed in the middle of the page, he lamented, and he felt that an illaudable ingenuity was shown in spotting the illustrations irregularly on the leaves and surrounding each with an annoying decoration in pale gray, in odd and unsymmetrical shapes. As for *Bugle Song*, it was worse: there was no discoverable unity even in the text, and the drawings ranged from mediocrity downwards. The *Nation*, though at times heavy-handed, was frequently refreshing in its frankness, and this splenetic outburst perhaps came close to a truth that contemporaries were loath to admit.

The major de luxe work for 1888 was something of a novelty, Victor Hugo's *Notre-Dame de Paris*, in both English and French versions. It was limited to five hundred copies, one hundred on Japan paper selling for $20 for two octavo volumes, the remaining four hundred on satin-finish paper at $12. In this venture E & L collaborated with H. R. Jenkins of New York, who was responsible for the French edition. It was a new translation by Abby L. Alger, graced with two hundred illustrations by Rossi, Bieler, and Myrbach, sixteen of them aquarelles printed in colors in Paris expressly for this edition. Hugo's death in 1885 had already brought forth new translations and new editions of his writings in the United States, notably by Little, Brown and Co., Crowell, and Routledge, all profusely illustrated; but, as the *Dial* remarked, the crowning compliment to Hugo was the issue of this *édition de luxe* by E & L.[76] For grangerites there were available sets of the plates in separate portfolios on Japan and satin-finished paper.

Other expensive books were *European Etchings*, comprising twenty etchings by French, German, and English artists, ranging from $150 downwards; a limited edition of George Eliot's *Poems;* *Recent Italian Art*, with the usual photogravures; and *The Napoleon Gallery*, a series of one hundred outline etchings by the French artist Reveil from paintings on the Napoleonic legend, in French galleries. These pictures were also available in sheets for those who wished to use them for extra-illustrating. The *Goupil Gallery of Photogravures*, a selection of ten recent Salon favorites, was followed by such gems as *Voices of the Summer, Song Birds and Seasons,* and Longfellow's *Maidenhood*. Several of these last were "delicately colored," and apparently the *Song Birds and Seasons* was quite attractive to the reviewer in the *Critic*.[77]

As is evident, 1888 was a full year for E & L, with generally good notices and undoubted commercial success. One novelty was apparent this year: instead of issuing a complete *édition de luxe* of Hugo and then parceling it out later in cheaper sets or in single, over-illustrated volumes, they reversed the procedure and planned to bring out the set a few volumes at a time. But the other method was still too profitable to abandon, so that, in the next few years, they mingled the two procedures.

After so successful a season, 1889 showed another slackening of pace, with a full resumption of vigor in 1890. There was the usual large-sized book of etchings, *Famous Etchers* this time, and the inevitable photogravures appeared in *Recent English Art*, with reproductions of paintings by Leighton, Leslie, and Alma Tadema. A new series, which was to be successful for years to come, began in 1889: this was *Goupil's Paris Salon of '89*, a sumptuous folio volume filled with photogravures of popular favorites in the Salon exhibition. These volumes had been appearing in French and were bought in increasing quantities in America. E & L took advantage of the well-advertised Paris Exposition of 1889 to bring out an English translation and, at the same time, bought exclusive rights to the French edition. The volume for 1889 comprised one hundred tinted photogravures, reproduced by the "unrivalled Goupil process," with descriptive notes. Bound in brilliant red, with a golden palette and colors stamped on the cover, the volume cost from $18 to $20, in either French or English. Yet it was undeniably handsome and E & L made the most of it for several years. The limited edition was almost completely subscribed by October 26 and was exhausted by December 1. The *Critic* thought it an admirable work in every way.[78]

Notre-Dame de Paris, which E & L made in de luxe form in 1888, appeared in a cheap, single-volume edition in 1889, a practice that would be followed in later years. Several reviewers noted that the plates were not as clearly printed in the cheap edition, even though there were still 175 illustrations.[79]

There was also an *édition de luxe* of Duruy's *History of Greece,* a much smaller work than his *History of Rome,* which won a medal at the Paris Exposition. In this instance E & L imported it from England, one thousand copies only, a hint that the Roman history had not been wholly successful. The *Critic* remarked that in the subscription sale of this work the West did as well as the East: Chicago subscribed for three hundred copies; St. Louis, 150; San Francisco, fifty; New York, 250; and New England, 250.

Most of the remaining books of 1889 were holiday books of previous years, either dressed up with new bindings or in cheaper editions, as was *The Earl's Return,* featured in 1886. These were a convenient filler for weaker years and were surely as good in one year as another. The *Publishers' Weekly* rated the 1889 holiday books highly, noting that E & L had spent a fortune in getting ready remarkable art works and praising them for their "tangible faith in the growing appreciation and culture of art in this country."[80]

The list for 1890 was long and impressive. There was only one large set this year but the number of single titles was unusually great, running to more than fifteen. Two novels were given first attention: *Romola* and *Hans of Iceland.* The first was a glorification of a volume from the earlier de luxe edition of George Eliot, but this time the illustrations were photogravures and were taken entirely from photographs of buildings, works of sculpture, and a few paintings. Dana Estes himself had made the selection in Florence and no doubt thought it a remarkably inexpensive way to present a gift book. The idea was not original with him, however, as the Riverside Press's fine edition of *The Marble Faun* in 1889 had been his model. As an amusing coincidence, both Porter and Coates, of

Philadelphia, and E & L brought out editions of *Romola* illustrated
by photogravures from actual photographs. The choice of pictures
was inevitably similar but fortunately not identical. E & L had two
editions of *Romola*: the "Florentine Edition," in two volumes, bound
in white vellum cloth with red and gold stamping, at $6; a limited
edition of 250 copies had the sixty photogravures and two additional etchings at $15. The limited edition was presented in a scarlet
box and scarlet slip covers; the vellum binding was illuminated
with scarlet and gold tracery and fleur-de-lis designs. The Philadelphia firm also had two editions and most reviewers found it difficult to choose between their books and E & L's, some preferring
the typography of Porter and Coates and the pictures of E & L.[81]
At any rate, the use of photogravures from photographs was an important innovation that would reduce illustration costs immediately. Also, the *Critic* noted that E & L's *Romola* was nearly sold out
by November 1, showing that the public was perfectly willing to
have this type of illustration.

It is impossible to do justice to the many titles published in
1890. *Hans of Iceland,* also translated by Abby L. Alger, was another de luxe edition, in the same style as *Notre-Dame de Paris*.
The translation was termed "admirable" and the numerous etchings, photogravures and half-tones were generally praised.[82] Charles
Reinick's *Night Song*, with pictures by Henry Sandham, was put
out to satisfy the sentimental trade, as was also *Dreams of the Sea,*
with tinted photogravures.[83] The *Critic* thought that the latter work
was rather presumptuously dedicated "to Him who rules the
waves."[84] *Our Great Actors* was a portfolio with six watercolors,
including Booth as Richelieu, Salvini as Macbeth, Jefferson as Bob
Acres, Coquelin as Mascarille, Barrett as Paolo da Rimini, and
Irving as Mephistopheles. Then there was Camille Flammarion's
Urania, a semiscientific romance, whimsical and fantastic. All reviewers praised this book for its fine translation and particularly
for its luxurious form—its illustrations by French artists, its
sumptuous binding.[85] A new asteroid discovered in 1890 was named
Iclea after the heroine of *Urania. The Eve of St. Agnes,* a revamped
edition in the "illuminated missal style," was called "unique" by
E & L and fortunately remained so. There was also a fine decorated
edition of Laura Richards' *Captain January,* and revivals of *Lalla
Rookh,* Tennyson's verses, and even Darley's *Pen and Pencil
Sketches,* now twenty years old.

Goupil's Paris Salon of 1890 was of the same style and price as
the successful work of 1889, and there was a *Goupil Gallery of Great
War Paintings,* a selection of battle scenes from recent Parisian

salons. One of the best books, however, was Samuel Adams Drake's *The Pine Tree Coast.* Everyone seemed to like it, noting the singular talents of the author for such a book and lauding its engaging style, which made the reader long to see the places described. It was full of local color; old salts and older wrecks, quaint figures of the past, old buildings; an antiquarian tour that was obviously a labor of love for the author. There were pictures for nearly every page, hundreds of them in all, new photographs and old woodcuts. Drake did not emphasize the resort areas but sought out places that other writers had passed over.[86] One can imagine the interest Dana Estes, himself from Maine, would take in this book, and he certainly gave it handsome presentation.

The year 1890 saw the start of a new series of de luxe editions of famous authors. The sets in the 1880's had also been de luxe editions, but these of the nineties were, to borrow the modern phrase, super de luxe, though not in the meretricious sense in which the term is frequently employed today. E & L had tested the American market steadily during the eighties for all types of special editions and it had responded beyond their expectations. Other American publishers had done the same, and the book-buying public seemed inexhaustible. It was only natural, therefore, for Estes to expand his subscription activities, and in Walter M. Jackson he had the ideal man for such business organization.

The set for 1890 was an *édition de luxe* of Dickens. As advertised by Estes, it was "the nearest approach to the highest ideals of perfection in book-making ever attempted in this country."[87] With new type and special paper, its chief novelty was, of course, the illustrations, which would be "incomparably superior to any ever issued in any edition printed in this country and only excelled—if at all—by the illustrations in the original parts." All the original etchings (four hundred) by Cruikshank, Seymour, Browne, Stone, Cattermole, Doyle, Leech, Maclise, Landseer and others would be re-etched from original proof impressions. The wood engravings for *Barnaby Rudge* and other novels would be done by electrotypes furnished by Dickens' original publishers, with both types of pictures reproduced on imperial Japan paper. There were also twelve portraits of Dickens by famous artists, in chronological order, which would appear throughout the set, thus showing his appearance at the time of writing his different works. This edition was limited to one thousand sets, twice as large as the limited editions of the eighties, and appeared in forty-five volumes, at the rate of two volumes a month. Bound in vellum, each volume cost $2.50, to be sold by subscription only, in complete sets. Here was a truly handsome set, with the illustrations almost entirely by the original artists, and not one of those hybrids, which Percy Fitzgerald condemned, with pictures from many eras dispersed through the set, artists of completely differing styles put almost side by side, and some pictures meant for a small page set lonesomely in the center of a large one.[88]

At this point it seems appropriate to discuss the subscription book trade in the 1890's. Twenty years before, the book trade had been notably uneasy, even anxious, concerning the inroads of subscription selling but by the nineties the subscription business was recognized as an important and useful part of the book trade. Most of the large houses now had subscription departments with large corps of commercial travelers, many of them selling directly to individual customers. Some distributing firms had as many as five thousand salesmen, and it was estimated that in Chicago alone there were as many as twenty thousand.[89] By the 1890's subscription selling grossed about 12 million dollars yearly, but much of this came from cheap books, not special sets. For the cheap sets and popular books on etiquette, Indians, travel, life among the Mormons, famous people, and history, large printings were a necessity: some publishers counted on selling a hundred thousand copies, and a marketing of fifty thousand sets was not unknown.

Adolf Growoll described three distinct classes of subscription books.[90] First came the fine-art works, containing etchings, photogravures, steel or copperplate engravings, and the large works of reference; most of them were among the choicest works from the American printer, usually expensive and appealing to the wealthy bookbuyer and to libraries. Many would not have sold well in the ordinary bookstore but would do well when pushed by shrewd salesmen. The second class comprised history, biography, memoirs, books of travel, atlases, all works of medium price for the general reader. The third class was made up of popular works, intended for the great multitude who never visited a bookstore.

Despite the appeal inherent in many of these books, it was the canvasser himself who made the success of subscription selling. The hawker of books, if sufficiently "posted" and skillful in conversation, could, with necessary perseverance, bring to his net the cultivated and wealthy reader as well as the man of moderate means. Growoll was sure that the America of the nineties was a nation of bookbuyers, strange as it might appear to the trade, but the books had to be sold by personal magnetism. When people who were successful in business were approached by a persuasive agent they were often seized by a desire for books, vaguely hoping to do something for their neglected education. They were usually familiar with names such as Scott, Thackeray, Dickens, Bulwer, and Eliot and would buy them in any edition offered. Some of these sets had clumsy volumes printed on spongy paper, costing double what they should, yet they were rammed through by the salesman who "knew the ropes."

Growoll believed that a different type of agent was needed to sell the fine-art works, the de luxe editions. There was, indeed, a distinct hierarchy among agents, for some would not handle low-priced books at all, and some subscription books were outrageously expensive. Good canvassers for costly books expected to make from $150 to $500 a month. For this sort of book the agent had to be a man of culture and agreeable manners, a gentleman, in short, and of good address, since he had to move in the best circles. He must have a fair education, be a good judge of human nature, and be aware of the variety of mankind. He must also be honest, quick-witted, intelligent, and he must know the work he tried to sell, be able to answer questions about it, and not lie about its merits. Such people, thought Growoll, were really doing missionary work by introducing good books and works of art in circles that otherwise would never have heard of them.

Thus, many big publishers allotted the largest share of their distribution budget to subscription selling, with lesser amounts for bookstore and direct-mail selling. Harper, in 1910, set aside fifteen thousand dollars for subscription books, twelve thousand dollars for bookstores and nine thousand dollars for direct mail.[91] Elbert Hubbard proved, of course, how profitable selling by mail could be, but the book agent was to remain supreme until World War I. Nor did he disappear after 1914; on the contrary, he is still with us, chiefly for encyclopedias and dictionaries now, but also for religious books, medical books, and the like. In the 1920's Frank Shay sold books from a bookmobile—an old Ford stuffed with tomes, which he called his "peregrinating palanquin of bibliopolic treasures," but this was in the crazy twenties.[92]

How did the folks in the nineties like the book salesman? Probably some did, and perhaps more didn't, but the following exchange of letters may offer a humorous sidelight to this noble art. It started with a circular letter sent by Funk and Wagnalls to a group of reviewers, one of them being Julian Hawthorne. After a few words about the book being sent for review, the letter continues:

> In these very hard times many worthy persons (very many more than usual) are compelled to make a living by book-canvassing—a means of livelihood that is surely

honorable, but one that has been made the butt of so many
jibes and jokes by the press that there has arisen an un-
due prejudice against it, so that earnest and honest men
and women who *must* canvass to supply themselves and
their families find that the burden of this task is made
much greater.

Very often the canvassers are young men, sometimes
young women, working their way through college. Society
is unintentionally doing an injustice to these people, and
may easily be doing a real injury to itself. The public
once welcomed the canvasser as a public educator. Has
not the pendulum swung too far to the other extreme?

Daniel Webster paid his second term's tuition at Dartmouth by canvassing for De Tocqueville's "America." In
the rooms of the Massachusetts Historical Society may be
seen a canvassing-book used by Longfellow, on one of the
leaves of which is his first draft of the poem 'Excelsior.'
Prince Bismarck, when a student at Heidelberg, during
a winter's vacation canvassed for one of Blumenbach's
handbooks. And George Washington tells us how, prior
to the Braddock defeat, he sold in the neighborhood of
Alexandria 200 copies of Bydell's 'American Savage.'
Said the Rev. John Todd: 'I am satisfied publishing and
selling books by subscription is yet in its infancy. I re-
joice in this carrying the waters of knowledge to the very
doors of the people and coaxing them to drink.' And says
Dr. Talmage, with that delightful emphasis of exaggeration that marks the oratorical temperament: 'I always
feel like lifting my hat to a book agent, because he is doing more good than I can ever hope to do. . . .'

Possibly you would be willing to help pluck a thorn
from the path of canvassers by adding a word or two in
their behalf?

Yours very respectfully,
Funk & Wagnalls Company.[93]

Julian Hawthorne, who knew nothing concerning the data presented in Funk and Wagnalls' letter, replied as follows:

Dear Sirs,
As to the thorn-plucking industry, I fear I cannot help
you. I have no desire to prolong the existence of book
canvassing. In spite of your formidable array of names,
I regard him and her as unmitigated evils and nuisances.
They are usually employed by publishers to work off
showy but worthless books which could not be disposed

of in the usual way—the legitimate way. They are trained to talk a man into a state of imbecility, and then, under the guise of giving him something he does not want, to rob him of his money. Some good books have been canvassed; so much the worse for them—though not, of course, for the pockets of the publishers, who (and not the canvassers) are the real beneficiaries. They grow rich by extortion, instead of by fair barter and sale. A good book will make its way through the ordinary channels of trade; a bad or indifferent book ought to be buried as soon as may be. A good book that sells more copies by canvassing than by advertising is, precisely to that extent, taking what does not belong to it . . . . When the country was crude and undeveloped there was some excuse for canvassing; but now, when the whole reading community can be reached by honest advertising, which leaves the public its peace, privacy and freewill, no pretext will serve.

I am willing to pardon George Washington for having been a book-canvasser because he was the Father of His Country, and may have thought himself justified in disciplining it; moreover, it disposes forever of that impression that he was incapable of telling a lie. Daniel Webster's subsequent career may perhaps condone the sin of his youth; but I dare say that, had he never been a book-canvasser, he would have been President. The fact that Longfellow wrote 'Excelsior' on the fly-leaf of the book he was trying to foist on the public proves that he had become aware of his degradation, and was resolved to get out of it, if it cost him his life. As for Bismarck, the success of his political career has been mainly due to his genius for being hectoring and disagreeable, and he perceived early that no training for such a life could be so efficient as that of a book-canvasser. I know nothing particular about the Rev. Mr. Todd; but I suppose it is only natural he should wish to 'coax the people to drink.' About Mr. Talmage I do know a little; he once sent me for review a subscription-book of his own manufacture; the prospectus declared that with that volume and the Bible a man could get through the world triumphant; though why he dragged the Bible in I know not. I am happy to learn that my opinion about canvassing and Mr. Talmage's are diametrically opposed. *Liberavi animam meam.*

Sincerely yours
J. Hawthorne

Probably Julian Hawthorne's viewpoint was only the exception that proved the rule, especially when we consider the enormous subscription-book sales in the nineties, but it was refreshing!

For E & L, the years from 1891 to 1894 were a continuation of the sumptuous publishing that had characterized most of the 1880's. The Panic of 1893, followed by several years of depression, effectively limited their business in luxurious books. By 1895 their production of such works had dwindled to a trickle, and they found it advantageous to revive old favorites from their list and to concentrate on cheaper editions. The stream was unchecked until then, however, and impressive and costly works were produced, some of them among their finest achievements.

The new sets of standard authors were clearly most important. A new *édition de luxe* of Thackeray was announced as early as January, 1891, and a similar edition of Bulwer-Lytton came in March. The set of Thackeray was advertised as having a new font of type especially cast for it, with paper that was durable but also light in weight, so that the volume would be easy to hold. There were 210 woodcuts from Thackeray's own drawings and photogravure reproductions from paintings of Millais, Barnard, and Luke Fildes; also, twenty original etchings plus twenty-five etchings after Cruikshank, and photogravures and half-tones from photographs of places, about eighty altogether. This Kensington Edition, limited to one thousand copies now that demand had enabled E & L to raise the goal above the smaller quantities standard in the 1880's, was, seemingly, over-illustrated, but the popularity of the de luxe Dickens, as E & L affirmed, had prompted this approach. Printed in thirty volumes, bound in English vellum cloth, "library style," with paper titles, uncut, this set cost the subscriber $2.50 a volume.[94] The set of Bulwer, which E & L called the "best and only elegantly illustrated library edition" of this author, though the distinction appeared to lie solely in the illustrations, possessed two hundred photogravures from paintings by "noted American illustrators" or reproductions of actual places. As in all their de luxe editions, the pictures were "proof impressions on imperial Japanese paper," a phrase which lends unquestioned dignity and some artistic merit. In this set, also, natural-tint laid paper was employed, similar to hand-made paper, with no clay or other filling. There were thirty-two volumes in the set of Bulwer, at the usual $2.50 per volume.

These editions were, of course, very fine, at least to the taste of most Americans in the 1890's; possibly the $2.50 charged for each volume was not ridiculous, but it was surely extravagant. Yet the glamour of the photogravures and especially of the etchings was almost irresistible to people who were not always competent to judge the worth of the text and who probably would not read these particular volumes anyhow. An edition of George Eliot was announced in June, 1891, as well as a truly sumptuous Scott, which I shall describe later. George Eliot de luxe included 125 etchings and photogravures, this time from drawings by American illustrators such as Dielman, Harper, Sandham, Taylor, Garrett, Merrill, and Champney, a group that E & L used constantly, as did many other publishers. The other pictures were the inexpensive sort reproduced from photographs of places. This set of twenty-four volumes sold at the uniform price, $2.50 each.

In 1892 there appeared an edition of Victor Hugo, which E & L declared was the first to include all the romances, travels, poems, and dramas. In format like the previous *éditions de luxe,* it was blessed with two hundred etchings and photogravures by French artists, most of the plates being reproduced by Goupil and Company of Paris. This was a set of thirty volumes. The year 1893 saw editions of Dumas and Scott. The Dumas was in forty volumes, by a group of translators, among them Katherine Prescott Wormeley, who had made such a reputation by her translation of Balzac, done for Roberts Brothers. The set was the "only finely illustrated edition of the principal romances," having two hundred etchings and photogravures by such artists as Neuville, Leloir, Bayard, Flameng, Lefort, and a group of American artists, with portraits and landscapes, some from photographs, as fillers. There was strong competition here from Little, Brown, Appleton, and Crowell, whose editions were all profusely illustrated.

Of the editions mentioned, only the Scott was truly superior in both text and illustrations. All the other sets had won favorable notice: the *Critic* had remarked that no works were better suited than Bulwer's for a luxurious format and that there were no sumptuous editions available at the time, especially when people were eager to own choice editions of such standard authors.[95] The *Literary World* expressed similar views about the sets of both Thackeray and Bulwer [96] though a little later citing a New York bookseller's disillusioned definition of an *édition de luxe*: "You know what a rabbit is; well, a donkey is an *édition de luxe* of a rabbit."[97] The *Critic*, however, felt that Boston was fortunate to have the distinction of publishing the finest edition of Scott.[98] Work started on the illustrations in 1891: Dana Estes himself made many of the arrangements in France for the etchings and photogravures and also selected many of the photographs of places which would appear in the set. E & L declared that they spent forty thousand dollars on proof impressions of the three hundred etchings and photogravures; many of these were from paintings by English, Scottish, and French artists, such as Millais, R. W. Macbeth, Gordon Browne, John Pettie, Lefort, and Lalauze. This time the text was outstanding, since all Scott's prefaces and notes were reprinted as well as introductions and notes to each work by Andrew Lang. The set, first called the International Illustrated Edition, was soon dubbed the Andrew Lang Edition, and quite appropriately. E & L, with characteristic bombast, termed it the "most magnificent edition ever made of the works of any novelist," but most people knew how to take such claims. The set was in forty-eight volumes, at the usual $2.50 per volume, but there was an even more limited edition (five hundred copies) on Holland hand-made paper, with fifty additional illustrations, at $5 per volume.

The *Critic,* in the same article, pointed out that the expenditure of time and money was clearly warranted by the demand of the public for such works. Americans would pay $120,000 for a thousand sets of Scott, not counting the more limited edition of five hundred copies, which would bring in an equivalent amount. Yet so eager were subscribers to obtain these sets that the fifteen hundred copies of Dickens sold within thirteen months of publication; the one thousand copies of Thackeray, issued in January, 1891, were gone by June; and three quarters of the thousand copies of Bulwer, issued May 1, 1891, were sold by June 6, 1891. And the last-selling copies were raised from $2.50 to $3.00 a volume! It was clear, said the writer, that these quick sales demonstrated the readiness of the public to expend money liberally for what pleased its artistic fancy. Unquestionably, the purchaser who could afford sets of this cost would have already in his library ordinary "working" sets of all the standard authors. When he asked E & L where most demand for such sets had been shown, he was pleased to learn, "to the credit of the West, which we are so apt to characterize as wild rather than cultivated," that one half of each edition had been taken by agents around St. Louis and Chicago. The Far West took only 5 to 10 per cent of the amount, the South practically none. And this new spate of de luxe editions came from E & L's taking over an incomplete Dickens from another publisher and turning it into a publishing triumph!

The *Critic* continued to rhapsodize over each new novel to appear in the set of the "Waverley Novels." The *Literary World,* upon the publication of *Waverley,* in 1893, noted that the English version of the set was called the Border Edition and was published by

Nimmo in London, but praised the superior typographical beauty of these large-paper volumes, printed by the University Press.

The reviewer especially admired the dark green binding with paper labels in red and black. Lang's introduction was "felicitous in style," and the reviewer gave several long quotations. He thought the illustrations the most successful ever done for Scott's novels.[99] The *Critic* was much more detailed in its praise. Lang's prefaces admirably fulfilled their purpose of giving the stories their historical setting by telling of the circumstances in which they were composed, explaining pertinent bits of Highland lore, telling what books Scott used for his background, and giving other bibliographical data. Lang drew heavily on J. G. Lockhart's biography but also utilized Scott's correspondence, kept at Abbotsford. The reviewer believed that most readers would enjoy Lang's comments, so good on Celtic genealogy and myth, and would only wish that they were longer.

The *Critic* was impressed by the artistic value of the illustrations. In *Waverley* there was an etched portrait of Scott, after a painting by Raeburn, then a series of etchings and photogravures such as R. W. Macbeth's "The Hold of a Highland Robber," Robert Herdman's "Prince Charles Edward in Shelter," John Pettie's "Disbanded," and others by Scottish and English artists, all on heavy Japan paper. The same admiration was offered *The Antiquary*, whose notes and pictures alike were thought very fine. The large number of pictures from the "Scotch School" was highly commended as giving popular flavor. There is no need to run through the remaining volumes: *Ivanhoe, Kenilworth, The Pirate*, all were admired. Toward the end, it was noted that the illustrations were not always uniform in quality, being the work of so many hands, and that the use of French illustrators, such as Lalauze, would inevitably clash somewhat with the Scottish style, but all felt that it was still the most sumptuous edition for the book lover.[100]

The gift books for these same years, 1891 through 1894, were nearly as sumptuous as the sets, although there were no more of those exaggeratedly limited editions costing as high as $150. They followed much the same pattern as before, the illustrated poems, the extra-illustrated novels from sets of authors to be published or already published, volumes of pictures (etchings or photogravures), with the major novelty a series of volumes on great cities. Thus, in 1891 appeared the Sterling Edition of Scott's *Lady of the Lake*, which all reviewers praised highly for its illustrations and its handsome format. The pictures were photogravures from photographs of Highland scenery, most of them unfamiliar and quite artistic. The volume was bound in white vellum cloth with gold stamping, protected by red slip covers. One of the most attractive of the season's books, was the judgment of the *Nation*, the *Critic*, and the *Literary World*.[101] Almost equal praise was showered upon *Rienzi* and *The Last Days of Pompeii*, each illustrated with fifty photogravures (tinted, alas!) from photographs. Most reviewers spent time extolling individual scenes, as well as the "faultless typography of the University Press."[102] *Arcadian Days*, made up of thirteen essays by W. H. Downes on American landscapes, won favor in Boston because the author was art critic of the *Boston Transcript*.[103] The travel book was Virginia W. Johnson's *Lily of the Arno, or Florence Past and Present*, an enthusiastic, gossipy work, illustrated with the inevitable photogravures, many personally selected by Estes himself.[104] All of these books were brilliantly bound, during the early nineties, usually in white vellum cloth with colored stamping in intricate arabesque designs, often very striking; these white bindings were protected by red slip covers and the books were often boxed as well. This book was quite a bargain at three dollars and the only expensive gift books this year were the novels by Bulwer, which ranged from six to fifteen dollars in a limited edition. It should not be forgotten, however, that Goupil's *Paris Salon*, which was now an annual feature, cost from fifteen to eighteen dollars, making it the really de luxe production. In 1892 Goupil published its own version in the United States, but E & L started a new series by Ludovic Baschet with the *Salon for 1892* and so on, selling at a slightly lower price than Goupil's.

For 1892, Virginia Johnson presented *Genoa the Superb, the City of Columbus*, largely because of the approaching Columbian Exposition. The *Lily of the Arno* had been very successful and E & L set out to exploit this new area, one that coincided with Dana Estes' new interests in European travel and archeological searching.[105] A new series, the "Exquisite Series," taken from French editions published by the distinguished Parisian bibliophile firm, Jouaust, with etchings chiefly by Lalauze, was much admired for its "dainty books."[106] They were, of course, small books of unusual taste in design, bound in half parchment and half silk, called "Editions Elzéviriennes" in Paris. The title for 1892 was *The Vicar of Wakefield*, and succeeding years saw such works as La Fontaine's *Fables* and *Paul and Virginia*.[107] Another novelty reflected Estes' interest in the Browning Society in Boston. As early as May, 1891, he had been on the executive committee, because of his undoubted administrative talent and energy, and had shared honors with such worthies as Thomas Wentworth Higginson as master of ceremonies at banquets. In 1892, E & L published Browning's *Prose Life of Strafford*, dividing the cost with the London Browning Society. The work was a curiosity, done in Browning's youth for *Lardner's Cabinet Cyclopaedia*, actually as a favor for John Forster who had fallen ill and could not fulfill his contract.[108]

The outstanding books for the next two years were the travel books, Clara Erskine Clement's *The Queen of the Adriatic, or Venice Mediaeval and Modern* (1893) and *Naples, the City of Parthenope* (1894). They combined history in popular style with rambles through the modern cities; they were lively and entertaining, full of anecdotes and quotations. The book on Venice took liberal slices from Gibbon, Hazlitt, Monckton Milnes, Helen Hunt, and Ruskin, with no lack of sometimes gushing comment by the author. Nevertheless, they were thoroughly readable, beautifully illustrated and richly bound—and not expensive![109] The volume on Naples was equally good, and on a city not so frequently described. The *Nation* thought it particularly fine, since the author was aware of her limitations and gave an accurate and tasteful survey instead of a pretentious hodgepodge.[110] So pleased were E & L with the success of the *Queen of the Adriatic* that they presented Mrs. Clara Clement Waters with a splendid, calf-bound copy, done expressly for her in London.[111] Mrs. Waters did volumes entitled *Constantinople, the City of the Sultans* (1895) and *The Eternal City, Rome* (1896), not quite so successful, perhaps, as the first two,[112] and these were followed by Eustace Reynolds-Ball's *Cairo, the City of the Caliphs*, all elaborately illustrated. In text and pictures these books were the equal of most volumes on cities and in format were more inviting than any rival volumes in the 1890's.

The other volumes of this period were largely the extra-illustrated "holiday editions" of novels. The Lang Edition of Scott provided a fruitful supply for several years, as did the editions of Hugo and Dumas. Thus in 1893 *Ivanhoe* was presented with twenty illustrations (twelve etchings, eight photogravures) by Lalauze in both trade and limited editions, the latter of 150 copies, and costing $15 for two volumes. *Les Misérables* appeared in five volumes, with 120 half-tones for a change, plus the usual etchings and photogravures; *Ruy Blas* was adorned by etchings after Adrien Moreau and was limited to five hundred copies. With the usual apparatus of lush bindings, slip covers and boxes, E & L were wisely utilizing their heavy outlay on the sets to make successful gift books. *Kenilworth, Heart of Mid-Lothian*, and *Hernani* were featured in 1894; *Rob Roy*, Dumas' *D'Artagnan Romances*, and Hugo's *Letters to His Wife* in 1895. Another series entitled "Masterpieces of English Literature" served to mine from the already published sets such books as *David Copperfield, Vanity Fair,* and the like, each published in two volumes, with ten full-page etchings, at $2.50 a pair. Still cheaper were the "Roxburghe Classics," including about one hundred titles from standard authors, priced from $1 to $2. By 1894 times were bad, and sumptuous editions could not be emphasized as before.

This fact is borne out even more clearly by the slim list offered in 1895, when there were only about three new works, with a dressing-up of former favorites to fill out the list, and most emphasis on children's books. Hugo's *Letters to His Wife,* translated by Nathan H. Dole, included much not found in any other edition, and was of real value for the text, not the pictures. A curious novelty was the frantic translation of Charles Nodier's *Trilby, the Fairy of Argyle* early in 1895, to capitalize on the vogue of Du Maurier's novel. E & L and Lamson, Wolffe and Company, also of Boston, raced to get out a translation first. E & L gave the task to Nathan Haskell Dole, who accomplished the work in four days: the copy was sent to the printer chapter by chapter, proof returned and plates cast, so that just five days after the French book had been handed to Dole the printed sheets were coming from the press. The bound copies were on sale five days later, just twenty hours before Lamson, Wolffe had their version available.[113] It hardly seemed worth the trouble but it was exciting!

The final years of E & L—to 1898, that is—had little new to offer. There were each year a few lush works, but so few in comparison to better days! Outside of the handsome volumes of Dumas or George Eliot or Scott there were a few books like the *Memorial Life of Victor Hugo* and Lloyd Mifflin's *At the Gates of Song,* a collection of sonnets which won reviewers' notice. These extra-illustrated novels were still sumptuous, as, for instance, Dumas' *Chevalier de Maison-Rouge,* with its buckram jacket of peacock green, its inner cover stamped in red and gold, its laid paper, uncut edges, gilt tops, and all the luxury of full-page etchings. George Eliot's *Adam Bede* was equally handsome and also limited to 250 copies, for the fastidious.[114] Some liked E & L's revival of the old stories by William Ware, *Zenobia, Julian,* and *Aurelian,* in profusely illustrated editions. Bulwer's *Paul Clifford* was tried, a rather unusual choice for a holiday book, and George Sand's *Consuelo* was handsomely featured in 1897.[115] More interesting was a book such as Thomas Steele's *A Voyage to Viking-Land* (1896), which the *Critic* thought the best popular account yet of a tour of Scandinavia, and which was illustrated with humble half-tones from the author's photographs. Except for children's books, however, illustrated holiday books were sadly in decline.

The last activity of the firm was in sets of standard authors, but cheaper sets now, until times were better. In 1897 E & L had put out an edition of Justin McCarthy's *History of Our Own Times*, with twenty-four photogravure portraits, in four volumes; also the Brontës' works, in a cheap edition. In 1898, just at the moment of the firm's reorganization, E & L took over the series of Cabinet Editions published by Merrill and Baker in New York, really a subsidiary enterprise of Walter Jackson, which reverted to E & L on his departure. Merrill and Baker had an imposing array of favorite authors published in moderately priced editions. The volumes were octavo in size, usually with cheap leather bindings though they were obtainable in cloth. There was always a photogravure frontispiece to each volume, which, in a final blow at good taste, was hand-tinted in excruciating shades; the remaining illustrations were fairly numerous woodcuts. These editions, though called "de luxe," were certainly not limited, as was obvious from the broken type and scarred illustrations. With decorative bindings they looked impressive on the shelves, and the corps of salesmen trained by Jackson had no difficulty selling them at $1.25 a volume. Each volume, by the way, usually included two volumes bound in one, so that the customer got fair value. Many of these sets were the old E & L plates of the 1880's, doing noble service years later; some were entirely new sets, planned by Jackson or his colleagues.

Thus E & L acquired the following new authors for their list: Washington Irving, in ten volumes; J. Fenimore Cooper, in sixteen volumes; and Ruskin, in thirteen volumes. The other names are familiar already from E & L's publishing: Dickens, Bulwer, Thackeray, George Eliot, Carlyle, Hume, Guizot's *France,* Dumas, Scott, Fielding, and Hugo. After the recent emphasis on luxury editions E & L had an opportunity to put their canvassers to work on these useful sets. The set of Dickens, for example, was clearly printed and had photogravure frontispieces and over two hundred illustrations on steel and wood: its fifteen volumes sold for only $18.75 in buckram, $22.50 in half seal morocco. The other sets were correspondingly priced, some of them, like the Ruskin, being real bargains. Such works were good for a depression, but Dana Estes, after the feast of splendor, must have found this fare drab enough.

Dana Estes and Co., during its span from 1898 to 1914, published many of the same types of illustrated books favored by E & L. Although there were gift books every year, among them the extra-illustrated classic or sentimental poem, the trend was more dis-

tinctly to works of description and travel, or even to Dana Estes'
first love, books on natural history. The most important illustrated
books were the sets of standard authors, which were renewed, reshuffled, and repriced to meet fresh demands. There are simply too
many of the average gift books during this period to make possible
any study of them. Just a few will be mentioned, to show the tone,
and I shall give more space to the sets, which were a lasting contribution.

For 1898 there were no real "gift books," unless one includes
a biography of Charles Carleton Coffin by his friend, William Griffis,
not an illustrated book in Dana Estes' sense of the word. By 1899,
however, came the final reincarnation of the famous edition of
Lalla Rookh, now reduced to half-tone reproductions of the original
photogravures and selling at only $2.50. The other books were
travels through China and Tibet or in East Africa, or even a
learned morsel such as Sextus Julius Frontinus' first-century account of Rome's water supply! In succeeding years there were rather sloppily sentimental volumes, such as *Among the Flowers,* but
more books on cities, histories, biographies, and nature studies
helped to balance the list. There were no more sumptuous portfolios of prints or super-limited editions; in fact, most of the gift
books were very reasonably priced. Some of the past favorites, like
the books on Venice, Florence, Genoa, Naples, and the rest, which
had done so well in the nineties, were presented in new editions, at
$1.50 each, in 1905. Mrs. Richards' *Journals and Letters of Samuel
Gridley Howe* was an example of the sober work more commonly
found in the list. In 1908 Dana Estes edited two "gift book" volumes
called "The Noble Thoughts Series," including *Thoughts of Marcus
Aurelius* and *Thoughts of John Ruskin.* After his death, in 1909,
the gift books became almost entirely works of travel, many of them
British imports. A few excellent nature books, especially those by
C. W. Townsend, fell into this category. During the firm's last years
there were series, "Beautiful England Series," "Estes' Rambles
Series," "Mountain Climbs Series," "Beautiful Ireland Series,"
"The World's Romances," "Beautiful Switzerland Series," and the
like, but all of these were foreign imports and showed no originality.

One must conclude that, following the breakup of E & L, Dana
Estes followed the line of least resistance in the preparation of
holiday books, attempting to make them less expensive, less pretentious and less conventional. Although many of the choices were
good, both before and after his death, they rarely bore any impress
of originality, and, in the last years, were simply borrowed wholesale from English lists. While Estes was interested in travel books

he never seemed able to attract any truly outstanding works to his list: most are pleasant and adequate, little more than ephemeral, books that still are found on library shelves but are obviously dated. E & L had established a reputation for sumptuous illustrating, the *édition de grand luxe,* but Dana Estes and Co. did not maintain this prestige, chiefly because the times no longer seemed propitious and also because Estes himself had wearied of it, at least as regards single volumes. Whatever energies he possessed were employed in the fashioning of his beloved sets.

It was perhaps characteristic that the first advertisement of Dana Estes and Co., in 1898, should feature Lang's edition of the "Waverley Novels."[116] This was not, of course, the de luxe edition of 1893 but what one may call a reshuffled version, bound in twenty-five volumes, with 130 etchings (the de luxe edition had three hundred) and selling at $1.50 a volume. It was called by Estes the Andrew Lang Edition. Then there was the Illustrated Cabinet Edition, which was to become a standard name for the more expensive sets. It presented the novels in forty-eight volumes, with 250 etchings, at $1.50 or $3, depending on the binding. By 1899, ten of these sets had been prepared, embracing Shakespeare (Hudson Edition), Eliot, Hugo, Prescott, Thackeray, Dickens, Scott, Ruskin, Bulwer, and Charles Reade. Prescott and Reade were new to Estes' list; the edition of Reade was first advertised, in fact, in September, 1899. In the description of the sixteen-volume set, the fine English deckle-edge paper, the eighty photogravures and etchings by Frank Merrill and others were celebrated, but nothing was said about new plates. In a set of Bulwer advertised at the same time, a "practically new set of plates" was mentioned, and the 125 photogravures and etchings were by the group that had worked on the de luxe edition of 1892.

All of these Illustrated Cabinet Editions were less sumptuous and, naturally, less expensive than the de luxe sets. Thus Bulwer's novels appeared in twenty-five volumes, with no limitation of numbers, whereas the de luxe set had included thirty-two volumes, with seventy-five more pictures, proof impressions on Japan paper, and similar niceties. Thackeray's works were in twenty volumes in the Cabinet Edition as compared with thirty volumes in the de luxe edition, and contained nearly as many pictures, lacking only some of the etchings. In the instance of George Eliot's writings, the volumes and number of pictures were identical in both sets. Purchasers of the Cabinet Editions were getting good value, at $1.50 a volume, and had sets that were just as readable and handsome as the others in all vital points.

From this time on there was a continued program of adding authors to the Cabinet Editions, usually one or two sets each
year. In 1900, Estes also inaugurated the Illustrated Sterling
Editions, which were cheaper versions of these same sets. Thus in
January, 1900, there were fourteen sets of this type, including
Dickens, George Eliot, Bulwer, Scott, Carlyle, Hugo, Guizot, Fielding, Hume, Cooper, Irving, Ruskin, Thackeray, and Dumas. These
were really the sets taken over from Merrill and Baker in 1898 and
given a new name; they now sold at $1 and $2, according to the binding, and contained some illustrations, including etching or photogravure frontispieces. The advertising stressed the larger number of
illustrations than in most inexpensive sets, and asserted that they
were superior in typography, paper, and binding to the ordinary
cheap set. Be that as it may, they were good values for the time and
were increased in number along with the Cabinet Editions, although
some different authors were included.

In 1900 appeared a small set of Melville's novels, in holiday
garb, later to be incorporated into the Sterling Edition. The revival
of Melville was apparently timed to benefit from increased interest
in the Pacific after 1898. A little later, the old set of books on
Napoleon, dating back to 1882 in E & L's list, comprising Hazlitt's
Life, Bourrienne's *Memoirs* and those of Mme Junot, were published in the Cabinet Edition, and two new authors, Marryat
and Eugène Sue, came out in large sets of twenty-four and twenty
volumes respectively. Soon after, Schiller, Goethe, and Green's
History of the English People were resurrected for the Sterling
Edition. So it went, undoubtedly a large-scale operation and a very
shrewd one, since it utilized all the hard work, not to say expense,
of the past, for very attractive large series that could be marketed
easily and for an indefinite period.

It is scarcely worth while chronicling the revival of the older
sets but it is appropriate to say a word about the new ones. Before
long, for nearly every author already published by E & L, there
were three editions: the Cabinet Edition ($1.50 per volume); the
Handy Volume Edition, usually in half the number of volumes of
the Cabinet Edition ($1.25 per volume); and the Sterling Edition,
often in still fewer volumes ($1 per volume). Plutarch's *Lives*
came out in three volumes in 1902. This was followed by Scott's
Poems in six, and Tennyson's *Poems* in twelve volumes—in Cabinet
Editions. In the case of Tennyson, the International Copyright Act
of 1891, for which Dana Estes had fought so energetically, served
to put a crimp in this edition, since Macmillan refused to give print-

ing rights, at any price, on some poems published after 1891. As the subscribers had been promised a complete Tennyson, Dana Estes had to buy sheets from Macmillan and inlay each sheet into the larger leaf of the Cabinet Edition.[117]

Saintsbury's translation of Balzac was published in 1903 in the Cabinet and Sterling Editions, in thirty-six and eighteen volumes, respectively. This was, of course, a fine version, perhaps not so brilliant as Miss Wormeley's, but one that has remained a favorite. A set of Edgar Allan Poe appeared in 1904, in six volumes, followed by the writings of Charles Lamb. The following year there was a new Shakespeare in the Cabinet Edition, edited by W. J. Rolfe, and a cheap Pocket Edition, edited by Israel Gollancz, which was widely advertised as a bargain, since its forty volumes cost only twenty-five cents each.

Other formats of Shakespeare were published in 1906 as was a revival of Guizot's *History of England,* which had not been on the firm's list for twenty years. There was also Dumas' *Celebrated Crimes,* another new work for Dana Estes. By this time the roster of sets had become most imposing and they were praised in the Christmas Number of the *Publishers' Weekly* for 1906.[118] A really original venture was the new translation of Tolstoy by Professor Leo Wiener of Harvard, a set of twenty-four volumes. There were introductions and notes by Dr. Hagbert Wright and Aylmer Maude, with a life of Tolstoy, bibliography, and general index, features not ordinarily found in these sets. The translations were advertised as "uncensored" and extra pains were taken with the transliteration of Russian names. There were seventy illustrations, either reproductions of paintings by Russian artists, facsimile pages from Russian books and manuscripts, or pictures by French artists such as Detaille and Desnoyers. Somewhat by exception this set also appeared in limited editions: the Connoisseur Edition was limited to 150 numbered sets, the Edition des Amateurs to fifty numbered sets. A few of the other Cabinet Editions were also available in this form, notably Scott and Carlyle; the name Connoisseur Edition was used for the 1893 version of Andrew Lang's "Waverley Novels," in a specially limited edition at $5 a volume. Another newcomer to the list was Jane Austen, whose novels, with introductions by William Lyon Phelps and illustrations by C. E. and H. M. Brock, were published in sets.

A series of "British Poets," in the Cabinet Edition, came out in 1908. The poets, Thomas Hood, Shelley, Keats, Scott, Gray, and Burns, and a book of *Great Dramatists,* made, in all, fifteen volumes. Four volumes were then added to the set of Dumas, making it next to the largest set in the Cabinet Editions, a total of thirty-eight volumes, exceeded only by the forty-five volumes of Scott. After Estes' death no new authors were added, although a few variations were made in the bindings and prices of the sets already established. Thus, in 1910, all of the Sterling Editions were available in another guise, bound in crash, at $1.25 a volume, under the name of New Imperial Library of Standard Sets. There were several colors to be had, and the sets were housed in neat wooden boxes, an attractive merchandising device. Now and then a single work was taken from a set for extra-illustration, as Goethe's *Faust* was illustrated by Willy Pogany in 1911. A little later the firm prepared Handy Volume Editions, in flexible leather bindings, of Rolfe's *Shakespeare,* Hugo's *Les Misérables* and favorite works by Ruskin, but the basic list of sets was as before. When Dana Estes and Co. were bought by L. C. Page in 1914, the long lists of both Cabinet and Sterling Editions were surely one of the major assets of the firm. In fact, many of these Illustrated Cabinet Editions are still found, with detailed descriptions, in the L. C. Page catalogue, and, scanning the pages of *Bessie Graham's Bookman's Manual,* one frequently discovers the only sets of famous authors still available are these veterans originally published by Dana Estes.

To give some idea of the array of editions for sale in 1914, I shall first list the Cabinet Editions and then the Sterling Editions, in tabular form. There were 480 volumes of twenty-two authors in the Cabinet Editions, with approximately two thousand etchings and photogravures, eight hundred full-page woodcuts and half-tone engravings and hundreds of text illustrations. The binding was in English silk-ribbed cloth, in duodecimo, with gilt tops, the price $1.50 a volume, the books being sold either in sets or separate volumes.

Illustrated Cabinet Editions

Austen	12 volumes	36 color prints
Balzac	36 volumes	139 etchings and photogravures
British Poets	15 volumes	45 etchings and photogravures
Bulwer	25 volumes	125 etchings and photogravures
Carlyle	26 volumes	130 etchings and photogravures
Cooper	32 volumes	100 etchings and photogravures
Dickens	30 volumes	336 etchings and woodcuts
Dumas	38 volumes	182 etchings and photogravures
Dumas, *Celebrated Crimes*	3 volumes	18 etchings and photogravures
Eliot	24 volumes	120 etchings and photogravures

Illustrated Cabinet Editions

Hugo	24 volumes	100 etchings and photogravures
Marryat	24 volumes	150 etchings and photogravures
Napoleon:		
Bourrienne	4 volumes	24 etchings and photogravures
Hazlitt's *Life*	6 volumes	36 etchings and photogravures
Mme Junot	6 volumes	33 etchings and photogravures
Poe	6 volumes	38 etchings and photogravures
Prescott	16 volumes	100 engravings and woodcuts
Reade	18 volumes	90 etchings and photogravures
Ruskin	26 volumes	288 full-page engravings
Scott	48 volumes	251 etchings and photogravures
Scott: *Poems*	6 volumes	35 etchings and photogravures
Shakespeare (Hudson)	12 volumes	36 etchings and photogravures
Shakespeare (Rolfe)	20 volumes	62 etchings and photogravures
Sue	20 volumes	92 etchings and photogravures
Tennyson	12 volumes	60 etchings and photogravures
Thackeray	20 volumes	266 etchings and woodcuts
Tolstoy	24 volumes	75 etchings and photogravures

Illustrated Sterling Editions

Balzac	18 volumes	93 illustrations
Bulwer	15 volumes	108 illustrations
Carlyle	10 volumes	74 illustrations
Cooper	16 volumes	64 illustrations
Defoe	8 volumes	36 illustrations
Dickens	15 volumes	300 illustrations
Dumas	15 volumes	106 illustrations
Eliot	8 volumes	52 illustrations
Fielding	7 volumes	48 illustrations
Goethe	5 volumes	20 illustrations
Guizot's *France*	8 volumes	200 illustrations
Guizot's *England*	4 volumes	84 illustrations
Hugo	10 volumes	50 illustrations
Lamb	5 volumes	37 illustrations
Macaulay	3 volumes	46 illustrations
Melville	4 volumes	20 illustrations

Poe	6 volumes	38 illustrations
Reade	12 volumes	76 illustrations
Ruskin	13 volumes	273 illustrations
Schiller	5 volumes	20 illustrations
Scott	12 volumes	124 illustrations
Shakespeare (Hudson)	10 volumes	40 illustrations
Smollett	6 volumes	24 illustrations
Thackeray	10 volumes	260 illustrations

It will be remembered that the volumes in the Sterling Edition cost one dollar each and that there was always a photogravure frontispiece, with woodcuts or steel engravings as the other illustrations. These were large books (5¾ x 8½), sturdily bound in cloth, and ordinarily containing the equivalent of two volumes in the Cabinet Edition; thus a typical volume might have 850 to 900 pages, on good, opaque paper, in clear, readable though undistinguished typography. They were really excellent bargains and many libraries still have these volumes on their shelves, doing service after all these years.

Such, then, were the sets in which Dana Estes took so much pride. They are representative of another age, when people read complete works of authors, not only individual classics; when sets of standard authors on the shelves were the delight of appreciative readers or the badge of respectability for the less sophisticated. Lucky the boy or girl who could browse in a library full of good sets! An omnivorous reader soon finds that other works than masterpieces give great pleasure, that Dickens or Thackeray or Eliot wrote more than three novels, that one may develop some critical judgment just by reading the great and the lesser works by a distinguished author. The modern home does not welcome sets of authors and a little verse by Ernest Elmo Calkins tells why:

> Dear Sir: How rash to wish for "sets"
> For if his shelf-room one forgets
> That wasted space will bring regrets.
> My Hugo stretches seven feet;
> One-third of him my needs would meet.
> My Balzac is "the works complete";
> The same for Hardy and Voltaire,
> Until I have no space to spare,
> And later more beloved books
> Are hidden in the strangest nooks,
> Nor can be found where'er one looks.[119]

Certainly, books that are not read should not deprive valued books of shelf space, although there is something to be said for the esthetic delight of a truly handsome, illustrated edition. Today, people prefer a single masterpiece to the set, and they are entitled to their preference, which may be a wise one. Nevertheless, although E & L's sets may not have attained the chaste perfection of a Gadshill Dickens, for example, most of them were artistic and readable editions of great writers, and it is certain that some private libraries still cherish them. Again, some of them are still purchased secondhand, if one may judge by dealers' catalogues and records of auction sales, which list them at rather high prices, even today.[120] Whether the vogue for such sets will ever return is difficult to say, but, in the meantime, Dana Estes' editions serve as a monument to a generation that was not afraid to read widely.

Chapter Seven

BUSINESS HISTORY OF ESTES AND LAURIAT AND DANA ESTES AND COMPANY

SINCE previous chapters have described E & L's ventures in publishing works of science, art books, history, and children's books and their temporary or continued success in these fields, this chapter will confine itself to the business aspects of the firm and to its relations with the book trade in general. Because none of the firm's records or correspondence have survived, it is impossible to give the desired details on the yearly changes, the policy decisions of the two partners, and the fluctuations of the business. Only by the external events do we perceive the vigorous direction of Dana Estes and the wise counseling of Charles Lauriat, yet the vigor and enterprise of E & L are obvious from the very start, and, if enterprise could do it, they were going to be successful. Viewing the first two decades of the firm's existence, they seem to have had more than their share of struggles and litigation, but a closer examination reveals that these "growing pains" were a direct result of the energy and tenacity displayed by the head of the publishing section, Dana Estes. Most of this chapter will be taken up with the firm's battles, many of which were directly concerned with the problems of international copyright. After the constant turmoil of the seventies and eighties, the years following 1890 seem placid indeed.

During the fall of 1872, when everything appeared so hopeful, came a narrow escape from complete disaster. On the night of November 9 fire broke out near the corner of Summer and Kingston streets, only a quarter of a mile distant, and within a few hours, despite heroic efforts by the small fire department, it became a major conflagration. Fed by a succession of large warehouses and fanned by a rising wind, the fire burned unchecked through the night, and next morning, on Sunday, it was threatening the business blocks near Washington Street. All through the night merchants, bankers, and householders had worked madly trying to salvage some of their belongings, and the partners of the new firm struggled to remove the choicest stock to a place of safety on Beacon Hill. Looking directly down Milk Street they could see the fire eating its way through the brick and stone buildings, melting the ironwork, and causing stones to explode like bombs. They could see the fire fighters perched dangerously on the roof of the Old South Church, determined to save that historic edifice if human power could do it. Some buildings across the street were blown up, in an attempt to stop the progress of the fire, and the windows of E & L's store were shattered and part of the woodwork destroyed. Some of their less expensive stock was ruined by this blast, and by the water and smoke that poured through the openings, but they could see, with jubilation, that the fire had been blocked by Washington Street and by the fire fighters' valiant defense of the Old South Church. Not until evening was the blaze really checked, but Estes and Lauriat could celebrate their fortunate escape from the Great Boston Fire, one of the worst calamities ever suffered by the city, and figure their losses as trifling indeed, in the general catastrophe.[1]

Many valuable collections of early printed books, illuminated manuscripts, theological works, early Americana, and modern authors had been housed in the burnt district, in fancied security, some in the very warehouses which gave the fire its start. Many of the book collectors, though overwhelmed by the suddenness of the disaster, determined to start again and welcomed the firm of E & L as an aid in carrying out their intention. Through such stimulus as this the bookstore acquired excellent London connections, importing the great Victorians, the finest secondhand items, especially the handsomely illustrated works on art, natural history, and travel which American readers were beginning to fancy. In June, 1873, Charles E. Lauriat made the first of his many trips to Europe to enrich his stock, bringing back numerous bargains in remainders, works from the Continent and particularly from Paris, where French publishers and illustrators were turning out an amazing quantity of sumptuous volumes. The early circulars and catalogues issued by the firm show the astounding bargains in old and contemporary works offered by E & L, and many collectors and many average book lovers made it a point to "drop in at Estes and Lauriat's."[2]

Two other well-known bookstores of this period, Bartlett's and Little, Brown and Co., catered to a somewhat limited range of interests, but E & L were on the lookout for a wider clientele and remained so until Estes and Lauriat became simply Charles E. Lauriat Co., after 1898. The young Charles Goodspeed knew Estes and Lauriat in the 1890's; it was at their shop, in fact, that he got his first notion of the magic of first editions by seeing the original chocolate-colored binding of Ruskin's *The Seven Lamps of Architecture,* taken from the safe by a salesman, as a great favor, since it was valued at seventy-five dollars.[3] But E & L aimed to supply not only the buyer of choice editions but also the person interested in bindings with armorial insignia from old English estates, the superbly illustrated works of English topography, the publications of English learned societies, famous sets of books, such as *Lodge's Portrait Gallery,* or even the magazines like *Vanity Fair,* with its portrait cartoons, and *Punch.* The works by the great illustrators were always featured, especially those by George Cruikshank. In addition, E & L dealt extensively in new books, so that their sales certainly exceeded those of their principal competitors.[4]

Even after 1898 there was little change in the basic nature of the stock. Among a series of sketches of Boston bookstores in the 1930's, printed in the *Boston Evening Transcript,* the sketch of Lauriat's, which was first in the list, emphasized the richness of its wares. The poor men sold their books on Cornhill for a pittance, but at Lauriat's private libraries were for sale. "Tall green Dickens. Tall blue Thackeray. Tall gray Ruskin. Leather novels. Leather essays. Leather memoirs. Novels, essays and memoirs that once stood in the wainscotted library and filled the walls to the frosted ceiling. . . . Here are five hundred beautiful volumes, full or half morocco, dated twenty-five years ago. . . . Yet as fresh as the day they were bought. . . . As fresh as the day they were bought for show to fill those walls to the frosted ceilings. Leather books unread. . . ."[5] There were private libraries on sale, intact, but there were also the materials to start a private library, the classics, the favorites of the day, Cather, Lewis, Leacock, Coué, Cabell, Lawrence. "Anything you want or we will order it for you. . . . But that's not what Lauriat really means. . . . It really means Leather."

From the very start both partners took an active part in outside activities, such as attending the spring and fall Trade Sales in New York or traveling about the country to sell their books. Lauriat's traveling, however, was more in Europe than in America, and his almost yearly trips abroad to get books for the bookstore gave him relief from the sometimes hectic periods of business struggle. Estes was the American traveler for the firm, especially in the early years, and went on long trips over the East and Midwest to present the firm's new books. Both Estes and Lauriat went to the Trade Sales, often alternately, and soon established great reputations. Estes was known for his lively presentation of the firm's books to this audience of booksellers and dealers, while Lauriat's reputation over the years ranked near the top for sound judgment and business acumen. When T. O. H. P. Burnham died in 1891, it was said of this distinguished bookman that, with the exception of Lee, of Lee and Shepard, and Lauriat, of Estes and Lauriat, no man's lead was more followed by booksellers at the Trade Sales.[6]

In the front-cover advertisement in the *Publishers' Weekly* for April 12, 1873, the first large advertisement in a national periodical, E & L described the business as "Booksellers, Publishers and Importers," mentioning also the agency service for W. F. Draper and the Salem Natural History Publications. Dana Estes had first represented E & L at a New York Trade Sale in September, 1872, and "Dana," such was his trading abbreviation, took an active part in the Spring Trade Sale, in April. Apparently he was the only buyer from Boston and brought back a long list of "extraordinary bargains," obtained through the ruinous prices common at these clumsy auctions, where publishers ruefully saw many of their books sold to bidders at less than half price, if the market was not propitious. E & L advertised the bargains brought back by the "Only Man from Boston at the New York Spring Trade Sale," selling many of the books at half price right near the offices of the unfortunate publishers, as in the case of Roberts Brothers' $2.25 book, *The World Priest*, where one could "save $1.25 and a flight of stairs."[7]

Throughout 1873, along with the works in science and religion, E & L began to branch out into other fields. Their first novel and first volume of poetry were published, also the first juvenile, a translation of three tales by George Sand, and the first travel book, Shaw's *Picturesque Tourist Guide to Great Britain and Ireland*, prepared expressly for American travelers, with colored plates and maps to give it charm. Most important was the publication of Guizot's *Popular History of France*. There were also trivial works of practical interest, such as Captain Crawley's *Whist for All Players*, and T. D. Hall's *Primary English Grammar*, for the Boston schools. Competing with older American houses, E & L published *Passages from the Life of Charles Knight*, although Putnam was bringing it out in New York, following an arrangement made by

George Haven Putnam on a recent trip to England. For the Christmas season, E & L prepared their first holiday book, *The Garland of the Year, or the Months, Their Poetry and Flowers,* a typically needless book, giving a historical account of each month with selections from standard British authors and twelve colored plates. To help in Christmas sales there was a new edition of Estes' *Chimes for Childhood,* at seventy-five cents, and a Red Line Edition of Keble's *Christian Year,* in a choice of bindings.

Such a generally mediocre list of books had some excuse in this year, 1873. The firm had lost, though not heavily, in the Great Boston Fire of 1872, and it was a loss that could be repaired only gradually. More menacing, however, was the general decline in business which culminated in the Panic of 1873, when Jay Cooke and Company closed its doors, on September 18, and the New York Stock Exchange remained closed until September 30. From this time onward, business, especially in the East, sank into a depression that lasted until 1878, with heavy losses to the book trade. As an added misfortune, Dana Estes suffered a severe accident which laid him up for almost three months, just when the fall list was under way. For a new firm, in such a year, it was important just to keep going, and this the partners were able to do, largely because of the wise combination of bookselling and publishing. At this moment, it was probably the bookstore which kept things running, but the publishing business, despite bad times, was soon to do its share, for Dana Estes was a man of immense energy and ingenuity.

As an instance of his eagerness to publicize the new firm, in 1873, "Dana" wrote a letter to the *Publishers' Weekly* defending publishers against the complaint that they were undercutting the retailers by sending books to customers by mail. Publishers would never send books by mail, he asserted, if dealers stocked the books that people wanted. The real trouble was the indifference and want of enterprise of some dealers, who sold croquet sets and notions rather than take a risk on new books. Dana knew personally of instances where *very important* books were announced for months and dealers were earnestly requested to send advance orders, and not *five* copies were ordered by the book trade of the whole country. Nor would many dealers allow the publishers to send them samples of new publications, to be paid for in their regular account. "What wonder that publishers are forced to seek their customers through the newspapers and the mails."[8]

Commenting editorially on this letter the *Publishers' Weekly* soothingly remarked that the American retail trade was not as enterprising as it might be, but that this was a reaction against the original evils of undercutting, and that the publishers were in a good position to start a reform. It noted also that the argument about the dealers' refusal to take risks should be considered in the light of the newness of the Boston firm, which had yet to make a reputation for its books.[9]

It was humiliating to get caught in a bibliographical error, but this happened early in 1874. E & L advertised *Adventures of an Attorney in Search of a Practice* by Samuel Warren, only to be reminded by a letter in the *Publishers' Weekly* from the Indianapolis Public Library that the work was really by Sir George Stephen, that this fact was generally known (see Allibone), and that it was not creditable to the bibliographical knowledge of the publishers that the mistake should be made twice within the same number of years, since a Chicago firm made the same error in 1872.[10] The mistake was tacitly corrected in E & L's next advertisement.

E & L's being a combination of bookseller and publisher involved a few apparent inconsistencies. In 1874, while trying to move more rapidly some of their weighty stock, such as Campbell's *Lives of the Chief Justices,* the publishing division advertised a "very liberal discount for quantities of this work, to especially interest dealers in pushing the same,"[11] whereas, a little later, the bookselling division signed a 20 per cent discount pledge with most other Boston firms.[12] At the first meeting of the New England Booksellers' Association, in October, 1875, Estes offered a resolution that the advertising or retailing of books at wholesale prices was an evasion of the spirit and letter of the constitution and by-laws of the Association and urged all members to refuse to sell to any person violating this rule. This was a year in which there was a great to-do about underselling, but no permanent benefit ensued. In fact, by the 1880's, E & L were tremendous price-cutters, so much so as to lead a bookseller to write the *Publishers' Weekly,* in 1886, bewailing the poor conditions in the book trade and declaring that these conditions were partly due to E & L's regular "special sales" and their widely circulated catalogues, which reduced retail to wholesale prices.[13] In 1875, however, E & L were not sufficiently established to buck the trade, whatever may have been their desires.

That the publishing side of the firm was growing more important was established by the change of title in the advertisements beginning with 1876, when it read Estes and Lauriat, Publishers and Importers, instead of Booksellers, Publishers, and Importers, as in 1873. From this time on the bookselling side was not mentioned in the advertisements of new books, although everyone knew of the prestige of the bookstore. This dual reputation was quite unusual, since relatively few publishing firms were as famous for their bookstores as for their publishing activities. Many times, in later years, when E & L were mentioned in notes on the Boston book trade, it would be either the bookstore or the publishers, rarely both together, with possibly more frequent mentions of the bookstore than the publishers. Certainly the prestige of both divisions was equally great after 1880.

The first opportunity to make a distinguished showing on a national scale came at the Centennial Exhibition of 1876. In the hall where the leading publishers of the country had their exhibit cases E & L were reported to have "an exceptionally attractive display in their simple but tasteful case at the eastern end." Guizot's *History of France* was most prominent, displayed in open volumes richly bound in calf, tree calf, silk-lined morocco, and other styles. Other sets, such as Knight's *History of England,* Austin's *Massachusetts,* the *Works of Count Rumford,* Campbell's *Lives of the Chief Justices,* were presented in ornate bindings, making a rich and dignified exhibit.[14] This display was characteristic, besides, of E & L's most successful offerings, several of them being subscription books. Although the Panic of 1873 had brought a clinging depression to most of the book trade, E & L had done very well, almost prospered, proving that the combination of publisher and bookstore, under vigorous leadership, was a winning one. E & L boasted of the revival of business long before the trade as a whole felt the upturn.[15]

E & L continued to exploit the Trade Sales with great shrewdness. At the spring sale in 1877 they made a particularly heavy purchase, "60 boxes of books at 40 to 60 per cent below publishers' prices. Now opening, the best collection of standard works ever purchased at the spring trade sale." Thus ran the triumphant advertisement in the Boston *Daily Advertiser,* and the *Publishers' Weekly* commented sadly that this was a regular house, not an interloper, and could not be blamed for patronizing the Trade Sales so long as publishers invited this slaughter.[16] A week later the Boston Letter of the *Publishers' Weekly* described the results: "The principal retail book business just now in Boston consists in selling at a ruinous rate the works of the best American authors, bought at the late trade sale. Somehow it is not highly amusing to the publishers."[17] Of course, it should not be forgotten that the publishing division of E & L had to undergo this slaughter at the Trade Sales, while the bookselling division recouped some of the loss by the losses of other publishers. Thus at the fall Trade Sale in 1877, many E & L publications went at less than half the retail price, including many novels and even the "Epochs of Modern History," which usually had better luck.[18]

And now, in this same year, 1877, begins the tale of *Chatterbox*. The merits of this famous juvenile have been described already, and it is the "*Chatterbox* Controversy" that I record here. In some respects it is the most interesting phase of E & L's history and serves as a cogent example of the troubles caused by lack of an international copyright law. More than that, however, the controversy reflected the fighting spirit of Dana Estes, who was willing to spend thirty thousand dollars, over a period of ten years, to win his point and to beat down those who tried to infringe on his business domain. Though the controversy was, basically, a copyright problem, it was also part of Estes' relentless pursuit of the cheap-reprint publishers who had ventured to print some of the firm's unprotected books and thereby incurred his hatred. Just why he was so bitter is hard to say, but there is no doubt about the vengeful tenacity which used up his energy and the firm's money over so many years. Yet he had the final joy of success, attended by the failure of several of those who had tried to compete, all of which must have given great satisfaction to this tough fighter from the state of Maine.

The start of the *Chatterbox* affair was signalized by an editorial in the *Publishers' Weekly*, for November 10, 1877,[19] captioned "American Enterprise." According to this account, the English publishers of *Chatterbox*—James Johnston, Limited, of London —had announced that the United States market was open to all dealers who ordered the book in quantity. E & L sent a check to their London agent with an order for a small number, with the understanding that they would cable larger orders if they found a demand. The English publishers were not interested in a small order which was received later than the final date advertised for orders and assured the agent that, had the order been for five thousand copies, they could not fill it. By the time the agent's reply reached E & L they had orders for more than five thousand copies and had "no resource but to reprint the book." They immediately contracted with S. S. Kilburn,[20] who put nearly forty wood engravers to work, and within two months they succeeded in reproducing over two hundred woodcuts, electrotyping the book, manufacturing over twenty-five tons of paper for it, and, through the efficiency of the University Press, printing and binding an edition of twenty thousand copies. This edition E & L distributed to the trade at less than the cost of the imported copies. They advertised *Chatterbox* for the Christmas trade as the "king of juveniles, the finest yet made." It was published in cloth at $2.50, in illuminated boards at $1.50.

This bold gamble paid off handsomely, so that in January of 1878 E & L began to advertise *Chatterbox* for 1878, to be reprinted from monthly parts. The announcement was made early, said the publishers, so that the trade would know that it could depend upon an ample supply of a "reprint in all respects equal and in some superior to the English copies, and at a lower price."[21] In May, E & L announced that they had written the English publishers, offering to pay a royalty on every copy sold in 1878, had written several times, in fact, but that the Englishmen had not had the courtesy to acknowledge the letters. As a result, they were prepared to reprint the work without British authority: "We confidently appeal to the American Trade to support us and our edition as against imported copies."[22]

The British publishers were dismayed at the prospect of another heavy loss in the American market and attempted to salvage something by getting Thomas Nelson, their authorized American agent, to make an agreement with E & L on a uniform price and simultaneous delivery for the Christmas trade.[23] E & L advertised *Chatterbox* this year as an exact reprint of the English edition, a "stronger bound and handsomer book than the English edition."[24] It was also cheaper, only $1.00 in the illuminated-board covers, and $1.50 in cloth. Estes was able to place twenty thousand copies during a trip through the West in early September, and the Eastern trade would naturally be many times larger.[25] The sales were so good that E & L and Nelson put out a joint advertisement promising that there would be no price reduction on *Chatterbox* before January 1, 1879.[26]

The success of *Chatterbox*, due not only to its inherent merits but to the vigorous advertising and marketing by E & L, was so great that Estes decided that it would be smarter to become the authorized American agent and corner the entire American market than to compete with another firm. Such a viewpoint led him to favor international copyright, a view he made public in an excellent, clear statement in the *Publishers' Weekly* for March 15, 1879.[27] This was the first of his many arguments for international copyright, which he had not championed before he glimpsed the business necessity of his own firm. Like many American firms, E & L had made royalty agreements with foreign authors and had paid them what E & L called "fair" amounts; sometimes these royalties were equivalent to those paid American authors, sometimes not. And there was no obligation to pay anything! Now, however, with the chance of making tremendous profits by energetic selling of *Chatterbox*, Estes was deeply concerned over the need for protection, so this man, who himself casually reprinted *Chatterbox* without permission, fought to prevent others from doing the same thing.

After considerable dickering, therefore, E & L were able to announce in August, 1879, an agreement with the English publishers which made them the sole American distributors. According to E & L's advertisement, the London owner of *Chatterbox* was a wealthy gentleman, not connected with the publishing business, who had spent vast sums on *Chatterbox* solely as an antidote to the "unhealthy sensational literature circulated so widely among our boys and girls."[28] Under this philanthropic aura E & L would reprint the volume from imported plates, with a new scale of prices, ranging from $1.25 to $2.25. As the *Publishers' Weekly* remarked, E & L had displayed generalship in arranging for the supply of the American market.[29] And since the success of *Chatterbox* had turned Estes' interests toward children's books, the whole affair proved momentous for the firm.

The success of *Chatterbox* this year came up to expectations. In September the *Publishers' Weekly* noted that E & L already had orders "running up to some fabulous number of thousands and are expecting twice as many more."[30] This was the year when E & L flaunted their advertisement headed "The Survival of the Fittest," a good section of which was devoted to praise of *Chatterbox* and the warning: "Booksellers and the public are cautioned against buying imitations of this book."[31] This warning, only two years after E & L had made a success by an imitation, seems rather humorous. In January, 1880, E & L triumphantly proclaimed their success in bold, black type: "We sold over 100,000 volumes and we believe this sale unprecedented in the annals of this class of books."[32] This was the year of *Zigzag Journeys in Europe*, which sold over eight thousand copies, but most of the other juveniles were not important, and several of them were also *Chatterbox* specialties, such as the *Original Chatterbox Picture Gallery* and the *Original Chatterbox Album of Animals*. Very clearly, it was *Chatterbox* that sold the lion's share and made a splendid profit for the firm.

More were sold during the special January discount sales, which became a regular feature with E & L. An advertisement in July claimed 150,000 volumes sold, with the demand not fully supplied by this enormous figure. The *Publishers' Weekly* noted that E & L were jubilant over increasing sales, reporting 80 per cent improvement over the preceding January and 40 per cent over February. With such generous profits looming up, E & L bought the adjoining store and enlarged their quarters by building a plate-glass front to both stores, with communication at the front and back of the stores. They now had numbers 299 to 305 Washington Street (there had been a postal renumbering a few years before) and really adequate quarters for both divisions of the business.[33]

Although most of E & L's books were very frankly published to make money, Estes brought out, from time to time, small books and pamphlets on topics of public interest, none of which could have had any commercial success. Thus, in 1875, he had published William G. Dix's pamphlet, *National Constitution the Only Road to National Peace*, and, in 1876, his *The American State and American Statesmen*. A few years later appeared a series of pamphlets by Charles Francis Adams. The first dealt with the public library and the common schools, discussing their relationship, the problem of fiction in the public library, and new developments in the public schools of Quincy. The second reprinted Adams' testimony before the Commerce Committee of the House of Representatives on bills to reorganize interstate railroad traffic and was entitled *Federation of the Railroad System*. Other pamphlets, some of them addresses at public celebrations, others on educational topics, in which Estes was particularly interested, and even a long series on imperialism, at the time of the Spanish-American War, came frequently enough to attest to Estes' public spirit. This was also made evident by his participation in numerous charity affairs, including book fairs for the Old South Church and numerous other Boston events, as well as in the establishment of the Hughes Public Library at Rugby, Tennessee. This was a library conceived by Dana Estes, "as a token of respect for Thomas Hughes," to be erected at the idealistic co-operative settlement in Tennessee planned by the author of *Tom Brown's Schooldays* in 1882. At a dinner for Hughes in Boston, Estes persuaded his brother publishers to contribute books for the library, all Boston publishers giving two hundred to five hundred books apiece (E & L gave two hundred). Estes became a trustee and handled the transportation of the books.[34] It is sad to relate the fiasco of the whole Rugby settlement because of the dishonesty of one of the promoters, but Estes' conception was a generous one.

Because of the great sales in 1879 even more extensive preparations were made for business in 1880: by July the many juveniles and other books for fall were running on twelve presses at the University Press, with a proportionately large share devoted to *Chatterbox*.[35] But the boasts of success with *Chatterbox* had attracted nationwide attention, and John W. Lovell, the famous cheap-book publisher, saw a chance for profits by reprinting *Chatterbox* himself. Lovell had already cut into E & L's profits by a cheap reprint of Knight's *Popular History of England,* two years before, and by 1880 the whole cheap-reprint movement was in full swing.

By November the *Chatterbox* Controversy began with a burst of denunciation in two advertisements, by E & L and John W. Lovell, back to back in the *Publishers' Weekly.*[36] There is not enough space to cite them in full, but I shall try to give something of their flavor by substantial quotations. Apparently Lovell brought out his reprint of *Chatterbox* early in November, whereupon E & L sought an injunction against Lovell in the U. S. Circuit Court of the Southern District of New York. At the beginning of the court proceedings E & L issued a circular of caution to the trade which read as follows:

Caution

To all whom it may concern:

Suit having been this day begun in the U. S. Circuit Court in the Southern District of New York against John W. Lovell and John D. Williams, for the infringement of our rights in *The Chatterbox,* all persons are hereby cautioned against buying, selling or assisting in the manufacture of any unauthorized edition of the book, as it is our intention to prosecute all persons who in any way infringe our rights in the book to the full extent of the law.

Boston
Nov. 15, 1880.

Estes & Lauriat
Assignees of the Proprietor of *Chatterbox*

Lovell, in his advertisement, declared that Judge Blatchford had immediately dismissed the case on the simple affidavits of the defendants, and roundly denounced E & L for their circular: "Issuing of the circular is therefore a gratuitous piece of impertinence on the part of Estes & Lauriat. They would only have been justified in taking such a course if an injunction had already been granted. The effort to destroy a rival's business by such misrepresentations and threats is as base as it is malicious and will certainly recoil on the perpetrators."[37] One may judge, by the heat of this denunciation, that E & L's circular had been quite effective in this period of Christmas buying.

Lovell went on to relate the previous history of *Chatterbox* reprints. In 1876 Appleton, not being able to make a satisfactory arrangement with the agents, reprinted and published an edition; in

1878, E & L, "who now set up such a cry for their 'moral rights,' as they call them, pirated this work and, to the great injury of the English owners, flooded the market with their edition." Lovell also publicized the complaint of the Reverend E. B. Tuttle, an Army chaplain, who asserted that *Chatterbox* for 1878 contained some of Tuttle's *Boys' Book About Indians,* of which Tuttle owned the U. S. copyright. Tuttle wrote E & L, threatening to get out an injunction, and E & L, "to prevent such action and to gain time to market their edition," wrote stating their willingness to make compensation. After Tuttle returned from England he called on E & L, but "their books being marketed and probably knowing that I was in no position to carry on expensive litigation, they failed to take any interest in my case," with the result that he received no compensation. Lovell thought himself entitled to the support of the trade, since its members never would support "monopolies."

E & L's rejoinder bore throughout an air of injured innocence. They defended their first reprint of *Chatterbox* in 1877 as they had done before, alleging the problem of orders to be filled, and they declared that Lovell was attempting to mislead the public into a belief that E & L had transgressed the moral rights of the proprietor of *Chatterbox* in order to justify Lovell's own attempt to sell an imperfect and garbled edition to the American trade. In fact, the English proprietor had been convinced by E & L's arguments and had acknowledged the justice of the case by making E & L his permanent representatives in the United States. As for Mr. Tuttle, E & L reiterated their willingness to make him compensation "if he could show legal or even moral claim," and had so declared to his attorneys, but they had never received any response.

The point of the suit against Lovell lay in the law of trademark. The proprietor had a good and valid trademark in the title *Chatterbox,* which could be defended in the United States, and E & L took an assignment from him with the avowed purpose of defending this right in American courts. The only reason that Judge Blatchford refused a temporary injunction against Lovell and Williams was that the proprietor of the trademark had not used due diligence in prosecuting infringements made before Lovell's, and the case was deferred for a final hearing.

As a final argument against Lovell, E & L observed that Lovell's reprint lacked twenty large illustrations and enough text to make sixty full pages, therefore the only complete and genuine *Chatterbox* was their own. "We appeal to all respectable members of the trade and all believers in fair dealing to support the only authorized and complete edition of this popular work."[38]

Apparently, E & L were irked that the *Publishers' Weekly* had not come to their aid early in the controversy and wrote to the editor to this effect. On the editorial page the magazine declared: "The *Publishers' Weekly* does not have to make its position clear in relation to the piracy of authorized publications. We gave our opinion unmistakably in the case between Roberts Brothers and Lovell and it has not changed since. It applies the same standard to the reprinting of *Chatterbox*, although the existence of a whole Chatterbox literature which had been left unmolested by special lawsuits or objections would seem an extenuating circumstance. The case shows that international copyright would after all be sound business law."[39]

By mid-December two unauthorized editions of *Chatterbox* had appeared. E & L issued another "caution" advertisement, alleging that one version used the title for a book in which not more than six pages of the 412 in the original were included. Another edition was called an American Reprint, having a cover which was an exact imitation of the original, with an imprint reading: Boston, A. W. Lovering, Washington Street. There was no such person as Lovering, and the name of the real publisher appeared in very small type below. This was Lovell's edition, with the large omissions noted above.[40]

Business was still excellent, however, for *Chatterbox* was not the only book on E & L's list, and the 1880 publications were unusually good. In June of the following year the Boston papers announced that Dana Estes had purchased the stone mansion and grounds known as Englewood, situated on Beacon Street and Englewood Avenue, Brookline. According to the newspapers it was considered one of the handsomest suburban residences in the vicinity of Boston.[41]

Since the legal mills ground slowly and a preliminary injunction had been denied, *Chatterbox* was open to attack from any quarter. Therefore the edition for 1881 included not only the English material but also a considerable amount of American copyrighted text, to thwart the pirates to some degree. There were many other good juveniles, the bookstore was thriving, and the genuine *Chatterbox* would always sell well, even at a slightly higher price.[42] In 1881 E & L published thirty-seven books, half of them juveniles and half adult works. On August 31, 1882, E & L completed the tenth year of their copartnership and could be congratulated, said the *Publishers' Weekly*, on having gained a position as one of the "leading importing and publishing houses of the country."[43]

In August, 1883, Dana Estes lost his wife, Louise Reid Estes, whom he had married in 1867. As the obituary notices pointed out, Mrs. Estes possessed excellent taste and judgment, qualities which made her a valuable counselor for her husband and a painstaking editor. Only two years before she had edited the successful gift book, *Nature and Art*, which had been highly praised for its selection of poems. For many years she had engaged in correspondence with prominent English authors, notably George Eliot, with whom she had a personal acquaintance. She had undoubtedly influenced the choice of literary publications of E & L, and Dana Estes, in later years, did not deviate markedly from the course already set.

As if to forget his loss, Estes plunged into an unusually vigorous fall campaign, advertising a tremendously long list of books, more than some of the big New York publishers. In March of 1884 he also published a long argument favoring international copyright, in company with other Boston firms.[44] In May he left for Europe, accompanied by Dr. Elliott Coues, and spent several months there visiting the firm's agents in London and Paris, on the watch for new material.

Finally, after long months of waiting, came the first legal victory in the suit against Lovell and Williams. Judge Wheeler, of the United States Circuit Court of the Southern District of New York, made the decision in equity on the following grounds. The English publisher, James Johnston of London, was first responsible for the success of *Chatterbox* both in England and in the United States. He assigned E & L the exclusive right to use and protect the name in America for ten years from January 1, 1880. Lovell and Williams issued books so similar in appearance and style as to lead purchasers to think them Johnston's *Chatterbox*. There was no copyright law to prevent imitations, of course, but the defendants tried to pass off their work as Johnston's, even though much of it was different from the English original. Therefore E & L, as Johnston's agents in this country, were entitled to relief, since the defendants unfairly represented that their work was Johnston's.[45] The *Publishers' Weekly* thought the grounds for decision somewhat vague but noted that the decision showed the desire of the court to offer some protection, if possible.

Following this decision, in late August, 1884, E & L sent out their first "Caution," warning against publishing or selling any book bearing the title *Chatterbox*, as all infringers of the trademark would be prosecuted.[46] The *Publishers' Weekly* thought that the courts would protect the originator of the combination of title, contents, and so on, known as *Chatterbox*, against books issued as imitations and in such guise as to persuade the public they were buying the publications of Johnston or his representatives.[47] The following week, however, Richard Worthington, a New York publisher, inserted a full-page advertisement in the *Publishers' Weekly* to the effect that his books, *American Chatterbox, Chatterbox Junior, Little Chatterbox, Chatterbox Picture Book, Chatterbox Quartette, Baby Chatterbox,* and others, did not fall within Judge Wheeler's decision, so that booksellers might safely buy his publications. He added that E & L had started no suit against him.[48]

This omission was soon rectified. The next week E & L published "Caution no. 2," repeating their same arguments and informing the trade that suits had been filed against Richard Worthington, Frank Leslie, and Belford, Clarke and Company.[49] The *Publishers' Weekly* sympathized with the retail dealers who, uncertain of their legal rights in this controversy, were ground between the upper and nether millstones, and hoped the suit would soon be decided.[50] Worthington boldly offered one hundred dollars' reward for information leading to the conviction of those who would reprint, publish, or offer for sale any of his *Chatterbox* books, declaring that the copyright and plates of these were his "sole and exclusive property."[51]

Late in December the same Judge Wheeler who had decided against Lovell and Williams granted an injunction against Belford, Clarke and Company in New York, and early in January, 1885, a similar injunction was granted in a Chicago court. E & L issued "Caution no. 3" against the sale of Belford, Clarke's imitation.[52] But success here was balanced by a setback from Worthington, also in January. Judge Wallace denied E & L's injunction on the grounds that E & L did not have too good a position in equity, having once refused to recognize Johnston's rights until they thought it profitable to become his sole representatives in this country and to obtain a monopoly in the use of the trademark.[53] Worthington jubilantly advertised this decision in a full-page spread in the *Publishers' Weekly*.

Amid this legal melee E & L were sued in equity by no other than Mark Twain, who sought to restrain them from further distribution of a catalogue in which they announced his forthcoming book, *Huckleberry Finn*, ready for sale at a price reduced from $2.75 to $2.15. Mark Twain alleged that E & L published this statement knowing it to be untrue and in order to hinder the sale of the book by subscription at $2.75; E & L had no copy for sale since the book had not yet been published. The book was to be sold only to subscribers and, even after publication, E & L could obtain it only by collusion with the plaintiff's agents, who would have to break their contract with Mark Twain to sell to E & L.[54] When trial was held, in the Circuit Court of Boston, with Judge Colt, E & L stated that they advertised *Huckleberry Finn* at $2.15 on the "probability" that some agent would break his agreement and sell to them at reduced rates.[55] Lauriat, Estes, and others connected with the firm submitted affidavits, denying having approached any agent to corrupt him. E & L said that, out of courtesy, they would not send out any more catalogues but good faith with their customers required them to fulfill the orders already received and to be received.[56] The court reserved decision at this time, but in February rendered a decision against Mark Twain, so that E & L could advertise that *Huckleberry Finn* was "now ready for sale at a price reduced from $2.75 to $2.15."[57]

In April, Mark Twain sent the *New York World* a very amusing letter concerning his troubles with *Huckleberry Finn* in Massachusetts. It was occasioned by the Concord Free Trade Club's electing him a member.

> It does seem as if Massachusetts were in a fair way to embarrass me with kindness this year. In the first place, a Massachusetts judge has just decided in open court that a Boston publisher may sell not only his own property in a free and unfettered way, but also may as freely sell property which does not belong to him but to me—property which he has not bought and which I have not sold! Under this ruling, I am now advertising that judge's homestead for sale, and if I make as good a sum out of it as I expect, I shall go on and sell out the rest of his property. In the next place, a committee of the public library of your town have condemned and excommunicated my last book, and doubled its sale. This generous action of theirs must necessarily benefit me in one or two additional ways. For instance, it will deter other libraries from buying the book, and you are doubtless aware that one book in a public library prevents the sale of a sure ten and possible hundred of its mates; and, secondly it will cause the purchasers of the book to read it out of curiosity, etc., etc., and find that there is nothing objectionable in the book after all.[58]

The *New York World* aptly captioned the letter: "Why Mark Twain is Happy."

At the same time that E & L were battling Mark Twain as well as the violators of *Chatterbox*, John B. Alden advertised a reprint of Guizot's *France* for eight dollars instead of the thirty-three charged for E & L's edition, and a little later, in March, 1885, issued a flamboyant advertisement entitled "Battle of the Books," listing several of E & L's favorite sets at greatly reduced prices, with sneers at "millionaire publishers." This advertisement was repeated several times, frequently turned sideways on the page to attract attention.[59] Belford, Clarke and Co., E & L's old adversaries, also introduced a reprint of Guizot. These reprints must have cut heavily into E & L's business. What with lawsuits and business worries, Lauriat had to take a January vacation on a farm, but Dana Estes was apparently unshaken. A momentary relief came from the failure of Richard Worthington, but the slippery Worthington was not down for long; he had gone bankrupt in 1876, and was an old hand at lawsuits, having spent much time, while doing business in Montreal, defending himself against charges of customs' infractions.[60]

So embittered was Dana Estes by the attacks on *Chatterbox* and the reprinting of many of E & L's sets that he set up a subsidiary firm, the Aldine Publishing Co., capitalized at $125,000, with shares allotted to the trade and to the largest dry-goods houses. "When rogues conspire, honest men should combine," he declared.[61] This was aimed particularly at Belford, Clarke and Co. and John B. Alden. The new firm prepared to publish "authorized and honestly-made cheap editions," and hoped that the public would support them in opposition to the pirates. By September, 1886, thirty-six volumes had been published, most of them novels from E & L's list of the 1870's, Gaboriau, Mrs. Oliphant, Whyte-Melville, and so on. Standard authors were published in sets, with very poor paper and binding, commonly called Boston Edition. These publications, many of them paper-covered books selling for thirty cents, were by little-known or anonymous authors, for the most part, and did not cause the pirates much concern. People were not interested in "authorized" books, only cheap books. The end of the Aldine Publishing Co. came in 1890, when their plates were turned over to the Lovell combine, whose aim was to stabilize the cheap-reprint business.[62]

Evidently more angered by Worthington than any of the others E & L issued "Caution no. 4," asserting that "certain notices and comments regarding our right to the trade-mark *Chatterbox* have been published in a form which we believe IS INTENDED AND CALCULATED TO DECEIVE" and noting that Judge Wallace denied a motion for a temporary injunction upon technical grounds only, so that a final injunction was certain, as in previous cases.

This was another warning against selling any other *Chatterbox* than E & L's, which, they probably hoped, would hurt Worthington's sales.[63] In August, "Caution no. 5" was issued, repeating the terms of the injunction against Belford, Clarke and Company. Worthington, however, continued to advertise his *Chatterbox* titles as if nothing had happened. All of this drove Estes to a stronger campaign for international copyright. Early in 1886 the *Publishers' Weekly* praised Estes for pricking some of the bupples in Roger Sherman's attack on copyright before a congressional committee.[64] Sherman was so annoyed that he wrote a letter to the magazine to refute the arguments of Henry Holt and Dana Estes. Although most of the letter concerns technical arguments about copyright, one point deserves mention. Estes, in his testimony before the Senate committee, had said that he had quite a few manuscripts of American authors in his safe which he was unwilling to publish because of the competition of foreign literature. Perhaps other publishers, remarked Sherman, felt like Estes, who published a de luxe edition of George Eliot and paid her heirs a large royalty but would not undertake publication of an American author whose reputation was not made. Sherman commended the business sagacity of Estes, but doubted his interest in American authors.[65]

Another injunction was won against Frank Leslie and the American News Co. in April, a permanent injunction against Belford, Clarke in May. The adding of the name of Frank Leslie to *Chatterbox* did not change the validity of the trademark.[66] In October, E & L announced that Belford, Clarke and Co. had again infringed their rights to *Chatterbox*, that suit had been brought against them, and another injunction obtained in the Circuit Court at Chicago, thus leading to "Caution no. 6" against all infringers.[67] E & L had demolished one adversary after another, but Worthington still remained a fierce thorn in the flesh. Just as E & L were advertising their triumphs over Leslie and Belford, Clarke, Worthington inserted a full-page advertisement facing one of E & L's in the *Publishers' Weekly*.[68] This advertisement was headed "Truth vs. Fiction," in large black capitals. It noted that the injunctions against Leslie and Belford, Clarke were granted because the defendants had tried to deceive the public into believing that their publications were the original *Chatterbox*.

> That the public may know what kind of men Estes and Lauriat are, I give the following extract from the testimony of Mr. Estes in their suit against me:
> Question: Was not the reprint of the *Chatterbox* of

1878 made by you in a form calculated to deceive the public?

Answer: Upon reflection, I should say it undoubtedly was.

Question: And was so intended?

Answer: Yes.

Worthington went on to describe Judge Wallace's refusal to grant an injunction and declared that dealers might buy his books in perfect safety.

E & L let loose a barrage of advertisements and "cautions," warning that there would be a final injunction against Worthington, even though the preliminary injunction was denied on technical grounds, that another New York firm had been enjoined by the same Judge Wallace, that a whole series of injunctions, beginning with that against Lovell, proved that E & L had the law on their side.[69] Worthington, whose *Chatterbox* sales must have been really very small, retorted with an advertisement asking booksellers who had received letters from E & L warning them against selling Worthington's books to forward all such communications to him. "Such warnings, coming from such traders in DECEIT, should receive no attention from respectable and intelligent booksellers."[70] Finally, Worthington was able to announce that, on October 29, 1886, Judge Wallace closed E & L's side of the case and a circuit court in Chicago refused to grant an injunction against his books.[71]

One can only imagine Estes' rage at this turn of events. While preparing to employ the full extent of the law against Worthington, for a principle—not commercial success alone—was now at stake, Estes sent advertisements all over the country. They read as follows:

The Genuine Chatterbox
Is
Always Sure To Sell.

Did You Ever Know It to Fail?
Then why order inferior and unsalable books when you can buy one on which *there is no risk*?

. . . .

Now that nearly all the spurious and illegal imitations of *Chatterbox* have been enjoined by repeated decrees of the U. S. and State Courts and suits against all others are being pushed forward, it is evident that with the dishonest competition removed, the genuine book will be the safest, best selling and most profitable of all juvenile books.[72]

This was a good advertisement and must have hindered Worthington's sales as well as given an added boost to *Chatterbox*'s already great popularity.

By December, E & L brought suit against George A. Leavitt and Co. of New York for sale of Worthington's *Chatterbox* books, and, on December 15, a preliminary injunction was granted against the Worthington Company. Although the injunction was undeniable, the wily Worthington quickly announced that the *Chatterbox* books in question did not belong to the Worthington Co. but to him personally, so that dealers could buy his books in safety. This legal technicality saved Worthington for the Christmas sales of 1886, but suit was immediately brought against him.[73] At last in May, 1887, Judge Shipman granted a final decree against Worthington and the long struggle was over. As the *Publishers' Weekly* commented: "The decision of Judge Shipman in the Estes vs. Worthington case of the great *Chatterbox* series, which, let us hope, is as profitable to the law book publishers as it is the contrary to the trade at large, strengthens very greatly the fortifications of copyright by trademark."[74] E & L issued a triumphant announcement of their victory, but it had been a costly fight: ten suits against infringers of copyright had cost E & L nearly thirty thousand dollars and the defendants had had to spend about the same amount. It is worth noting that *Chatterbox* was never bothered again during its long career, though this was due, as well, to the fact that it was protected by international copyright after 1891. It was just such cases as *Chatterbox*, however, so tremendously publicized, that helped swing publishers and congressmen to the side of international copyright.

After the *Chatterbox* controversy, times were less exciting but more prosperous for E & L. With no competition, *Chatterbox* sales justified all of Estes' hopes; in late December, 1888, E & L reported that they had sold out their first "enormous" edition of *Chatterbox* and that a new edition was just off the press in time for Christmas.[75] *Chatterbox* remained a staple throughout the firm's existence; later on, colored pictures were added and the price reduced, but the quality of the publication continued high right into the twentieth century, even after it ceased to be published by Estes.

That the firm had prospered was proved by the reorganization of E & L, which took place in 1886. In June, five new partners were admitted, since, as was announced, the old partners believed that with the infusion of new and younger blood the firm would be strengthened and its business greatly enlarged, with assurance of its ability to eclipse its successful record of the past thirteen years.

The strain of running such a large business had been heavy, especially upon Lauriat (Estes seemed indefatigable), and the notice intimated that Lauriat, having recovered his health and spirits by extended vacations in Europe and the South, would devote at least half his time to the interests of the business. The five new partners were assigned the following duties: Charles E. Brown, as before, was in charge of the wholesale department and represented E & L as a traveler; Walter M. Jackson, only twenty-two years old, was in charge of the manufacturing and publishing department, a post which testified to his unique abilities; Isaac R. Webber conducted the library department, Seneca Sanford the retail department; Asa H. Walker, who had had a great deal of experience in the subscription-book business and had just retired from the vice-presidency of the Jones Brothers Publishing Co. of Cincinnati, was given general management of the subscription department. Some, like Brown and Sanford, had been with the firm from its beginning; Walker, on the other hand, retired after seven months, and the youthful Jackson took over his responsibilities.

Estes' vigorous leadership drew strong men into the publishing division, men who were given enough opportunity and leeway to start separate careers for themselves along with their valuable services to E & L. In this fashion E & L became a training school for young publishers, particularly in the subscription-book field, just as the bookstore became a school for the book trade in general, one of its most distinguished graduates being Frederic G. Melcher. Walter Montgomery Jackson was easily the most distinguished of those who worked in the publishing division. Born in Massachusetts in 1863, Jackson entered E & L as a boy and soon made his talents known. He was particularly attracted to the subscription department, which E & L were expanding so rapidly in the early eighties. That he could be made a member of this prosperous firm at the age of twenty-two speaks clearly enough of his ability: he was a young man of active imagination and unusual vision, keen-eyed and quiet in manner yet decisive and possessed of excellent business judgment.[76] Jackson was probably chiefly responsible for the nationwide distributing system that marketed E & L's historical works and later the fine library sets of famous authors. By the nineties his active imagination was producing so many new publishing ideas that he made an agreement with E & L to have part of his time to himself, to devote to subsidiary firms. There was first Merrill and Baker, in New York, who utilized plates of E & L's de luxe editions of the eighties to turn out a whole series of standard authors at moderate prices. In 1895 he joined with Francis A.

Nichols to form the Grolier Society, which began by publishing sets of *Secret Court Memoirs* and the like, largely because of the current interest in Napoleon. Nichols also had published, in Boston, sets of court memoirs, for subscription agents, apparently as a subsidiary of E & L, after working in E & L's subscription department for some years.

Jackson's success in selling John Clark Ridpath's histories, in conjunction with newspapers, and his spectacular marketing, through the medium of the London *Times,* of the *Encyclopaedia Britannica,* much to the dismay of many Britishers, are part of his later history. By the late nineties it was obvious that his wide-ranging interests exceeded even the liberal confines of E & L, and his departure from the firm was inevitable, but this is anticipating. E & L gave him almost twenty years of unequalled opportunity in the field of subscription selling, with mutual profit.

Another graduate of the subscription division was R. H. Hinckley, who saw the possibilities of a subscription edition of the Bible. His fourteen-volume set was printed at the Merrymount Press, then rising to fame, and was illustrated with etchings, as the fashion dictated. It was the King James version printed without verse numberings and available in several bindings, but notably in full pigskin, to give the medieval flavor. He later became a South American representative of Jackson's Grolier Society.[77]

Herbert M. Caldwell, who was a salesman for trade books, developed his own imprint on a series of standard classics, mostly of English novelists, and published fifty-cent books to compete with the Burt Home Library, distributed by the A. L. Burt Co. of New York. Caldwell's books were more attractive in appearance than the Burt classics, and he later brought out little gift volumes, such as *The Lady of the Lake,* which were turned out in varying gay bindings from year to year. Caldwell's firm was a subsidiary of E & L, just as were the C. J. Jewett Publishing Co., which took over the historical subscription books in 1886, the Aldine Publishing Co., the Fine Art Publishing Co., the Cassino Art Co., and the Meisterschaft Publishing Co., which Estes initiated in 1882 to publish a self-instruction series of pamphlets in French and German. Last among those trained by Estes were the Page brothers, Lewis Coues Page and his brother, George. Dana Estes married Grace Coues Page in 1884, and his two stepchildren went to work with E & L after finishing Harvard, Lewis in 1891 and George in 1893. Lewis remained less than a year, then joined Joseph Knight in the Joseph Knight Company, also linked to E & L; his brother remained with E & L until 1896, when he joined Lewis in the new L. C. Page and

Company, formed after the retirement of Knight, with Lewis Page as president, George Page as treasurer, and another brother, Carl, as secretary.[78]

Both Estes and Lauriat celebrated the *Chatterbox* victory by extended trips abroad. Mr. and Mrs. Estes were entertained by Tennyson, Thomas Hughes, the Earl of Lytton (Owen Meredith), and others, both at their homes and at dinner parties in London to meet leading literary people. Estes was one of the American publishers who paid generous royalties and was *persona gratissima* to the British, who were attracted by his warm personality and his magnetism. He was a tall, strongly built man, always very erect, with a resonant and commanding voice. His full beard, carefully trimmed and combed, only added to his impressiveness, of which he was fully aware.[79]

Because of his personality and because of the long battle for protection of literary property which he had waged with *Chatterbox* it was inevitable that he should play a prominent role in the local copyright association, later called the International Copyright Association of New England. The first meeting, of over fifty people, took place at the Parker House on December 27, 1887. The gathering included such celebrities as James Russell Lowell, Charles W. Elliot, James Parton, Edward Everett Hale, H. O. Houghton, J. T. Trowbridge, R. A. Dana, B. H. Ticknor, Arlo Bates, John D. Long, and Curtis Guild. Both Estes and Lauriat were present, and Estes called the meeting to order, starting it off with a brief historical sketch of copyright activities. Lowell, who was elected temporary chairman, praised Estes' statement of the case and urged the meeting to elect Estes temporary secretary, which was done. An organizing committee selected Charles W. Eliot as president; John Lowell, Francis Parkman, and H. O. Houghton, vice presidents; Thomas Bailey Aldrich, treasurer; and Dana Estes, secretary. The officers were elected by acclamation and the meeting then adjourned.[80] Shortly afterward, Estes was elected to the Executive Committee of the American Publishers' Copyright League and helped prepare an address on international copyright.[81]

Estes continued his active participation in copyright activities. Along with most firms, E & L listed the books by American authors in their catalogue: there were 105 titles, many of them juveniles, a rather surprising number for a firm that published so much European material.[82] Estes was appointed one of a committee of three to appear before the committees of the Senate and House in the interest of the copyright bill then before Congress. At the local meeting, Estes voiced his hope for a copyright measure soon, though declaring that the demands of the typographical unions were a little exasperating.[83]

A writer in the *Critic* declared that Estes was nothing if not energetic and that the new copyright association had achieved more in four weeks than the Publishers' Copyright League had achieved in two years.[84] The Boston association sponsored authors' readings to gain funds and to publicize the copyright dilemma and these were held in March, 1888, in a Boston theater, with Dana Estes presiding.[85] But the copyright bill did not pass, so that more authors' readings were held in 1889; at one meeting, Estes gave the final speech, summing up copyright affairs. When the bill was finally passed, in April, 1891, Dana Estes took part in the gala celebration held by the American Authors' Copyright League at Sherry's in New York. In this large gathering, with many speakers, Estes spoke following E. C. Stedman and G. H. Putnam, an indication of the distinguished place he had won in American publishing as well as a tribute to his share in winning the battle for international copyright.[86]

With the ever-increasing press of business Estes felt that the firm's quarters on Washington Street were not large enough to serve both the publishing and the bookselling departments. In 1889, therefore, he set about the construction of the Estes Press Building, which was completed at the end of the summer. This was located in the heart of the business district, at 192 to 202 Summer Street, about a quarter mile from the Washington Street store. Bounded on all sides by streets or alleys, it had light and air in every direction. It was really two buildings, joined together by a heavy fire wall, connected outside by massive balconies. The south building, fronting on Summer Street, commanded an extensive view of the harbor from the upper windows and enjoyed uninterrupted sunlight all day long. It was built of yellow fire brick, trimmed with brownstone, and was a thoroughly impressive structure. This south building was given over to the wholesale department of E & L, and contained the offices and warerooms needed for their increasing business. Other firms had space here too, among them the subsidiary firms, such as the Cassino Art Company, the Aldine Publishing Company, and the Meisterschaft Publishing Co. The celebrated engravers, John Andrew and Son, had their studios on the top floor. The north building, on Aldine Street, Estes and Gilbert Places, was devoted to manufacturing, chiefly in connection with book publishing. This section was served by large elevators and a new system of ventilation. Here were located printing concerns, both regular and fine-arts printers, who did much of their work for E & L, and the old bookbinding firms of Fleming and Co. and Macdonald and Sons.

Because of the removal of the publishing department the old quarters on Washington Street became roomier for the bookstore. All the space occupied by the publishing branch was fitted up with shelves, making it a really sumptuous store. There were no further physical changes until after the dissolution of E & L, in 1898. For eight more years the old quarters sufficed for the bookstore, then, in 1906, the largest store in the building at 385 Washington Street was remodeled for the use of the Charles E. Lauriat Company.

As was incumbent for an important American publisher, E & L sent a display to the Paris Exposition of 1889. The (London) *Bookseller*, which gave an elaborate description of the American exhibits, did not think much of E & L's. This publisher, they commented, sent twenty works, thirteen of which were not American. First on their list was the *History of Rome*, by Duruy, a French Academician, edited by a Dublin professor, with plates made in England (this was untrue), and the chief illustrations made and printed in France; the whole work projected and produced by Mr. Kelly, of London (true only in part). "Do Messrs. Estes and Lauriat suppose the French jury is composed of babes and sucklings?" It was a relief, said the *Bookseller,* to turn to the cases of Houghton, Mifflin, Appleton, Lippincott, the Century Company and other truly American firms. "Large-paper editions of nothingness and *rechauffés* of German, French and English originals are not the sort of things that win the admiration of a jury of experts. They may be well enough to sell, but it is stupid to exhibit them in Paris, with a Didot and Delalain as judges. For books and printing, Houghton, Mifflin are first, and the rest nowhere."[87]

There was more than a grain of truth in this criticism, and it was borne out by the award of the Diploma of Honor to the Century Co., gold medals to Appleton, Houghton, Mifflin, Lippincott, and Merriam, and silver medals to nine firms, including E & L. It should be noted, however, in all fairness, that, as bookmaking, E & L's volumes were of very high quality, even though they were not distinctly American in inspiration. At the Columbian Exposition of 1893 E & L received more favorable mention. Not only were they the first publishers to have their exhibit ready, which gave them one of the choice locations beside Harper, Scribner, and Century, but there was general praise of their display, which was in an enclosure fitted up with ebony-black cases and tables which featured mostly their de luxe editions. The major display was the fine new set of Sir Walter Scott and examples of the Connoisseur Edition, limited to seventy copies, of various authors. On the walls were hung framed original etchings and other illustrations from their books. There was also an exhibit of rare books in fine and historic bindings, which advertised the qualities of the bookselling department. This elaborate exhibit won a medal, the highest honor, and twelve awards for the display of art publications, fine bindings, and illustrations.[88]

The lawsuits which had so occupied E & L in the 1880's played little part in their business affairs in the 1890's. There were only three cases of any publishing importance, and E & L won all three. The first was a suit to restrain E & L from selling another subscription book, *The Ebers Gallery*, and, as in the case of *Huckleberry Finn*, E & L won out.[89] Another concerned a complicated contract involving copyright, and this was won by E & L, since the plaintiffs had suffered no damage.[90] The third case, against the famous General Ben Butler, was for breach of contract, because Butler withdrew his book from the C. F. Jewett Publishing Co. (owned by E & L) after they had already done work on the manuscript, and transferred it to A. M. Thayer and Co. The suit was interesting chiefly because of the testimony of several publishers concerning the marketing of books. H. O. Houghton declared that nine tenths of the books published in regular trade channels brought their publishers no profits, whereas subscription books had a greater sale than any trade books. Mr. Knight, of the Methodist Book Concern, thought that it was the ability of the canvassers and the amount of pushing done by the publishers rather than the fame of the author that regulated the number of copies a book would sell. Butler finally had to pay damages of $2,500 to the Jewett Publishing Co.[91]

In the firm itself, Charles E. Brown retired in 1891 and Seneca Sanford died in 1897. Also in 1897 a group of young men were admitted as partners: Frederick Reid Estes, Francis H. Little, and Charles E. Lauriat, Jr., along with Eugene C. Belcher, who had been head accountant since 1872. Frederick Estes was Dana Estes' eldest son, who had been working in the retail and subscription departments for some years; Francis Little had been in charge of the manufacturing department for about eight years. This change brought E & L up to the size it had attained in the big reorganization of 1886, but several of the experienced oldsters had departed and Walter Jackson was increasingly absorbed in activities outside the firm.

The main business of the company, in the 1890's, was in art books, juveniles, and the elaborate sets of standard authors. In

1892, the *Publishers' Weekly* noted that E & L's specialties were fine-art books and juveniles and that their productions in both lines, for the fall season, were up to their "well-known average of quantity and quality."[92] Despite the Panic of 1893, which hit the publishing and bookselling business very hard, E & L continued their fine publications without much abatement. The publishing department was in worse straits than the bookstore, for the subscription department, which had so greatly expanded and was selling through regional agencies, was having difficulty in collecting the sums due. The financial losses were tremendous, but not catastrophic, for the partners were able to rally enough credit to continue.[93] The admission of new partners in 1897 was intended to strengthen the firm, but the split between the publishing and bookselling divisions had widened, especially since most of the financial weaknesses appeared in the subscription branch.

When Walter M. Jackson announced his withdrawal from E & L, in March, 1898, in order to devote himself to the Grolier Society and its publications, the break was inevitable. It was he who had been chiefly responsible for the immense expansion in the subscription department, and the removal of this major figure left a gap impossible to fill.[94] Jackson sold his interests to Dana Estes and his son, Frederick R. Estes, and soon it was rumored that the retail business would be separated from the publishing business, with a consequent reshuffling of partners.[95] In June came the final separation: the publishing firm became Dana Estes and Co., with headquarters in the Estes Press Building; the bookselling department became the Charles E. Lauriat Co., remaining at Washington Street. Dana Estes, Frederick Estes, E. C. Belcher, and F. H. Little became partners in Dana Estes and Co., taking over control of all the stock, the publishing plant, and all rights and contracts pertaining to this aspect of E & L. Charles E. Lauriat, his son, and Isaac R. Webber were partners in the Charles E. Lauriat Co., and purchased the retail business, although Estes still retained an interest in it.[96]

The *Publishers' Weekly*, early in July, 1898, published a long historical sketch of E & L, which was mainly a biography of Dana Estes.[97] It recounted the many successes of the firm, as seen through the eyes of Dana Estes, who obviously had a hand in compiling the notice, and by its length testified to the prestige of the firm. Dana Estes received an honorary A.M. degree from Bowdoin College on June 23, at the same time that Herbert Putnam was granted a Litt.D. degree.[98] Thus, in this same year, two distinguished Boston firms which had first won success under the same roof on Washington Street departed from the scene, Roberts Brothers, for good, in May, E & L in June, to be continued in two distinct firms. Both had achieved brilliant success, one as a literary publisher of high quality, the other as an active and efficient commercial organization, brimming with new ideas and emphasizing sales and profits. Although E & L would be continued by Dana Estes and Co., the great days of publishing were over, and E & L's prestige was not to be duplicated in the newer imprint.

The pattern of publishing in Dana Estes and Co. differed but little from that of E & L, especially during Estes' lifetime. The same classes of books published in the last years of E & L, fine-art books, travel, de luxe editions of authors, and juveniles appeared on the list of the new firm. There were perhaps more books on travel, as a result of Estes' increased interest in the field because of his own extensive journeys in Europe and Africa. Even after his death there was little change, perhaps hesitation rather than change. Some good books were published during the years 1898 to 1914, but it was no longer the output of a firm bursting with vitality.

The business of Dana Estes and Co. was not so extended as that of E & L, so Estes had more time for outside activities of personal interest. He had always taken a leading part in trade activities and was frequently called upon for important services, as during the campaign for international copyright. He was a leader among Boston publishers and especially sought as chairman of meetings of the trade. An example may be found in the meeting of booksellers, in 1895, held to offer a tribute of respect to H. O. Houghton, who had just died.[99] He was also a member of a host of associations and clubs, such as the Bostonian Society, the American Archeological Institute, the American Association for the Advancement of Science, the Boston Memorial Association, the Browning Society, and the Pine Tree State Club. He was active in town affairs in Brookline, where he had his home, and was much interested in national politics, as is shown by the pamphlets published on such varied topics as schools, disenfranchisement of Negroes, American imperialism, and railroad financing.

It was his interest in travel that evidently absorbed his final years. This was not the leisurely travel one might expect in a man of his years but rugged and adventurous exploring. His interest in archeology led him first to travel in Italy, then in Egypt. In 1904 he made an extensive trip, beginning in Egypt, where he collected antiquities of one sort or another, which were presented to the Walker Art Museum of Bowdoin College, then proceeding up the Nile to Uganda and the Congo. Much of the trip was accomplished on the gunboat Nafir, which traversed the whole of the navigable river, ramming all obstructions and establishing a record for this type of exploration. In August, 1908, Estes started on another journey, touring Italy, the Dalmatian coast, where he was arrested on suspicion of being a Servian spy when he tried to take photographs, and then Egypt. He next sailed down the east coast of Africa and landed at Mombasa, finally going south through Rhodesia and arriving at Cape Town late in December. This 2,500-mile African trip, almost the same as that taken, a few months later, by Theodore Roosevelt, another believer in the strenuous life, greatly weakened Estes' health. On his return to Brookline, in March, 1909, he became ill and, after a sickness of about ten weeks, died June 16. If it had not been for this unusually difficult trip, on which he suffered many hardships, he might have lived for many more years, with corresponding benefits for Dana Estes and Company, but such was not to be. And probably this vigorous man, so temperamentally akin to T. R., would not have foregone the pleasure from his beloved travel except through dire weakness. Thus he led a life active to almost the last moment and carved a reputation as an explorer, a field in which he would find few competitors among publishers.

With Dana Estes' death the firm reverted to his sons, to whom he left the majority of his property. Many of the antiquities and curiosities acquired on his tours were left to institutions, and $2,500 was appropriately bequeathed to his native town of Gorham, Maine. His interests in the publishing business were left to Frederick Reid Estes, Dana Estes, Jr., and Philip S. Estes. Of these sons, only Frederick had shown any interest in publishing, and, while he had good literary taste, he lacked the drive and business shrewdness of his father. Estes bequeathed his interests in the Meisterschaft Publishing Co. to his clerk, Ludwig Erhard, and his stock in the Marshall Jones Publishing Co. to his nephew, Albert Marshall Jones.

The firm, under the new management, continued much as before. The same lines of books were published, but no large-scale projects were started. The books on travel increased, if anything, but they were almost entirely British imports; the same was true of the fine-art and gift books. More novels appeared, again mostly British and some of them good, but the juveniles began to slacken, and by 1913, had dropped almost to the vanishing point, a rather strange circumstance for this firm that had so prospered through juveniles. In 1912 the firm published forty-eight titles and advertised briskly, but in 1913 there was a marked drop, both in quality and quantity.

It was no great surprise to the trade to learn that the Page Co. (formerly L. C. Page and Co.) had bought out Dana Estes and Co. on March 25, 1914. Lewis Page was already a very successful publisher, with the "Little Colonel" books among others, and it was no great problem to induce Frederick Estes to relinquish a job he found increasingly distasteful. As a result, Lewis Page got the assets of Dana Estes and Co. at a bargain, including the plates of the many subscription sets so prized by Dana Estes and many of which still figure on Page's list. During 1914 the lists of Dana Estes and Co. and the Page Co. were run separately, but, in the year following, the Page Co. had only one list.[100]

As the *Publishers' Weekly* noted, the Page Co. thus acquired a business in which two of the Page brothers had made their start in publishing. The notice listed some of the books which had sold so well, such as Miss Parloa's cookbooks, of which about one million volumes had been marketed, and Mrs. Richards' *Captain January,* with nearly two hundred thousand in sales, not to mention *Chatterbox.* Yet most of the big sales were made under E & L, though Mrs. Richards' books sold very well after 1898, of course. The Page Co. featured practically none of the recent titles from Dana Estes and Co. in their advertising; only one recent book, Townsend's *Sand Dunes and Salt Marshes,* "a really excellent book from the Estes list," was advertised, and this was, indeed, a fine work.[101] For the fall, *Chatterbox* was praised, as was natural, and a new collection of short stories by Mrs. Richards, but the bulk of the Estes books dropped out of sight, even though quite a few juveniles have continued in the Page catalogue up to the present and have had a continuous sale. By the purchase the Page Co. acquired the premises of Dana Estes and Co. in the Estes Press Building and practically their entire force, including their traveling salesmen. Few people know that many of the sets of authors still presented in the Page catalogue were originally the work of Dana Estes and were responsible for a good share of the success of Estes and Lauriat; L. C. Page must surely have found these, along with Mrs. Richards' stories, the major assets from Dana Estes.

CONCLUSION

THE foregoing pages have attempted a survey of the publishing achievements of Estes and Lauriat and Dana Estes and Co. It is clear that E & L were not what one would call a "literary house." Yet they were truly famous in the nineteenth century—famous for their vigorous direction, their efficiency in marketing, and their tenacious exploitation of such angles as the country-wide selling of sets of standard authors.[1]

A productive comparison can be made between E & L and their closest neighbor in publishing—on the floors above—Roberts Brothers. The superiority of Roberts Brothers was more than physical: it lay primarily in the unfaltering good taste of their director, Thomas Niles. He, like Dana Estes, was a superb man of business, but Roberts Brothers never achieved the immense financial triumph of E & L because Niles possessed certain standards of publishing which he refused to lower, whereas Dana Estes, though eager for distinction in his book list, simply did not have the literary judgment to implement his desires. As a result, Roberts Brothers' list was filled with excellent poets, essayists, historians, scholars, and novelists, and E & L had relatively few new writers of distinction and fell back upon the authors whose reputations were already made. In other words, Roberts Brothers provided a sympathetic outlet for living authors, European and American, while E & L put their energies into the widest possible selling of books by famous authors, usually deceased, thereby promoting popular culture.

Dana Estes, from the start, tried to link his yearning for great business success with an educational philosophy of publishing. His presentation of popular science, during the first years of the firm's history, is clear evidence of this, to be followed immediately by the subscription marketing of Guizot's histories and the many sets of standard authors. Yet Estes was no Charles Knight, seeking truly inexpensive publications which all could buy; from the very first he published works that are expensive even by present-day standards and were de luxe indeed for those decades. E & L, whatever may be said of the money-making proclivities of their directors, tried valiantly to produce books in the handsomest style possible in that typographically dull age, and their continual striving for excellence in printing and illustration should be credited to them. That they were able to make a great deal of money on these expensive items is a tribute to their business acumen. There was distinct snob appeal in E & L's publications, of course, particularly the severely limited editions of lavish gift books and profusely illustrated sets of authors, but they were adjudged magnificent, by contemporary standards, and were prized by lovers of fine books and by those who, less certain in their taste, deemed such works a badge of respectability. The wide dissemination of some of the beautiful art gift books and the sets of authors, all of them eminently worth reading, surely had a beneficial effect on that segment of the American public that was too wealthy to bother with the cheap editions. Dana Estes himself was closely akin to this increasing group of *nouveaux riches* and was temperamentally fitted to cater to their tastes.

E & L's two really important fields were illustrated books, whether sets or single volumes, and juveniles, themselves copiously illustrated. E & L's juveniles, while not as distinguished as those of Roberts Brothers' Louisa May Alcott, were not far behind with Laura E. Richards; and the delightful "Zigzag Journeys," the "Knockabout Club Series," and the "Three Vassar Girls Series" were a major contribution to pleasurable reading for young folks. Characteristically, the educational slant was very strong in most of Estes' juveniles, from Miss Yonge's histories, in the seventies, to James Otis' stories of American history later on. Their juveniles were invariably handsome, some, like the "Zigzag Journeys," being truly superb. Mrs. Richards' stories were immensely and justly popular—she was, in fact, a fine successor to Miss Alcott—and represent one of the more lasting contributions in this area. Most of the children's books, it must be granted, were basically contemporary in their appeal, as were so many of E & L's publications; they demonstrated Estes' keen perception of what would sell in abundance. Although E & L made money in several other lines, notably subscription sets and gift books, it was the triumph in juveniles that really set off the period of prosperity that began with the eighties.

E & L, and, to a lesser extent, Dana Estes and Co., were firms more respected in the trade for their technical competence than for their literary distinction. I have tried to show that the literary value of their products was not negligible, but there is no reason to underestimate publishing that won its fame through choice of contemporary favorites and through superb and often original techniques of distribution and selling. E & L, particularly, demonstrate, by their success, the skill with which Dana Estes, aided by his associates, sensed the taste of the times, prepared books to satisfy it, sold these books to the public, and, withal, brought fresh elements of typographical beauty and refinement in illustration for the improvement of their readers. If they had done nothing more than publish the "Zigzag Journeys," Mrs. Richards' stories, and the handsome sets of historians, novelists, and poets, E & L would have performed a valuable service for American readers.

NOTES

Chapter One

1 G. H. Sargent, *Lauriat's* (Boston: Privately printed, 1922), p. 13.

2 *Ibid.*, p. 15.

3 *Publishers' and Stationers' Weekly Trade Circular*, 2 (1872): 292.

4 *Ibid.*, p. 334.

5 Information concerning Dana Estes' early career is derived from the *Dictionary of American Biography*, VI, 188–89; the *Publishers' Weekly*, 54 (1898): 9–10; and obituary notices in the *Boston Evening Transcript* and the *Boston Globe* at the time of his death, June 16, 1909.

6 Sargent, *op. cit.*, pp. 15–16.

7 *Ibid.*, p. 16. They claimed 1792 as their foundation date.

8 Information about Lauriat has been derived not only from Sargent's book but also from obituary notices in the *Boston Evening Transcript*, the *Boston Globe* and the *Boston Herald*, all of February 13, 1920. There is no sketch of Lauriat in the *Dictionary of American Biography*, although Estes is included.

9 F. L. Pattee, *A History of American Literature since 1870* (New York: Century, 1916), Chap. 1.

10 *Ibid.*

11 Barrett Wendell, *A Literary History of America* (New York: Scribner, 1917), p. 438.

12 Samuel Longfellow, ed., *Life of Henry Wadsworth Longfellow* (Boston: Ticknor, 1886), II, 308.

13 Van Wyck Brooks, *New England: Indian Summer, 1865–1915* (New York: Dutton, 1940), p. 84.

14 *Ibid.*, pp. 84–85.

15 Pattee, *op. cit.*, Chap. 1.

16 Philip Rahv, *Discovery of Europe* (Boston: Houghton, Mifflin, 1947), pp. xii-xiii.

17 *Ibid.*, p. xvi.

18 W. D. Howells, *A Woman's Reason* (Boston: Ticknor, 1882), pp. 142–43.

Chapter Two

[1] Allan Nevins, *The Emergence of Modern America, 1865–1878* (New York: Macmillan, 1927), pp. 281–89.

[2] Van Wyck Brooks, *New England: Indian Summer, 1865–1915* (New York: Dutton, 1940), p. 102.

[3] *Ibid.*, p. 109.

[4] *Scribner's Monthly*, 6 (1873): 608 From Whitelaw Reid's commencement address at Dartmouth College, entitled "The Scholar in Politics." Cited by F. L. Mott, *A History of American Magazines* (Cambridge: Harvard Univ. Press, 1938), III, 104–7.

[5] *Ibid.*

[6] Van Wyck Brooks, *op. cit.*, p. 110. Brooks suggests that the refusal of this series by Ticknor and Fields and its subsequent publication in New York by Appleton indicated the passing of Boston as the intellectual center of the country, since all the later bulk of scientific publication, which was to dominate the thought of the next quarter century, came from New York.

[7] *Publishers' and Stationers' Weekly Trade Circular*, dated September 27, 1872, 2 (1872): 334.

[8] *Ibid.*, p. 405.

[9] *Atlantic*, 31 (1873): 759.

[10] *Lit. World*, 3 (1873): 140.

[11] *Ibid.*, 5 (1875): 140.

[12] Quoted by *Pub. Weekly*, 7 (1875): 447.

[13] C. C. Chatfield Co. in 1873. Presumably most of these series got their titles from Charles Knight's celebrated "Half Hours with the Best Authors."

[14] *Lit. World*, 4 (1873): 129. The *Atlantic* called it a "charming volume," with "never a dull line," and went on to say: "In fact, it is a model scientific book; it is based on firm facts, the deductions are wise, novel and temperate, and the style is at-tractive as well as intelligible" (34 [1874]: 116–17).

[15] *Ibid.*, 3 (1872): 110.

[16] Six steel plates and two hundred and fifty woodcuts.

[17] Among reviews, *Scribner's Monthly*, 4 (1872): 645, summed up its popular value very well. The *Atlantic* gave it an enthusiastic notice, calling it the first systematic manual, unique in conception and execution (31 [1873]: 746–47). Note also *Dictionary of American Biography*, IV, 465–66.

[18] See *Pub. Weekly*, 5 (1874): 57.

[19] *Lit. World*, 4 (1873): 44.

[20] *Atlantic*, 34 (1874): 626.

[21] *Ibid.*, 33 (1874): 496–97.

[22] *Ibid.*, 40 (1877): 380; *Lit. World*, 7 (1877): 116.

[23] *Pub. Weekly*, 7 (1875): 433; *Lit. World*, 5 (1875): 183.

[24] *Nation*, 20 (1875): 335.

[25] *Ibid.*, 26 (1878): 63–64; *Lit. World*, 6 (1876): 103; and *Pub. Weekly*, 9 (1876): 305.

[26] *Pub. Weekly*, 10 (1876): 19.

[27] *Dictionary of American Biography*, IV, 465–66.

[28] *Pub. Weekly*, 11 (1877): 588.

[29] *Atlantic*, 36 (1875): 365–68. *Birds of the Northwest* first appeared as a government document, one of the volumes in the famous Hayden Geological Survey, published in 1874. The *Atlantic* review is of the government publication, whereas most other reviews dealt with E & L's republication.

[30] *Dictionary of American Biography*, IV, 465–66. See also *Scribner's Monthly*, 18 (1879): 313–14.

[31] *Scribner's Monthly*, 16 (1878): 298. It was well illustrated from the author's own sketches, and contained an ornithological calendar for Boston, making it a true field book. See also *Pub. Weekly*, 11

(1877) : 524; *Nation*, 23 (1877) : 388.

32 *The Month at Goodspeed's*, 25 (1954) : 106–7.

33 *Atlantic*, 42 (1878) : 780; *Lit. World*, 11 (1880) : 296.

34 *Lit. World*, 12 (1881) : 55.

35 *Pub. Weekly*, 18 (1880) : 309.

36 *Ibid.*, 19 (1881) : 42.

37 *Ibid.*, p. 363. A reviewer in the *Critic* noted that Marion Harland derived an income of $2,500 a year from her cookbook and thought Miss Parloa might do as well (1 [1881] : 52).

38 Isaac Sprague was already well known as the illustrator of certain works by Asa Gray and George B. Emerson.

39 *Lit. World*, 12 (1881) : 264.

40 Note especially the laudatory notices in the *Atlantic*, 39 (1877) : 245–46; and 40 (1877) : 761.

41 *Lit. World*, 13 (1882) : 218.

42 *Ibid.*, 15 (1884) : 216.

43 *Dictionary of American Biography*, IV, 465–66.

44 *Critic*, 44 (1904) : 95.

45 *Nation*, 85 (1907) : 450; *New York Times*, 12 (1907) : 434.

46 *Dial*, 49 (1910) : 526; *New York Times*, 15 (1910) : 409.

47 *Nation*, 97 (1913) : 545.

48 *Dial*, 55 (1913) : 153; *Lit. Digest*, 47 (1913) : 692; *Springfield Republican*, September 11, 1913.

49 *Pub. Weekly*, 85 (1914) : 1235.

Chapter Three

1 Mary Abigail Dodge, *Twelve Miles from a Lemon* (New York: Harper, 1874), p. 21. Her pseudonym was Gail Hamilton.

2 *Ibid.*, pp. 30–31.

3 *Ibid.*, p. 30.

4 Donald Sheehan, *This was Publishing* (Bloomington: Indiana Univ. Press, 1952), p. 190.

5 F. E. Compton, *Subscription Books* (New York: New York Public Library, 1939), p. 34.

6 L. T. Dickinson, "Marketing a Best Seller: Mark Twain's 'Innocents Abroad,'" *Papers of the Bibliographical Society of America*, 41 (1947) : 107–22.

7 Compton, *op. cit.*, p. 34.

8 *Ibid.*, p. 36.

9 *Publishers' and Stationers' Weekly Trade Circular*, 2 (1872) : 93–94.

10 *Ibid.*

11 Dickinson, *op. cit.*

12 *Publishers' and Stationers' Weekly Trade Circular*, 2 (1872) : 94.

13 *Lit. World*, 5 (1874) : 40.

14 *Ibid.* There is a good description of the methods of subscription-book salesmen in Frederick B. Perkins'

Scrope, or The Lost Library, published by Roberts Brothers in 1875.

15 *Pub. Weekly*, 4 (1873) : 239.

16 *Ibid.*, 3 (1873) : 375.

17 *Ibid.*, pp. 381–82.

18 *Ibid.*, 4 (1873) : 645.

19 Advertisement in the *Publishers' Trade List Annual* for 1880.

20 Henriette Guizot de Witt, *Monsieur Guizot in Private Life, 1787–1874* (Boston: Estes & Lauriat, 1881), pp. 253, 254–55.

21 "For several years he was wont to collect his grandchildren at five o'clock every day in his library, where he gave them a simple sketch of their country's history. His aim was to awaken their intelligence rather than to load their memories. . . . In quoting the old chroniclers he translated and commented upon them in the style which made him so admirable a story-teller, and while his grandchildren listened his daughters followed him in shorthand." From an article on Guizot in *Littell's Living Age*, 123 (1874) : 757.

22 De Witt, *op. cit.*, pp. 344–45.

23 Advertisement of the work in *Publishers' Trade List Annual* for 1876.

24 *Ibid.*

25 *Atlantic*, 36 (1875): 121, *Scribner's Monthly*, 16 (1878): 443; *Lit. World*, 7 (1876): 135; *No. Amer. Review*, 123 (1876): 145–51.

26 *Popular History of France*, I, 5–8.

27 Edward A. Freeman, the noted British historian, remarked: "M. Guizot might not have taken it as praise, but we mean it as no slight praise when we say that we have scarcely ever seen a book written by a Frenchman on a French subject which was so little French in its spirit. . . . The book is a noble one; it would be well if the history of every nation could be told in the same calm and judicial spirit, with the same loftiness of moral tone" (*British Quarterly Review* [January, 1877]).

28 Gustave Lanson, *Histoire de la littérature française* (Paris: Hachette, 1902), p. 1004.

29 Charles K. Adams, *Manual of Historical Literature* (New York: Harper, 1889), pp. 325–26. He thought the translation rather poor in places, but most reviewers deemed it satisfactory.

30 *Lit. World*, 7 (1876): 135.

31 The sales of the French edition totaled 100,000 copies by 1876 (*Pub. Weekly*, 9 [1876]: 305).

32 Yet C. K. Adams called it "probably the best popular history of England for the general reader, after Green's." He thought the illustrations unusually fine, since they were for elucidation as well as for embellishment. It was "not profound but healthful in tone," not at all superficial or partisan but concerned with a broad survey of all levels of English life (Adams, *op. cit.*, pp. 470–71).

33 *Harper's Mag.*, 49 (1874): 744–45.

34 *Nation*, 18 (1874): 31; *Lit. World*, 4 (1874): 157.

35 Adams, *op. cit.* p. 466; W. C. Smith, "John, Baron Campbell," *Encyclo-paedia Britannica*, 9th ed. (Philadelphia: J. M. Stoddart, 1875–90), IV, 669–71.

36 *Nation*, 19 (1874): 27.

37 *Lit. World*, 5 (1874): 76.

38 *Nation*, 19 (1874): 255; *Scribner's Monthly*, 9 (1874): 122; *Harper's Mag.*, 50 (1875): 600.

39 See the reviews of A. H. Johnson's *The Normans in Europe* in the *Nation*, 28 (1879): 221; and R. W. Church's *Beginning of the Middle Ages, Nation*, 27 (1878): 200. See also G. M. Dutcher, *A Guide to Historical Literature* (New York: Macmillan, 1931), p. 68, note.

40 See the reviews in the *Nation*, 25 (1877): 108–9, 306–7, for example; but the *Lit. World*, 11 (1881): 442, considered the series excellent, especially the volume on Troy by S. G. W. Benjamin.

41 *Pub. Weekly*, 6 (1874): 436.

42 *Ibid.*, 9 (1876): 501.

43 Adams, *op. cit.*, p. 468.

44 *Lit. World*, 12 (1881): 43. The translator was highly praised by all reviewers.

45 *Scribner's Monthly*, 22 (1881): 474–75; *Atlantic*, 48 (1881): 412-14.

46 *Pub. Weekly*, 6 (1874): 455. Yet a later note in the same magazine (10 [1876]: 470), discussing the works displayed at the Centennial Exhibition in Philadelphia, pointed out that *Picturesque America* was a success only by dint of vigorous canvassing.

47 Subscriptions were taken only for the complete work, and each part was payable on delivery, the "Carrier" not being permitted to give credit or receive money in advance.

48 See *Lit. World*, 9 (1878): 82, and 10 (1879): 125.

49 *Nation*, 24 (1877): 249.

50 *Lit. World*, 5 (1875): 172; *Pub. Weekly*, 7 (1875): 357.

51 See Camille Jullian, *Extraits des historiens français du XIXe siècle* (Paris: Hachette [1896]), pp. lviii-lix; and C. K. Adams, *op cit.*, p. 327. Martin's continuation cost $16.50 in the cloth binding, making Guizot and Martin together a heavy

$49.50 for the reader interested in French history.

⁵² Gustave Masson was a professor at Harrow, and later wrote *The Story of Mediaeval France* for Putnam's "Story of the Nations Series." He wrote well and accurately, although his books did not contain much original research.

⁵³ *Lit. World*, 12 (1881): 159. This book, by exception, was criticized for being poorly printed, apparently because the plates were made in England.

⁵⁴ Adams, *op. cit.*, p. 326.

⁵⁵ Quoted from the E & L advertisement in the *Publishers' Trade List Annual* for 1883.

⁵⁶ Adams, *op. cit.*, pp. 122–23. See also Dutcher, *A Guide to Historical Literature*, p. 190.

⁵⁷ *Pub. Weekly*, 27 (1885): 62, 286, 314, 357. Alden's set, however, was in a much smaller format and completely lacked the beauty and impressiveness of E & L's large volumes.

⁵⁸ *Ibid.*, 30 (1886): 526.

⁵⁹ See *Lit. World*, 5 (1874): 11.

⁶⁰ *Ibid.*, 15 (1884): 110.

Chapter Four

¹ *Pub. Weekly*, 3 (1873): 133. There was crudeness and irregularity in the page and the letters, but it was a "great mechanical triumph," said the Boston Letter.

² *Lit. World*, 3 (1873): 140.

³ *Ibid.*, 4 (1873): 15; *Pub. Weekly*, 3 (1873): 556.

⁴ *Nation*, 19 (1874): 11.

⁵ *Lit. World*, 5 (1874): 11; *Pub. Weekly*, 5 (1874): 369.

⁶ *Pub. Weekly*, 6 (1874): 158.

⁷ S. M. Ellis, *Wilkie Collins, Le Fanu and Others* (London: Constable, 1931), p. 124; F. L. Mott, *Golden Multitudes* (New York: Macmillan, 1947), pp. 142–45.

⁸ There is an interesting account of Mrs. Riddell and her writings in S. M. Ellis, *op. cit.*, pp. 266–335.

⁹ *Atlantic*, 35 (1875): 628.

¹⁰ *Ibid.*, p. 623.

¹¹ *Nation*, 20 (1875): 381.

¹² *Atlantic*, 37 (1876): 239.

¹³ *Pub. Weekly*, 9 (1876): 627. The list of novels appears in the same volume on pp. 684–95.

¹⁴ *Ibid.*, 10 (1876): 1047.

¹⁵ *Ibid.*, 11 (1877): 56–57. Lucy H. Hooper, Philadelphia-born, had been assistant editor of *Lippincott's Magazine* until 1870, then went to Paris, where she served as corres-

pondent for various newspapers and made several translations, while her husband was vice-consul general in Paris.

¹⁶ *Ibid.*, p. 83.

¹⁷ Pierre Martino, *Le naturalisme français* (Paris: Colin, 1923), p. 153, quoted from Daudet's *Trente ans de Paris*.

¹⁸ *Pub. Weekly*, 11 (1877): 154, quoted in E & L's advertisement.

¹⁹ *Atlantic*, 38 (1876): 248–49; 40 (1877): 111.

²⁰ *Nation*, 24 (1877): 282, also by T. S. Perry.

²¹ *Lit. World*, 7 (1877): 139.

²² *Pub. Weekly*, 11 (1877): 142.

²³ Pseudonym of Mary Abigail Dodge.

²⁴ *Pub. Weekly*, 11 (1877): 498.

²⁵ *Ibid.*, p. 607; *Atlantic*, 40 (1877): 11–12; *Nation*, 25 (1877): 185; *Lit. World*, 8 (1877): 30.

²⁶ *Pub. Weekly*, 12 (1877): 120; *Nation*, 25 (1877): 274; *Atlantic*, 38 (1876): 250, French edition; *Lit. World*, 8 (1877): 64. Some critics felt that so clever a writer as Daudet need not have exaggerated the evil to such a degree, thus making the tale gloomy.

²⁷ E. Werner was the pseudonym of Elizabeth Bürstenbinder, a voluminous writer.

28 *Atlantic*, 40 (1877) : 764. Also *Nation*, 25 (1877) : 185.

29 *Pub. Weekly*, 11 (1877) : 683.

30 *Nation*, 25 (1877) : 275; *Lit. World*, 8 (1877) : 64.

31 Although these novels had a steady sale they did not fare well at the New York Trade Sales in 1877, which indicated that buyers were not sure of their future popularity.

32 *Pub. Weekly*, 12 (1877) : 228, 403, 425.

33 *Ibid.*, 13 (1878) : 2.

34 *Ibid.*, pp. 3, 12.

35 *Lit. World*, 8 (1878) : 164.

36 *Pub. Weekly*, 13 (1878) : 183, 197.

37 *Atlantic*, 42 (1878) : 298–99.

38 *Ibid.*, 49 (1882) : 846–51; *Century*, 26 (1883) : 498–509.

39 *Atlantic*, 49 (1882) : 851.

40 Altogether *Dosia* sold 39,000 copies in France by 1883.

41 *Nation*, 27 (1878) : 199; *Atlantic*, 42 (1878) : 301–2

42 Apparently Mme Durand did not care for the English translation of *Dosia* and made a statement, in 1879, that previous translators— meaning Mrs. Sherwood—had abridged and mutilated her work, coloring it with their own ideas (*Pub. Weekly*, 15 [1879]: 584).

43 *Nation*, 27 (1878) : 244.

44 This was the title used in the Little, Brown edition of Daudet's novels.

45 *Pub. Weekly*, 15 (1879) : 441.

46 *Ibid.* This was from Colman's poems, published in 1873.

47 See Régis Massac, *Le "detective novel" et l'influence de la pensée scientifique* (Paris: Champion, 1929), pp. 495–523; H. D. Thomson, *Masters of Mystery: a Study of the Detective Story* (London: Collins, 1931), pp. 92–108.

48 *Pub. Weekly*, 15 (1879) : 368.

49 *Nation*, 19 (1874) : 207.

50 *Lit. World*, 10 (1879) : 281.

51 *Pub. Weekly*, 17 (1880) : 443–45.

52 *Ibid.*, 18 (1880) : 190.

53 *Nation*, 31 (1880) : 176.

54 *Lit. World*, 11 (1880) : 197–98.

55 *Ibid.*, 12 (1881) : 181. The *Nation* was not so favorable this time.

56 *Ibid.*, 13 (1882) : 267; *Pub. Weekly*, 22 (1882) : 222.

57 H. M. Caldwell did his publishing of Gaboriau after E & L stopped in 1898, and continued into the early years of the twentieth century. (Apparently Dana Estes no longer desired to handle the Gaboriau novels.)

58 The Library of Congress Catalog lists seventeen different titles by Gaboriau, only nine of which represent original French works, and this list does not include all of E & L's publications.

59 *Lit. World*, 9 (1878) : 120.

60 *Pub. Weekly*, 24 (1883) : 374.

61 Will(iam) Allen Drumgoole was her real name.

62 See the Preface to the translation of *Jörn Uhl*, written by F. S. Delmer.

Chapter Five

1 *Lit. World*, 9 (1878) : 123. Reprintings of this book on the average of every two years in the 1870's, less frequently in the 1880's, indicated that it had sales appeal.

2 F. J. H. Darton, *Children's Books in England* (Cambridge: Cambridge Univ. Press, 1932), pp. 277–78.

3 *Athenaeum*, no. 2040 (December 1, 1866) : 716.

4 Darton, *op. cit.*, pp. 277–78.

5 *Ibid.*, p. 300.

6 *Pub. Weekly*, 12 (1877) : 554.

7 *Ibid.*, 13 (1878) : 2.

8 *Ibid.*, 12 (1877) : 643.

9 *Ibid.*, 14 (1878) : 672.

10 *Ibid.*, p. 284.

11 *Ibid.*, 16 (1879) : 666.

12 *Dial*, 1 (1880) : 164.

13 *Frederic G. Melcher, Friendly Reminiscences of a Half Century among Books and Bookmen* (New York:

Book Publishers' Bureau, 1945), p. 3.

14 *Critic*, 2 n. s. (1884): 282.

15 *Lit. World*, 16 (1885): 446. In 1884 the reviewer called *Chatterbox* "a perfection of a scrap-book for young eyes" (15 [1884]: 414).

16 *Ibid.*, 17 (1886): 433. *Young America*, the cheap reprint, was sold for 75 cents as compared with $1.25 for *Chatterbox*.

17 *Ibid.*, 18 (1887): 426.

18 *Ibid.*, 19 (1888): 426.

19 *Ibid.*, 10 (1879): 139.

20 *Ibid.*, *Nation*, 28 (1879): 375. The *Publishers' Weekly* considered the pictures better than those usually found in such works (15 [1879]: 299).

21 *Nation*, 29 (1879): 354.

22 The *Literary World* thought she did more writing-down than was necessary (10 [1879]: 139).

23 *Nation*, 28 (1879): 375.

24 *Lit. World*, 12 (1881): 119.

25 Robert M. Lovett, "A Boy's Reading Fifty Years Ago," *New Republic*, 48 (1926): 334-36.

26 *Pub. Weekly*, 16 (1879): 377.

27 *Ibid.*, p. 479.

28 *Ibid.*, 17 (1880): 16.

29 I wish to acknowledge here my continuing debt to the pages of Virginia Haviland, author of "The Travelogue Storybook of the Nineteenth Century," which appeared in *The Hornbook Magazine* from March to August, 1950. I have constantly drawn interesting facts from her articles.

30 Barrett Wendell, *A Literary History of America*, pp. 337–38.

31 Oliver Optic's "Young America Abroad" started as early as 1868.

32 Lovett, *op. cit.*, pp. 334–36.

33 Rodolphe Töpffer, *Oeuvres complètes: Voyages en zigzag* (Geneva: Pierre Cailler, 1945), Vols. XVIII, XIX.

34 Ralph Davol, "Hezekiah Butterworth, A Sketch of His Personality," *New England Magazine*, 33 n. s. (1906): 507–17.

35 *Ibid.*

36 Cited by Virginia Haviland from

Howe's *A Venture in Remembrance* (Boston: Little, Brown, 1941).

37 Davol, *op. cit.*

38 *Ibid.*

39 *Pub. Weekly*, 16 (1879): 240–41.

40 *Ibid.*, p. 189.

41 *Ibid.*, pp. 506, 582.

42 *Nation*, 29 (1879): 427. The *Nation* also reviewed Knox's *Boy Travellers in the Far East*, the rival work, and liked it too, though there was "something occasionally to be desired on the score of refinement," such as some pictures of torture. Otherwise, it was irreproachable (29 [1879]: 392).

43 *Lit. World*, 10 (1879): 360.

44 There was even an eighteenth book, *Zigzag Stories of History, Travel and Adventure* (1896), a selection of the best stories from the entire series.

45 Haviland, *op. cit.*, p. 217.

46 *Lit. World*, 12 (1881): 11.

47 *Nation*, 31 (1880): 462.

48 *Dial*, 2 (1881): 184.

49 *Critic*, 2 (1882): 38.

50 Lovett, *op. cit.*

51 Haviland, *op. cit.*, p. 117.

52 Cited by Haviland, *op. cit.*, p. 215.

53 Lovett, *op. cit.*

54 Nixon Waterman in *Boston Transcript*, September 6, 1905.

55 *Lit. World*, 20 (1889): 425.

56 *Ibid.*, 13 (1882): 434; 16 (1885): 438; 17 (1886): 432; 19 (1888): 422; 21 (1890): 472; 24 (1893): 419.

57 *Nation*, 37 (1883): 493; 33 (1881): 478; 35 (1882): 513; 39 (1884): 487; 43 (1886): 505; 47 (1888): 440; 55 (1892): 416.

58 *Critic*, 12 (1889): 282. Also 2 n. s. (1884): 282; 8 (1887): 89; 10 (1888): 257; 14 (1890): 308; 21 (1894): 71–72.

59 Preface to *Zigzag Journeys in the Occident*, 1882.

60 *Nation*, 35 (1882): 513.

61 Haviland, *op. cit.*, p. 220.

62 *Pub. Weekly*, 18 (1880): 56.

63 *Ibid.*, p. 510.

64 *Lit. World.*, 11 (1880): 298.

65 *Pub. Weekly*, 19 (1881): 42.

66 *Ibid.*, 20 (1881): 815.

67 *Nation*, 33 (1881): 400, 478.

68 *Lit. World*, 12 (1881): 449–50.

69 *Nation*, 39 (1884): 487.

70 *Ibid.*, 33 (1881): 160.

71 *Lit. World*, 12 (1881): 201.

72 *Nation*, 34 (1882): 84–85.

73 *Critic*, 2 (1882): 7; also *Lit. World*, 13 (1882): 27.

74 *Nation*, 35 (1882): 552.

75 *Lit. World*, 14 (1883): 58.

76 *Ibid.*, 13 (1882): 458.

77 *Ibid.*, 12 (1881): 425. Bernard A. Weisberger, in his *Reporters for the Union* (Boston: Little, Brown, 1953), sneers at Coffin apparently because he was stirred by emotion in his reporting instead of remaining brutally realistic. Since Coffin ventured, in accord with the spirit of the times, to include moral reflections as well as stories of events, he is termed "a solemn, jaundiced Yankee" or "the godly Coffin," wallowing in bathos when he describes the dying words of a young soldier. Such history-writing can be, in kindness, called nothing but inept.

78 *Herald Tribune Book Review*, 31 (1954): no. 12, p. 4. Review of Lovell Thompson's *Youth's Companion*.

79 Lovell Thompson, ed., *Youth's Companion* (Boston: Houghton, Mifflin, 1954), p. 70.

80 *Ibid.* It is a strange omission in this same book that Butterworth is not even mentioned, since it is certain that his many contributions were more popular to readers of the eighties and nineties than the unusual contributions from famous people which fill the pages of this anthology.

Note also the tribute to Stephens by Mark Antony De Wolfe Howe, quoted in Virginia Haviland's article: "It is a strange circumstance that Charles Asbury Stephens had in the hollow of his hand the *Youth's Companion's* wide audience, at its height some 550,000, was probably more read than any other author, and yet failed to achieve any recognized place in what is known as

'American literature' " (Haviland, *op. cit.*, p. 222).

81 Thompson, *op. cit.*, p. 608.

82 *Lit. World*, 4 (1873): 107.

83 *Critic*, 1 (1881): 369.

84 *Lit. World*, 12 (1881): 327.

85 *Ibid.*, 13 (1882): 434–35.

86 *Nation*, 35 (1882): 513.

87 *Ibid.*, 37 (1883): 434.

88 *Lit. World*, 14 (1883): 58.

89 Haviland, *op cit.*, pp. 223–24. Virginia Haviland tries to make a dry-as-dust out of Ober; this is not borne out by the books themselves nor by the contemporary reviews, except for the *Nation*, whose reviewer was distinctly prejudiced.

90 *Nation*, 51 (1890): 485.

91 *Ibid.*, 47 (1888): 440.

92 *Critic*, 8 (1887): 298.

93 *Ibid.*, 10 (1888): 275.

94 *Lit. World*, 18 (1887): 424; 19 (1888): 421.

95 *Critic*, 12 (1889): 268.

96 *Ibid.*, 14 (1890): 294.

97 *Ibid.*, 16 (1891): 317.

98 Haviland, *op. cit.*, pp. 224–30.

99 *Ibid.*, p. 229.

100 *Dial*, 3 (1882): 177.

101 *Nation*, 41 (1885): 450.

102 *Ibid.*, 37 (1883): 434.

103 *Ibid.*, 39 (1884): 487.

104 *Lit. World*, 13 (1882): 433; 14 (1883): 416; 15 (1884): 414.

105 *Ibid.*, 16 (1885): 438.

106 *Ibid.*, 17 (1886): 432; 18 (1887): 424; 19 (1888): 422; 20 (1889): 424; 21 (1890): 472.

107 *Dial*, 3 (1882): 177; 4 (1883): 203; 5 (1884): 220; 6 (1885): 222.

108 *Critic*, 16 (1891): 317.

109 *Nation*, 35 (1882): 552; 37 (1883): 508; *Lit. World*, 18 (1887): 454.

110 *Critic*, 3 (1883): 521.

111 *Ibid.*, p. 522; *Nation*, 37 (1883): 508.

112 See *Lit. World*, 15 (1884): 414.

113 *Ibid.*, 14 (1883): 58.

114 *Pub. Weekly*, 22 (1882): 724, 856.

115 *Lit. World*, 13 (1882): 434.

116 *Ibid.*, 15 (1884): 414.

117 *Ibid.*, 16 (1885): 446.

118 *Critic*, 4 (1885): 282.

119 *Ibid.*, 6 (1886): 271; 12 (1889): 229–30; 14 (1890): 276.

120 *Ibid.*, 2 (1884) : 274.
121 *Lit. World*, 15 (1884) : 413; *Nation*, 39 (1884) : 443.
122 *Critic*, 8 (1887) : 271; 10 (1888) : 286; *Lit. World*, 19 (1888) : 424.
123 Nation, 47 (1888) : 504.
124 *Lit. World*, 18 (1887) : 423; *Critic*, 8 (1887) : 246, 298.
125 *Critic*, 10 (1888) : 301.
126 *Lit. World*, 19 (1888) : 469; *Pub. Weekly*, 34 (1888) : Christmas Number, 65–67.
127 See especially the warm tributes in the *Horn Book Magazine* (17 [1941] : 245, 247–55), by Anne Eaton and Bertha E. Mahony.
128 Laura E. Richards, *Stepping Westward* (New York: Appleton, 1931).
129 Alice M. Jordan, *From Rollo to Tom Sawyer* (Boston: The Horn Book, 1948), p. 17.
130 Richards, *op. cit.*, p. 156.
131 *Ibid.*, p. 323.
132 *Lit. World*, 12 (1881) : 11.
133 *Nation*, 31 (1880) : 462.
134 *Critic*, 1 (1881) : 338.
135 Richards, *op. cit.*, p. 323.
136 *Lit. World*, 12 (1881) : 478.
137 Cornelia Meigs, ed., *Critical History of Children's Literature* (New York: Macmillan, 1953), p. 257.
138 Edmund L. Pearson, *Books in Black and Red* (New York: Macmillan, 1923), pp. 62–64.
139 Richards, *op. cit.*, p. 324.
140 *Critic*, 4 (1885) : 262; *Nation*, 41 (1885) : 407; *Lit. World*, 16 (1885) : 446; *Dial*, 6 (1885) : 222; *Pub. Weekly*, 28 (1885) : Christmas Number, 70.
141 Quoted from L. C. Page catalogue, 1950–51.
142 *Critic*, 12 (1889) : 271; *Nation*, 49 (1889) : 483; *Lit. World*, 20 (1889) : 422; *Dial*, 10 (1889) : 224.
143 *Nation*, 55 (1892) : 456.
144 *Critic*, 24 (1895) : 426.
145 *Lit. World*, 22 (1891) : 472; 23 (1892) : 480; 28 (1897) : 478; 29 (1898) : 457.
146 *Dial*, 23 (1897) : 342; 25 (1898) : 467.
147 Richards, *op. cit.*, p. 324.
148 Meigs, *op. cit.*, pp. 379–80.
149 Richards, *op. cit.*, p. 325.
150 Theodore Roosevelt, *An Autobiography* (New York: Macmillan, 1913), pp. 19–20. He, like Pearson, was convinced that children's books, to be good, should be of a kind that grown-ups could enjoy.
151 The *Nation* gave the collection unstinted praise (51 [1890] : 464).
152 Richards, *op. cit.*, p. 326.
153 *Nation*, 51 (1890) : 464.
154 *Lit. World*, 22 (1891) : 43.
155 *Dial*, 11 (1890) : 253.
156 Quoted from L. C. Page catalogue, 1950–51.
157 *Dial*, 15 (1893) : 349; *Lit. World*, 24 (1893) : 419; *Critic*, 20 (1893) : 396.
158 *Pub. Weekly*, 46 (1894) : 340.
159 *Nation*, 61 (1895) : 393; *Dial*, 19 (1895) : 393.
160 *Dial*, 21 (1896) : 391.
161 *Ibid.*; *Lit. World*, 27 (1896) : 457.
162 *Lit. World*, 24 (1893) : 450; *Critic*, 21 (1894) : 324.
163 *Critic*, 20 (1893) : 413.
164 *Lit. World*, 27 (1896) : 479. The Series included: *Teddy and Carrots*, *Jerry's Family*, *The Boys' Revolt*, and *The Princess and Joe Potter*.
165 *Critic*, 24 (1895) : 369.
166 *Dial*, 25 (1898) : 407.
167 *Nation*, 55 (1892) : 461; *Critic*, 18 (1892) : 343.
168 Richards, *op. cit.*, pp. 329–30.
169 *Outlook*, 99 (1911) : 390.

Chapter Six

1 It should be noted that Retzsch's drawings, done in the 1830's and 1840's, were outline drawings, which are supposed to have exerted some influence on Darley's similar work.

2 Cited from the back cover of Part III of this set.

3 Frank Weitenkampf, *The Illustrated Book* (Cambridge: Harvard Univ. Press, 1938), p. 162.

4 Cited from the advertising on the back cover of Part III.

5 A book such as Pugin's *Glossary* sold for only sixteen dollars at a trade sale in April 1877. As the *Publishers' Weekly* remarked: "The bidding was low in spite of the excellent presentation of the stock by Dana Estes" (11 [1877]: 427).

6 *Lit. World*, 9 (1878): 123.

7 The *Literary World* gave it a long notice, filled with congratulations, and the *Publishers' Weekly* gave it a separate review in the Holiday Number, reproducing two pictures (*Pub. Weekly*, 14 [1878]: 640).

8 The *Nation* thought that the *Beaconsfield Cartoons* were poorly reproduced by a process called "chemical engraving," but admitted that the series was more up-to-date than any other (27 [1878]: 350).

9 *Pub. Weekly*, 14 (1878): 252.

10 The prospectus is given in the *Publishers' Weekly*, 16 (1879): 582.

11 *Lit. World*, 10 (1879): 184.

12 *Ibid.*, p. 386.

13 *Nation*, 28 (1879): 366; 29 (1879): 438.

14 *Pub. Weekly*, 17 (1880): 565.

15 *Lit. World*, 11 (1880): 291 and 12 (1881): 244-45, are notable.

16 *Pub. Weekly*, 16 (1879): 807.

17 *Ibid.*, 18 (1880): 665.

18 *Lit. World*, 12 (1881): 456.

19 S. G. W. Benjamin, *The Life and Adventures of a Free Lance* (Burlington, Vt.: Free Press Co., 1911), p. 313. Elsewhere he castigates public art taste of this period, the refusal to go beyond prudishness in most art publications, and the sneering criticism which, in one case, using a slight defect in a wood block as an excuse, blamed an engraver for putting a pimple on a nymph's thigh.

20 F. L. Mott, *A History of American Magazines*, (Cambridge: Harvard University Press, 1938), III, 185-86.

21 *Dial*, 1 (1880): 86-87.

22 Weitenkampf, *op. cit.*, p. 186.

23 *Dial*, 1 (1880): 86-87. See also *Nation*, 32 (1881): 266.

24 *Lit. World*, 11 (1880): 266.

25 *Ibid.*, 10 (1879): 413. The work was highly commended for its rich illustrations and useful text.

26 *Pub. Weekly*, 18 (1880): 56-57.

27 The *Literary World* noted that the new edition of Thackeray had proved itself by selling 1,000 sets by November 1 (12 [1881]: 425).

28 *Pub. Weekly*, 20 (1881): 315.

29 *Lit. World*, 12 (1881): 448-49. The same critic, perhaps a friend of the family, called the book "extremely gentlemanly, or rather ladylike, out of respect to its compiler." See also *Dial*, 2 (1881): 173.

30 *Pub. Weekly*, 20 (1881): 316.

31 *Dial*, 2 (1881): 174-75; *Lit. World*, 12 (1881): 350-51.

32 The *Dial* gave the book great praise, also noting "just the right size and weight" (2 [1881]: 178).

33 *Lit. World*, 13 (1882): 458.

34 *Dial*, 3 (1882): 174-75.

35 *Ibid.* These books were noticed quite favorably by this magazine and several others.

36 The *Nation* gave it a most favorable review, 35 (1882): 511, as did the *Literary World*, 13 (1882): 458, and the *Dial*, 3 (1882): 171. The *Critic* felt that Linton damaged his cause by his violence, when moderation might have won almost everyone to his side (3 [1883]: 10). See also the *Publishers' Weekly*, 24 (1883): 200.

37 *Lit. World*, 13 (1882): 423. The set of Goethe was also published by S. E. Cassino, who had published scientific works jointly with E & L, and by Crowell in New York.

38 This edition was published on fine paper made especially for it by Tileston and Hollingsworth, the 350 illustrations were by Sir John Gilbert, and the volume was a royal octavo in size. It was so popular that there were soon four styles available, ranging in price from $3 to $5.

39 *Bookbuyer,* 1 (1884) : 300.
40 *Dial,* 4 (1883) : 199, 239; *Lit. World,* 14 (1883) : 449, *Pub. Weekly,* 24 (1883) : 47.
41 *Lit. World,* 15 (1884) : 110.
42 *Nation,* 38 (1884) : 349.
43 *Ibid.,* 39 (1884) : 467.
44 *Dial,* 4 (1883) : 201.
45 *Nation,* 41 (1885) : 379.
46 *Critic,* 1 n. s. (1884) : 114.
47 Estes had sent his original letter to the *New York Tribune,* and a copy to the *Critic,* which accounts for the appearance of the letter and the criticism of it in the same issue.
48 *Critic,* 1 n. s. (1884) : 114.
49 *Ibid.,* 2 n. s. (1889) : 304, also *Pub. Weekly,* 24 (1883) : 374, 26 (1884) : 417, and *Lit. World,* 15 (1884) : 416.
50 This *édition de grand luxe* was also available in six cloth portfolios at five dollars each.
51 *Lit. World,* 15 (1884) : 169; *Pub. Weekly,* 25 (1884) : 599, 619.
52 *Pub. Weekly,* 27 (1885) : 363.
53 *Ibid.,* p. 564.
54 *Critic,* 4 (1885) : 260–61; *Lit. World,* 16 (1885) : 442; *Pub. Weekly,* 28 (1885) : Christmas Number, 42. Only the *Nation,* whose reviewer blasted almost all the gift books this season, had no use for the *Eve,* "more misdirected effort and useless expenditure" (*Nation,* 41 [1885] : 488).
55 *Lit. World,* 16 (1885) : 429.
56 *Pub. Weekly,* 28 (1885) : 900. At this date only four copies of the satin remained, nine copies of the Japan paper, and thirteen of the vellum paper.
57 *Lit World,* 16 (1885) : 463.
58 *Critic,* 4 (1885) : 296; *Nation,* 41 (1885) : 488.
59 *Critic,* 4 (1885) : 260–61; *Lit. World,* 16 (1885) : 435–36. Both periodicals gave it long, highly favorable reviews.
60 *Critic,* 4 (1885) : 260–61. Only the *Nation* disliked it, remarking that it was not attractive, that many illustrations were clumsy and in harsh colors. The reviewer found merit in the pictures by Kenyon Cox and Will Low, which appeared nearer to what was "simple and truthful in design." This same reviewer had no use whatever for the authentic Persian designs—they were "assuredly not decorative." The whole book was an imitation of a French fashion, and not a good imitation (*Nation,* 41 [1885] : 472).
61 I own a copy of *Lalla Rookh,* which I found in a second-hand bookshop for fifteen cents; though slightly battered, it was still intact, and its lowly price was a good reflection of the change in taste. In all honesty it was worth more than fifteen cents, but the crossed-out prices ranging downward from five dollars indicated its humiliating descent.
62 *Lit. World,* 17 (1886) : 461.
63 *Ibid.,* p. 422.
64 *Critic,* 6 (1886) : 276; the *Nation,* 43 (1886) : 482; praised especially the emblematic title page.
65 *Dial,* 6 (1886) : 194.
66 *Critic,* 6 (1886) : 269. See also praise from *Lit. World,* 17 (1886) : 432; *Nation,* 43 (1886) : 482; and the *Dial,* 6 (1886) : 195, whose reviewer said that "the book will shine with a modest light amid the host of more showy volumes."
67 *Critic,* 5 (1886) : 64.
68 *Ibid.,* 10 (1888) : 295–96.
69 *Pub. Weekly,* 32 (1887) : Christmas Number, 42. The *Düsseldorf Gallery* was highly lauded in this issue.
70 *Lit. World,* 18 (1887) : 421.
71 *Pub. Weekly,* 34 (1888) : Christmas Number, 40–41: Estes and Lauriat have so many beautiful books that words fail in attempting to do them all justice."
72 *Lit. World,* 19 (1888) ; 413.
73 *Critic,* 10 (1888) : 255.
74 *Ibid.,* p. 285; *Lit. World,* 19 (1888) : 421; *Dial,* 9 (1888) : 209.
75 *Nation,* 47 (1888) : 381.
76 *Dial,* 9 (1888) : 207.
77 *Critic,* 10 (1888) : 254. Fine engravings after Giacomelli, he thought, and particularly poetic in conception.
78 *Ibid.,* 12 (1889) : 202.

79 *Lit. World*, 20 (1889) : 421; *Nation*, 49 (1889) : 351.

80 *Pub. Weekly*, 36 (1889) : Christmas Number, 53.

81 *Lit. World*, 21 (1890) : 426–27; *Dial*, 11 (1890) : 246; *Nation*, 51 (1890) : 343, 361; *Critic*, 14 (1890) : 221, 272.

82 *Critic*, 14 (1890) : 221; *Lit. World*, 21 (1890) : 434; *Dial*, 11 (1890) : 246; *Pub. Weekly*, 38 (1890) : Christmas Number, 29.

83 Reinick's *Night Song* had only twelve lines, but Sandham made sixteen illustrations for it, in royal quarto format (12 x 15). The cover was pale blue, with a tracery design of vines surrounding a golden lyre. Each line of the verse was printed over a pen and ink sketch and the photogravures were on facing pages. The *Critic* felt that, though some of the pictures were not bad, Sandham's reputation would suffer if he did much of this sort of work (14 [1890] : 273). See also *Lit. World*, 21 (1890) : 432.

84 *Critic*, 14 (1890) : 273; also *Lit. World*, 21 (1890) : 434, "one of the crudest in its selection of verses and artistic quality." Yet the *Dial* rhapsodized over the book (11 [1890] : 246).

85 *Critic*, 14 (1890) : 273; *Nation*, 51 (1890) : 343; *Dial*, 11 (1890) : 248; *Lit. World*, 21 (1890) : 434.

86 *Lit. World*, 21 (1890) : 469; *Critic*, 15 (1891) : 165; *Nation*, 51 (1890) : 427–28, a long review full of praise.

87 *Pub. Weekly*, 37 (1890) : 38; *Lit. World*, 21 (1890) : 14.

88 Percy Fitzgerald, *The Book Fancier* (London: S. Low, Marston, 1914), p. 201. E & L undoubtedly were guilty of this practice in some of their sets, but in this set of Dickens all the artists were contemporaries at least, even though of differing styles.

89 Donald Sheehan, *This Was Publishing* (Bloomington: Indiana Univ. Press, 1952), Chaps. 7, 8, particularly.

90 Adolf Growoll, *The Profession of Bookselling* (New York: Publishers' Weekly, 1893), pp. 143–47. All the information he supplies is very much to the point, and comes from a master in the book trade.

91 Sheehan, *op. cit.*, p. 197.

92 *Herald Tribune Book Review*, 30 (1954) : no. 25, p. 2.

93 *Critic*, 25 (1894) : 44. Many of the facts in Funk and Wagnalls' epistle were somewhat askew. There was grave doubt that Washington and Bismarck ever served as book canvassers; there was no foundation at all for the story about Longfellow; Webster graduated from Dartmouth in 1801 and Tocqueville's *America* was published in 1835. But taking the facts as correct made Julian Hawthorne's letter the more humorous (*Critic*, 25 [1894] : 77).

94 Such a set appears now and then in booksellers' catalogues, priced from $25 to $40. The Smith, Elder, *Thackeray*, without any over-illustration, usually brings a higher price, which shows the durability of true quality.

95 *Critic*, 15 (1891) : 75.

96 *Lit. World*, 22 (1891) : 133.

97 *Ibid.*, p. 262.

98 *Critic*, 15 (1891) : 301. The writer of the article was C. E. L. Wingate, who usually wrote the "Boston Letter" for the magazine.

99 *Lit. World*, 24 (1893) : 85.

100 *Critic*, 19 (1893) : 252; 20 (1893) : 35, 357; 21 (1894) : 110, 272; 22 (1894) : 273, 348, 25 (1896) : 74, etc., *Lit. World*, 24 (1893) : 85, 413.

101 *Nation*, 53 (1891) : 428; *Critic*, 16 (1891) : 332; *Lit. World*, 22 (1891) : 462. This book was available in two bindings at $1 and $4.

102 *Nation*, 53 (1891) : 428; *Critic*, 16 (1891) : 316; 17 (1892) : 144; *Lit. World*, 22 (1891) : 462; *Pub. Weekly*, 40 (1891) : Christmas Number, 31.

103 *Critic*, 16 (1891) : 336; *Lit. World*, 22 (1891) : 433.

104 *Lit. World*, 22 (1891) : 465; *Critic*, 16 (1891) : 332.

105 The work on Genoa was highly praised, though some thought it possibly too poetic. *Lit. World*, 23

(1892): 438; *Critic,* 18 (1892): 341–42; *Pub. Weekly,* 42 (1892): Christmas Number, 31, 53.

106 *Pub. Weekly,* 42 (1892): Christmas Number, 53.

107 Particular praise was given the *Fables* in Elizur Wright's translation, with thirteen fine etchings by LeRat. See *Lit. World,* 24 (1893): 470; *Dial,* 15 (1893): 345.

108 *Critic,* 18 (1892): 357; *Pub. Weekly,* 42 (1892): 466. There were other handsome books, such as a de luxe edition of William Ware's old novel of *Zenobia;* picture books such as *Recent International Art, American Etchings,* Thomson's *Seasons, Parisian Photogravures;* but nothing of outstanding originality.

109 *Critic,* 20 (1893): 407; *Lit. World,* 24 (1893): 416; *Dial,* 15 (1893): 345. It is rather amusing to observe that every reviewer expatiated more on the covers than the text of these books. Clara Erskine Clement was the pen name of Mrs. Clara Clement Waters.

110 *Nation,* 59 (1894): 487; *Lit. World,* 25 (1894): 422.

111 *Critic,* 21 (1894): 29.

112 *Lit. World,* 27 (1896): 451. This reviewer thought the book admirable, however.

113 *Critic,* 23 (1895): 249, 265.

114 *Lit. World,* 27 (1896): 411.

115 *Dial,* 25 (1898): 401; 15 (1893): 348.

116 All following details of books published by Dana Estes & Co. were derived from the firm's advertisements in the *Publisher's Weekly* and the *Publisher's Trade List Annual.* It does not seem necessary to give a citation for each reference to an advertisement but there will be a few references to items of unusual interest or to other sources of information.

117 Communication from Frederic G. Melcher to me.

118 *Pub. Weekly,* 70 (1906): Christmas Number, 109–10.

119 *Herald Tribune Book Review,* 29 (1953): no. 21, p. 11.

120 It is impossible to do more than hint at the evaluation of these sets in the last ten or fifteen years, judging from *American Book Prices Current.* Some of them have sold at auction at very high prices: Tolstoy, in morocco, brought from $160 to $220; Waverley Novels (1893), morocco, $150 to $280; Dickens (1882), $70; Dumas, $180 and $60; Carlyle, $16 to $125, in various bindings; George Eliot (1894), $50, $30, and $13; Eugène Sue, $18.50; Ruskin, $32; Thackeray, $75 to $125; Bulwer, $20 to $145. Most of those bound in cloth went very cheap, especially when the covers were faded, as is usually the case. The leather bindings raised the price materially, and some of the rigidly limited sets are still considered valuable.

Chapter Seven

1 G. H. Sargent, *Lauriat's* (Boston: Privately printed, 1922), pp. 21–23; *Pub. Weekly,* 54 (1898): 9–10; Russell H. Conwell, *History of the Great Fire in Boston* (Boston: B. B. Russell, 1873), *passim.*

2 Sargent, *op. cit.,* pp. 23–27.

3 C. E. Goodspeed, *Yankee Bookseller* (Boston: Houghton, Mifflin, 1937), p. 14.

4 *Ibid.,* p. 27.

5 Clifford B. Orr, *An Inside View of the Retail Book Stores of Boston* (Boston: *Boston Evening Transcript* [1933]), n. p.

6 *Pub. Weekly,* 40 (1891): 955.

7 *Ibid.,* 3 (1873): 415 (April 26).

8 *Ibid.,* p. 375.

9 *Ibid.,* pp. 381–82.

10 *Ibid.,* 5 (1874): 138. Two years later E & L's trade catalogue was criticized, along with others, as

"singularly arranged, a peculiar classification." Examples were given to prove the point, with the added sneer that many books somewhat hard to classify were thrown into the "Miscellany" section. Very few trade catalogues were given good ratings, however (9 [1876]: 706).

11 *Ibid.*, 5 (1874) : 369.

12 *Ibid.*, 7 (1875) : 208 a.

13 *Ibid.*, 29 (1886) : 278. In 1888 E & L, in a discussion on underselling in the *Publishers' Weekly*, indicated that they bought in such large quantities that they were forced, by the nature of the trade, to give larger discounts to their regular customers. This was one of the advantages of the large bookseller, they asserted (*Pub. Weekly*, 33 [1888]: 398).

14 *Ibid.*, 10 (1876) : 19.

15 *Ibid.*, 13 (1878) : 310; 15 (1879) : 472.

16 *Ibid.*, 11 (1877) : 470.

17 *Ibid.*, p. 498.

18 *Ibid.*, 12 (1877) : 368.

19 *Ibid.*, p. 554.

20 S. S. Kilburn advertised in the 1870's that he was "prepared to undertake the pictorial department of any book, however illustrated, or to furnish the whole illustration of a pictorial newspaper, both in designs and engravings, with the promptitude the press requires." Ray Nash, *Printing as an Art* (Cambridge: Harvard Univ. Press, 1955), p. 20, note 21.

21 *Pub. Weekly*, 13 (1878) : 2.

22 *Ibid.*, p. 494.

23 *Ibid.*, 14 (1878) : 97. This agreement was indicated by a joint advertisement by Nelson and E & L in July.

24 *Ibid.*, p. 252.

25 *Ibid.*, p. 284.

26 *Ibid.*, p. 816. Dated December 1, 1878.

27 *Ibid.*, 15 (1879) : 307. Since so few letters of Dana Estes have been preserved I am quoting one found in the R. R. Bowker Collection of the New York Public Library. This probably gives a typical specimen of Estes' epistolary style.

ESTES & LAURIAT.
Publishers, Booksellers and
　Importers
301 Washington Street.
Publishers of the American Art
　Review.

Boston, Oct. 29. 1880

Dear Mr. Bowker.

I post you the impressions of the Fletcher Harper which you desire, and am glad to hear your good opinion of the Review.

The late numbers we think are particularly fine, and we are now going in for a limited edition de luxe. The Appletons' are to drop the Art Journal with the end of this year, and that will probably help us considerably. I thank you for the suggestion to Mr. Pascoe about which he wrote us. I have been so busy I have not been able to give him a detailed answer, though I have acknowledged his offer. I do not exactly see how he can act for more than one publisher without clashing of interests, but possibly he can arrange it in that way.

Yes, we are having a great success with our Juveniles. Indeed, we find it almost impossible to get them manufactured as fast as we can sell them this year.

Yours faithfully,
Dana Estes,
Per Stenographer.

I am laboring on the International Copyright question. Saw the Harpers & Mr. Evarts last week. If the opposition of the Philadelphia Idiots, & others of their class does not kill the matter we may succeed this time. I have also another matter in hand in which you would be interested. I am getting up a free library for Tom Hughes' Tenn. Colony Rugby. Have already 3400 vols. subscribed by the trade. How would it do to ask for contributions from the English Publishers? I will send you more details of it later on, as it progresses.

Yours Truly
D. E.

28 *Pub. Weekly*, 16 (1879) : 186.

29 *Ibid.*, p. 189.

30 *Ibid.*, p. 377.

31 *Ibid.*, p. 479.

32 *Ibid.*, 17 (1880) p. 16.

33 *Ibid.*, p. 301.

34 *Ibid.*, 22 (1882) : 457.

35 *Ibid.*, 18 (1880) : 110. According to the *Literary World*, 11 (1880) : 266, 298, E & L were preparing about 200,000 volumes of juveniles, with 100,000 for one of them alone, and were regretful they could not print 20,000 more.

36 *Pub. Weekly*, 18 (1880) : 827-28. These were full-page advertisements, cleverly spaced to attract the reader's eye.

37 *Ibid.*, 18 (1880) : 828.

38 *Ibid.*, p. 827.

39 *Ibid.*, p. 836. The "Chatterbox literature" mentioned is the various collections of pictures, verses, etc., drawn from the magazine and sold separately from the annual, and usually at a cheaper price. The case of Roberts Brothers and Lovell was the reprinting, by Lovell, of the poems of Jean Ingelow, whom Roberts Brothers had made famous in the United States by their wide advertising. Because of Lovell's competition Miss Ingelow's royalties were greatly reduced.

40 *Ibid.*, p. 844.

41 *Ibid.*, 19 (1881) : 695. At the same period Lauriat had gone to the Maine woods "to recruit his health."

42 *Ibid.*, 20 (1881) : 400. An article on "Boston Book-Makers" noted that "the elegant bookstore of Estes & Lauriat [is] now perhaps the largest general bookstore in Boston." It contrasted the elegant front of E & L with the dingy signboard of Roberts Brothers, in the entry beside E & L.

43 *Ibid.*, 22 (1882) : 320.

44 *Ibid.*, 25 (1884) : 301.

45 *Ibid.*, 26 (1884) : 231.

46 *Ibid.*, p. 287.

47 *Ibid.*, p. 339.

48 *Ibid.*, p. 445.

49 *Ibid.*, p. 552.

50 *Ibid.*, p. 564.

51 *Ibid.*, p. 576.

52 *Ibid.*, p. 972; 28 (1885) : 251.

53 *Ibid.*, 27 (1885) : 19.

54 *Ibid.*, p. 9.

55 One suspects more than probability here, since E & L were old hands in the subscription-book trade and must have known what the exact chances were. In 1886 there was comment on Mark Twain's difficulties in keeping his subscription editions out of the hands of the trade in *Pub. Weekly*, 30 (1886) : 204–5.

56 *Pub. Weekly*, 27 (1885) : 52–53.

57 *Ibid.*, p. 213.

58 *Ibid.*, p. 490.

59 *Ibid.*, pp. 62, 286, 314, 674.

60 *Ibid.*, p. 74, also 6 (1874) : 212.

61 *Western Bookseller*, (1885) : 275; *American Bookseller*, 17 (1885) : 276.

62 R. H. Shove, *Cheap Book Production in the United States, 1870–1891* (Urbana: Univ. of Illinois Library, 1937), p. 97.

63 *Pub. Weekly*, 27 (1885) : 171.

64 *Ibid.*, 29 (1886) : 277. See also an interesting letter from Estes to R. R. Bowker, dated February 16, 1886, which shows in detail the important role Estes was playing in the battle for international copyright (R. R. Bowker Collection, New York Public Library).

65 *Ibid.*, 29 (1886) : 600.

66 *Ibid.*, pp. 138, 615.

67 *Ibid.*, 30 (1886) : 506.

68 *Ibid.*, pp. 578–79.

69 *Ibid.*, pp. 606–7, 619, 634.

70 *Ibid.*, p. 635.

71 *Ibid.*, p. 660.

72 *Ibid.*, p. 664, (November 6.)

73 *Ibid.*, pp. 962, 968.

74 *Ibid.*, 31 (1887) : 661–62.

75 *Ibid.*, 34 (1888) : 1025.

76 Biographical sketch issued by the Grolier Society. See also *Pub. Weekly*, 103 (1923) : 951, 1079–81.

77 Communication from Frederic G. Melcher to me.

78 *Pub. Weekly*, 49 (1896) : 863.

79 Communication from Frederic G. Melcher to me.

80 *Pub. Weekly*, 33 (1888) : 70–75.

81 *Ibid.*, p. 76.

82 *Ibid.*, pp. 99–100.

83 *Ibid.*, pp. 448–49, also 76.

84 *Critic.*, 9 (1888): 30.

85 *Pub. Weekly*, 33 (1888): 517.

86 *Ibid.*, 39 (1891): 562-72.

87 Cited from *The Bookseller* of July 5, 1889 in the *Publishers' Weekly*, 36 (1889): 195.

88 *Pub. Weekly*, 41 (1892): 850; 44 (1893): 10, 713.

89 *Ibid.*, 33 (1888): 496–97.

90 *Ibid.*, 48 (1895): 716.

91 *Ibid.*, 42 (1892): 632, 1023; 43 (1893): 504; 44 (1893); 711.

92 *Ibid.*, 42 (1892): 383.

93 Communication from Frederic G. Melcher to me.

94 *Pub. Weekly*, 53 (1898): 560.

95 *Ibid.*, p. 741.

96 *Ibid.*, p. 905 (June 4.)

97 *Ibid.*, 54 (1898): 9–10 (July 2.)

98 *Ibid.*, p. 12. Estes was immensely proud of this degree and never failed to append it to his name, whenever possible.

99 *Ibid.*, 48 (1895): 308.

100 *Ibid.*, 85 (1914): 1098–1100.

101 *Ibid.*, p. 1235.

Conclusion

1 See Helmut Lehmann-Haupt, *The Book in America* (New York: Bowker, 1939), p. 201.

INDEX

233